THE ENCLOSED GARDEN

*The Tradition and
the Image in
Seventeenth-Century
Poetry*

Stanley Stewart

THE ENCLOSED GARDEN

The Tradition and the Image in Seventeenth-Century Poetry

The University of Wisconsin Press

Madison, Milwaukee, and

London, 1966

Published by the University of Wisconsin Press
Madison, Milwaukee, and London
U.S.A.: Box 1379, Madison, Wisconsin 53701
U.K.: 26–28 Hallam Street, London, W.1
Copyright © 1966 by the Regents of the
University of Wisconsin
Printed in the United States of America
by The Colonial Press Inc., Clinton, Mass.
Library of Congress Catalog Card
Number 66–13808

To Barbara

Acknowledgments

I wish to express my appreciation for the help and encouragement of friends and colleagues during the years this study was being prepared. H. T. Swedenberg, Jr., John J. Espey, Hugh G. Dick, Robert L. Peters, and Robert F. Gleckner read portions or all of the manuscript and offered useful advice.

Rosemond Tuve's *A Reading of George Herbert* (1952) and Louis L. Martz' *The Poetry of Meditation* (1954) helped me more than the notes may show; my deepest debt is to the authors of these two books.

I wish also to thank the Research Committees of the University of California at Los Angeles and at Riverside for their consistent generosity, which allowed me to spend one summer at the Pierpont Morgan Library in New York City and two others at the Henry E. Huntington Library and Art Gallery in San Marino, California. I am grateful to these libraries, and to the New York Metropolitan Museum, for permission to reproduce a number of graphic works.

Over a period of years the fine staff of the Henry E. Huntington Library has extended many kindnesses, which I appreciate.

S. S.

University of California, Riverside
April, 1965

Contents

The illustrations follow page 114.

Introduction

The art and culture of almost every civilization which has left any trace reveal an interest in the garden. The garden is what we might call a primeval event, an archetypal fact of life, and naturally so. For there is at least one sense in which the garden is the sine qua non of civilization. Agriculture, one of the features commonly used to distinguish man from related animals, must be distinguished from enterprises like berry-gathering and grain-reaping, in which several of the so-called lower primates have shown themselves to be quite proficient. In fact, even the squirrels and birds harvest the fruits of the earth. Wilderness in the broadest sense of the term must be distinguished from the plots laid out and cultivated by man for the purpose of harvesting more than he can eat today, so that he may have food enough tomorrow. But despite the obviousness of this common-sense distinction, it is not surprising that Freudians, neo-Freudians, Jungians, neo-Jungians—and archetypalists in general—find themselves fascinated by the meaning of that interest in the garden. For them, there is one and only one garden image hovering in some limbo of the human unconscious, though that single Form has many manifestations.

It is perfectly right and proper that these excursions into the unconscious continue in order that some key to the recurrence of mankind's interest in particular forms may some day be found. But the purpose of this book is not to inquire into the garden image per se. Indeed, no matter how hard we hang on to the single, synthetic Form, it always (with our present state of knowledge) changes in our grasp. Apollo, Osiris, and Christ are not the same, no matter how many similarities among them we may list. Further, it is through the apprehension of dissimilarities existing within a body of similar expressions that the critic grasps the meaning of a particular text. This book, then, is not concerned with the figure of the garden, for treatment of that subject would require many volumes, some of them dealing with archeology, Egyptology, chemistry, and so on. Rather, the subject of this book is the figure of the enclosed garden, as it was used during the late sixteenth and early seventeenth centuries. Admittedly one can do little more than make an arbitrary slice out of the history of the use of a figure. But this does not change the fact that the enclosed garden written of by men like St. Bernard and Bishop Hall differs in significant details from Claudian's Garden of the Hesperides. The meaning of the former image must be considered in the context which informed the use of it by men like Hall, Vaughan, and Marvell, and which was, in turn, enriched by their use.

Thus, the purpose of this book is to assert the meaning of the enclosed garden as it functions in the imagery of seventeenth-century poetry. But as the title suggests, the focus is on a literary rather than a poetic context. If the purpose is to explicate particular poems, Marvell's "The Garden" for example, the means to that end is to identify and describe the relevant context. As we become familiar with the context of the enclosed garden, we find occurring within it a cluster of images, in prose as well as poetry. When apposite uses are juxtaposed, they shed light on their shared meanings; and such comparison also isolates important differences with respect to the complexity of particular utterances. Though the aim of this study in certain respects resembles that of the lexicographer, for the most part the lexicographer limits his investigation to the immediate context of a word within a phrase. Thus, in a dictionary, the item at the left is juxtaposed to a list of potentially relevant experiences, which demonstrate the occurrence of different (or the same) words in similar sentential contexts. In short, the dictionary describes the functional synonymy of words. Unfortunately, such a rendering often fails the literary student in his moment of greatest need; at least it may be safely said that even possession and faithful use of the OED does not guarantee a dependable paraphrase of such a complex utterance as Marvell's "The Garden." The point is (and this holds for both grammarians and

lexicographers) that the linguist describes the language as it is
normally used (in spite of the fact that he may cite poets as examples when no others exist), while the job of the literary critic
is often to describe the language as it is not normally used. Yet
unquestionably all three are concerned with linguistic contexts.

All meaning is contextual, therefore historical: every printed
poem was written in the past. Though the amount of data shrinks
as we go further into the past in our effort to understand the meaning of utterances, the method does not change. Nor is this statement intended as a defense of history against criticism. It is rather
the statement of what E. D. Hirsch recently called "a brute onto-
logical fact." [1] It is true that focus on the text is absolutely necessary if we would understand the meaning of a particular poem. But
this admission simply lends authority to the irrelevant (because
universally accepted) imperative, viz., if you would understand a
given poem, read that poem. It is a curious fact that in some circles
this imperative is honored as the almost hallowed formula for the
promulgation of right thinking in literary studies. Supposedly, to
ignore this imperative is to engage in the destructive act known
as historical research. Let it be said at the start, then, that even
though the aim of this study is to explicate particular poems within
a class of apposite expressions, there has been no conscious intention of denigrating any work of art. On the contrary, by examining the historical usage of the figure of the enclosed garden, it is
hoped that we may unfold the meaning of a shared linguistic culture, and thereby enrich our enjoyment of the poetry of that culture. This essay was written with the belief that aesthetic values
exist, and exist preeminently in such works as Marvell's "The Garden." But poetic value does not depend on the apotheosis of an
imperative, or on the mystique of poetry in which the meaning
must be held inviolate and unique. In fact, the argument here will
be that ad hoc, impressionistic approaches to Marvell's poem may
fail properly to value the poem because of ill-founded hypotheses
about its meaning.

The proper context of Andrew Marvell's "The Garden," and of
such works as Richard Rowlands' "Hortus Conclusus," Herbert's
"Paradise," Joseph Beaumont's "The Gardin," and William Prynne's
"Christian Paradise," is the tradition of the enclosed garden, which

flourished in literary and artistic circles throughout the Middle Ages and the Renaissance. Its norms, based on the allegorization of the Song of Songs, were known and used by poets of such diverse temperaments and interests as Robert Grosseteste, Guillaume de Lorris, Chaucer, William Nevill, Dunbar, James VI of Scotland, St. Teresa, and St. John of the Cross. As this study intends to show, this tradition was very much alive in English literature in the early seventeenth century.

THE ENCLOSED GARDEN

*The Tradition and
the Image in
Seventeenth-Century
Poetry*

CHAPTER I

The Song of Songs

THE LYRIC

By the beginning of the seventeenth century, reaction against the supposed licentiousness of secular lyrics had resulted, if publication may be taken as a reliable index of interest, in considerable success. Lily Bess Campbell's well-documented book, *Divine Poetry and Drama in Sixteenth-Century England*, offers a detailed history and analysis of the development of religious poetry during the sixteenth century.[1] At least one highly interesting fact emerges from this study: the piously inclined poet saw verse paraphrases of the Bible as the logical answer and divine alternative to the love lyrics found in the popular miscellanies of the time. Competition developed between the songs of the courtly lover and the lyrics of Solomon and David. Those lyrics, it was believed, resembled the sonnets and pastorals known to have so undermined English morality. Solomon and David, like Wyatt and Surrey, wrote songs of love, the paraphrase of which offered the English poet his best hope of routing bawdy court lyrics. After all, wrote the Fenners and the Baldwins, *The Court of Venus* (1539) treated of love in only an occult and perverted sense: the true author of the Psalms and the Song of Songs was Love Incarnate. The modern critic might be tempted to dismiss this controversy with the exorcism of a semantic label; and it must be admitted that the quarrel was over the meaning of the word "love." But for many writing in that day, the ambiguity of this word was more than a linguistic curiosity; that confusion blurred an irrevocable and terrible possibility, the circumvention of which rested entirely on a proper understanding of the correct (because divinely ordained) meaning of love.[2]

Opinion was sharply divided during the sixteenth century as to just what role the Song of Songs should play in this love debate. From earliest rabbinical days, the language of the Song of Songs caused a minority of readers to be uneasy. Some of these, like Castalio, passed from that uneasiness to the certainty that the work did not belong in biblical canon. Their argument was simple enough: the unabashed eroticism of the Song of Songs was not consonant with divine inspiration. But St. Bernard advanced the more influential view that Solomon's Song was the most elevated and distinguished of all biblical lyrics, more exalted even than the Psalms of David. The other songs in Scripture were written for special occasions, such as military victories. But the title "Song of Songs" had been given by the Holy Ghost in testimony to its "unique excellence," [3] or as St. François de Sales—a great admirer of St. Bernard—preferred to say, to its "excellent sweetnesse." [4]

According to tradition, the Song of Songs was an epithalamion sung at the wedding of Solomon and the daughter of Pharaoh. Richard Sibbes writes that such songs were particularly appropriate to occasions of celebration. In other words, the lyric conceptualization of the Song of Songs voiced by St. Bernard and others was taken quite literally, for no more joyful occasion could be named than *"The Intercourse betwixt Christ the Highest Lord of Lords, and his best beloved contracted Spouse."* [5] The title of Michael Drayton's verse paraphrase of the Canticles (as it first appeared in 1591) testifies not only to the same lyric understanding but also to the conventional interpretation of the "Bride and Bridegroom." Drayton's "Harmonie of the Church" is one of a number of verse paraphrases of Old Testament and Apocryphal books; its subtitle carries through the lyrical motif. Not only were these lyrics "meete to be read or sung, for the solace and comfort of the Godly," but they were the "spirituall songes and Holy Hymnes, of Godly Men . . . All, Sweetly Sounding, to the Praise and Glory of the Highest." In a piously intoned dedication to Lady Jane Devereux, Drayton claims for the authority of his poems the inspiration of Scripture itself, for his paraphrases should be read "not as poems of poets, but praiers of prophets." [6] At the same time, Drayton disclaimed the ambitions of the "gracelesse parasite" found plying his trade at court. Indeed, Drayton's sole aim was the advancement of God's glory and the edification of the Church.

Drayton's thinly veiled attack on court poets points up the recognized parallelism and competition between the verse paraphrases of the Song of Songs and secular lyrics. In his address to the reader, Drayton makes his intention even more explicit when he writes: "I speak not of Mars the god of wars, nor of Venus the goddesse of love, but of the Lord of Hostes that made heaven and earth; not of toyes in Mount Ida, but of triumphes in Mount Sion; not of vanitie, but of veritie; not of tales, but of truethes." [7] It is with this parallelism in mind that we should understand such a work as Henry Ainsworth's *Annotations* (1627). [8] Incorporating the earlier *Solomons Song of Songs in English Metre* (1623), the work reiterates the seriousness with which the title of the Song of Solomon was understood. Ainsworth's immensely popular work is divided into three parts. First, a prose translation closely follows the King James Version. In the opposite column runs the author's verse paraphrase. While the translation of the title, "The Song of Songs, which is Solomons," departs but little from traditional English equivalents of the vulgate "Canticum Canticorum Salomonis," the verse rendition reads: "This may be sung as the 55 or 86 Psalme." As in the Middle Ages, so in Ainsworth's time, the Song of Songs found its way into the musical literature of devotion. Ainsworth's explanation for this setting of the Canticles is close to Sibbes': he reminds his reader that "Songs and Psalmes are for the most part arguments of joy and gladness in them that sing." This view was shared by Catholics as well as Protestants; the eminent devotional writer Luis de la Puente states that "Spirituall Canticles, are affections of spirituall joy, & alacritie, rejoicing that God is who hee is"; [9] and Casimire Sarbiewski calls his paraphrases of the Song of Songs "Odes out of Salomons Sacred Marriage Song." [10]

The ironic fact is that (the anxiety of men like Castalio notwithstanding) the Song of Songs was sung in church as a hymn. Joseph Beaumont's "Jesus inter Ubera Maria" was set "To a Base and 2 Trebles." [11] The seven groups of seven songs in William Loe's verse paraphrase were all meant to be sung. We know this because the work is "set to the tune of, *Blessed are they that perfect are.*" [12] In a dedication to William Christmas prefixed to the poems, Loe defends his musical setting as justified by the true subject of Solomon's Song: the mutual love between Christ and his Spouse. To honor this union, the Congregation lifted a joyful noise unto the Lord. We see in the title of the chosen melody, "Blessed are they that perfect are," the general failure of those frontal assaults on the authenticity of the Song of Songs. That title may be seen, in fact, as a truncated commentary on the true nature of Solomon's "nuptial love song," whose expression was appropriate to be sung in church. We may believe that many of the paraphrases of the Song of Songs were so performed.

Many of the verses in George Wither's "The Song of Songs," for example, are scored for musical performance. These songs are included in Wither's *The Hymnes and Songs of the Church* (1623).[13] Falling within a dual classification of biblical lyrics, "The Song of Songs" could "properly be sung, with some other ancient Songs and Creeds." Commenting on these Old Testament lyrics, Wither insists that it is a mistake to consider them "impertinent to these later Ages of the Church." Because its subject matter was both historical and relevant, the Song of Songs in particular was vitally pertinent to the daily life of the reader. As for its eroticism, this quite properly stimulated the human affections. Rather than being a hindrance to devotion, as Castalio and others believed, this eroticism employed normal human propensities to a profitable end. The sole contingency of this benefit concerned man's understanding; "*divine Love,*" the true subject matter of the Song of Songs and whatever eroticism was to be found in the work, was the proper vehicle to reach man's highest faculty with truth: "Such is the mercy of God, that hee taketh advantage, even of our naturall affections to beget in our soules an apprehension of his love, and of the mysteries, which tend to our true happinesse." [14] It was with a knowledge of the limitations of human potentialities that the Holy Ghost spoke through Solomon, appealing to "the strongest, the commonest, the most pleasing, the most naturall, and the most commendable of our *Affections.*"

This lyric conceptualization of the Canticles represents a continuation of the reaction traced by Miss Campbell to its source in the Great Bible (1539), where the translator altered the title of the Song of Songs in such a way as to suggest a lyric or musical piece.

Thus, "Canticum Canticorum Salomanis" became "Ballet of Balettes of Salomon." [15] Here, as in William Baldwin's *The Canticles or Balades of Salomon* a decade later, we find the unmistakable imitation of the title of the secular *Boke of Balettes*. The avowed purpose of Baldwin's paraphrase was twofold: first, he wished to dispel the error of those who denied the divine authenticity of the Song of Songs. More important for our purpose, he wished also to offer the honest layman a song to sing other than those secular outrages which appeared on every hand. In short, he openly offered his paraphrase in the hope of driving "out of office the baudy balades of lecherous love that commonly" were "indited and song of idle courtiers in princes and noblemens houses." [16] In just the same way, Jude Smith believed such works as his *A misticall devise* (1575) would take the place of secular ballads, whose popularity he thought only temporary. In the preface to Smith's work, John Wharton castigates the readers of Ovid and Chaucer for dallying with "stale tales," [17] urging them to join the Psalmist in inspired song. Later, William Loe dedicates his paraphrase of the Canticles as the divine alternative to the hedonistic values of carpe diem:

> I have ever hated Epicurean resolution Let us eate, & drinke to morrowe we shall dye. But I have ever loved entyrely Christian exhortacion. Let us pray, & praise god, To morrowe we shall live For to love, is to live, ... If we love god, we shall live in him by our prayers, ...[18]

Toward the turn of the seventeenth century, competition between divine and secular lyrics often found expression in the form of paraphrase. Devotional writings might imitate the language of love poetry, confronting readers with a choice between alternatives which touched the worlds of both art and life. In Richard Rowlands' openly recusant volume of lyrics, which includes poems on the names of Mary and fifteen lyrics on the Rosary, this pattern of paraphrase reaches even into cradle songs. One poem, sung by the Virgin to her Son, develops the paradox of a situation in which the Mother nurses and comforts the source of all life and comfort. After several stanzas, the poet invokes erotic language, as the reader hears the ringing answer to passionate shepherds and their loves:

> My sweetnesse and the sweetest moste,
> That heaven could earth deliver
> Soule of my love, spirit of my lyf,
> Abyde with mee for ever.
>> Sing lullaby, &c. . . .
>
> Live stil with mee, and bee my love,
> And death wil mee refraine,
> Unlesse thow let mee dy with thee,
> To live with the [sic] againe.
>> Sing lullaby, &c.[19]

The appearance of this poem with several others on the names of Mary (all drawn from the Song of Songs) explains, in part, the convergence of erotic and devotional motifs. In the Song of Songs, the poet found divine sanction for his Marlovian echo, which would become part of the tradition: "Come live with me, and make this heart, thy Home." [20]

Perhaps the most interesting example of the competitive spirit of these paraphrases is found in the little work which is the source of the preceding quotation, Francis Quarles' *Sions Sonets* (1625). For a half century or longer the sonnet form had all but monopolized the lyric efforts of English poets. At the turn of the century, however, poets like William Alabaster, Henry Lok, Donne, and Herbert turned the sonnet to the expression of religious feeling. But Quarles did not stop here; he proceeded to make content rather than form the defining characteristic of the sonnet. A good part of the interest in his "sonets" derives from their odd shape. Varying in length from eight to ninety-six lines, these "sonets" in no case adhere to established norms. Yet the title is clearly meant to invite comparison. These are the "sonets" of "Sion," and their subject is the accepted theme of sonnet sequences, namely, erotic love. Perhaps even this divergence from the fourteen-line, iambic pentameter form in both its Petrarchan and English variations fits the purpose of Quarles' work. The term "sonet" refers, not to the formal arrangement of the poems, but to their thematic material.[21] That arrangement, moreover, is a mirror image of the subject matter of secular sonnets. This is not to say that the form of the poems is of no importance, for even here Quarles' lyrics must reveal some distinguishing feature. Thus, the apparent weakness of the sequence is its truest strength; the effect of the title is rhetorical. Like the title of Baldwin's paraphrase, it reminds the reader of the ambiguity involved in the contemplation of love. The love of God lent itself to the treatment of the richly erotic figures of the Canticles, and these, in turn, certainly resembled the traditional figures of the sonnet cycles. But the form of these divine "sonets," like their essential characteristics, was wholly different.

Careful reading of the numerous paraphrases of the Song of Songs will show that the desire to present an English audience with biblical lyrics is only half the story. These paraphrases are often so far removed from the original text as to require our consideration of the seventeenth-century concept of paraphrase. Here we find an almost universal acceptance of the view that the meaning of Scripture exists perfectly only in some nonlinguistic Form. There are three ways to make this Form known: through translation, paraphrase, and explication. Some writers, John Weemes, for instance, limited the means to only two. First, since not all men could read Greek and Latin (at least with sufficient ease to understand their original meaning), translation was of paramount importance. The second was paraphrase: "The second way how God maketh the Scripture plaine unto us, is by paraphrasing it, which goeth in a larger circuit of words than a translation doth, and this is called *tirgam* a Paraphrase." [22]

It seems clear that the poet who paraphrased the Song of Songs was at the same time explicating Scripture. In fact, so immersed in the allegorical meaning of the text could he become that in his fervor he might forget (as does William Loe) long passages. Of course, most paraphrases are apocopated in one way or another, even when they are much longer than their original. In *Microbiblion* (1629), for example, Simon Wastell allows his amplification of a single verse to stand as his entry for the Canticles.[23] Furthermore, nearly all paraphrases are preceded by explanatory prefaces, or, as in the case of Wither and Quarles, accompanied by marginal glosses. Ainsworth's *Annotations* openly represents the convergence of three genres: translation, verse paraphrase, and commentary. Understandably, a full appreciation of the way in which paraphrase functioned as a vehicle for biblical commentary (and with it an understanding of the influence of these paraphrases on the lyrics of the time) depends upon a knowledge of that exegetical tradition at large. And this is no simple matter, even when discussion is limited to the literature of the early seventeenth century. Nevertheless, important aspects of poems like Herbert's "Paradise" and Marvell's "Garden" are not fully understood until seen in the context of the allegorical tradition of the Song of Songs. Though that tradition finds its clearest expression in the sermons and treatises on the Canticles, it extends also into the graphic arts, into architecture, and into gardening. This of course is not surprising, for it is only to say that language is part of the life of a culture. Until we grasp the fuller implications of that part of the culture which concerns us, such truncated forms of that culture as are found in poetry will always appear crabbed and problematic. As we shall see, the language surrounding the Song of Songs, though a part of what we think of as seventeenth-century English, has certain particularities of its own.

INTERPRETATION OF THE SONG OF SONGS

The Song of Solomon[24] begins with an invitation: "Let him kisse mee with the kisses of his mouth: for thy Love is better then wine."[25] Typical in its syntactic shift, the passage shrouds the speaker's identity while revealing at once the poem's concern for the physically erotic. The speaker invites the kiss of a man whose love tastes better than wine. The next verse is in praise of the lover's name, which "is as ointment powred forth." We learn that he is beloved of the virgins. In the fourth verse, we come upon another shift, this time from direct address ("Draw me, we will runne after thee") to narrative. The King has brought the woman to his house, where they enjoy themselves. She and her friends (apparently the virgins) will remember him in the way they remember wine. At this point, the speaker pauses to describe herself:

> I am blacke, but comely, (O ye daughters of Jerusalem) as the tents of Kedar, as the curtaines of Solomon.
> Looke not upon me because I am blacke, because the Sunne hath looked upon me: my mothers children were angry with

me, they made me the keeper of the vineyards, but mine owne vineyard have I not kept.

Another break ensues in which the speaker once more addresses the lover, this time to inquire where he rests with his flock at noon. It would appear that the object of her affection is a shepherd. This question, occupying two verses, is followed by the shepherd's reply. He tells her to seek him among the hills, "beside the shepheards tents." There she is to rest the goats which have been placed in her care. After this the shepherd breaks into the first of a number of lavish descriptions of his beloved. She is like a company of horses; her cheeks are lovely and richly jeweled. Her neck glitters with golden necklaces.

The woman responds, praising her lover as a "bundle of myrrhe," promising that the night will be spent in love. Several problematic lines follow. But it seems safe to say that the chapter ends in another passage of hyperbolic praise of the beloved:

> Behold, thou art faire, my love: behold, thou art faire, thou hast doves eyes.
> Behold, thou art faire, my beloved; yea pleasant: also our bedde is greene.
> The beames of our house are Cedar, and our rafters of firre.

Chapter two begins with praise for the woman, who, compared with her sisters, is a lily among thorns. During the remainder of the chapter she returns this praise. Several verses here were of great importance to garden imagery:

> As the apple tree among the trees of the wood, so is my beloved among the sonnes. I sate downe under his shadow with great delight, and his fruit was sweete to my taste.
> Hee brought me to the banketting house, and his banner over mee, was love.
> Stay me with flagons, comfort me with apples, for I am sicke of love.

The woman describes the consummation of love: "His left hand is under my head, and his right hand doeth imbrace me." Later, she cautions her friends not to awaken her lover, who has fallen asleep. But even as she speaks she hears his voice as he comes running from the hills like a swift and agile young deer. He appears behind the lattice of the window, while she tells of his desire in this most celebrated passage:

> My beloved spake, and said unto me, Rise up, my Love, my faire one, and come away.
>
> For loe, the winter is past, the raine is over, and gone.
>
> The flowers appeare on the earth, the time of the singing of birds is come, and the voice of the turtle is heard in our land.
>
> The fig tree putteth foorth her greene figs, and the vines with the tender grape give a good smell. Arise, my love, my faire one, and come away.

Assuring herself that she and her lover belong together ("My beloved is mine, and I am his"), the woman calls upon the departed lover to hasten his return.

Chapter three relates the search of the beloved for her lover, whom she misses in her bed during the night. Failing to find him nearby, she ventures through the streets of the city, asking watchmen if they have seen him. They have not, and she continues until at last her search is rewarded. The lovers embrace, and in a state of excitement return to the house of the woman's mother. Having found her lover, the woman is reluctant to let him go. She again warns her friends not to awaken him; he has fallen asleep. The following verse seems to indicate another shift:

> Who is this that commeth out of the wildernes like pillars of smoke, perfumed with myrrhe and frankincense, with all powders of the merchant?

The answer to this question is somewhat oblique: "Behold his bed, which is Solomons: threescore valiant men are about it, of the valiant of Israel." The chapter ends with a description of the King's chariots, and the announcement of his marriage.

Chapter four begins with a repetition of lines in chapter one: "Behold, thou art faire, my love; behold thou art faire." This description, however, is more lengthy. The lover issues praise for the separate parts of the woman's body: for her eyes, hair, lips, breasts. Her neck is like the Tower of David, built for an armory "whereon there hang a thousand bucklers, all shields of mightie men." Because she is without spot, the lover invites her once again to leave with him from Lebanon, and to look down with him from the mountain of leopards. He has been ravished by her beauty:

How faire is thy love, my sister, my spouse! how much better is thy love then wine! and the smell of thine oyntments then all spices!

Thy lips, O my spouse! drop as the hony combe: hony and milke are under thy tongue, and the smell of thy garments is like the smell of Lebanon.

It is in this context that we first encounter the text which is of the greatest importance to this study:

A garden inclosed is my sister, my spouse: a spring shut up, a fountaine sealed.

The figure of the enclosed garden is developed in detail to the end of chapter four, and into chapter five:

Thy plants are an orchard of pomegranates, with pleasant fruits, Camphire, with Spikenaed [sic].

Spikenard and Saffron, Calamus and Cynamom, with all trees of Frankincense, Mirrhe and Aloes, with all the chiefe spices.

A fountaine of gardens, a well of living waters, and streames from Lebanon.

Awake, O Northwinde, and come thou South, blow upon my garden, that the spices thereof may flow out: let my beloved come into his garden, and eate his pleasant fruits.

Now there is another shift. The woman has been sleeping, though not soundly, when she hears her lover knocking at the door and calling to her. Chilled and damp from the night air, he asks admittance to her chambers. Dripping perfume and moved with pity, the woman opens the door only to discover that her lover has gone. Again she searches the city streets for him, but this time success eludes her. In desperation she instructs her friends to carry the news to him that she is "sicke of love." The friends wonder why they should so trouble themselves over this particular lover. The woman explains: "His hands are as gold rings set with the Berill: His belly is as bright ivorie, overlayd with Saphires." His kiss, again, is sweet, and he is altogether lovely: "This is my beloved."

At the beginning of chapter six the "daughters" or friends of the Bride offer to join her search for the Bridegroom. Where should they go to seek him? In verses which became familiar in both literary and graphic sources, the Bride answers:

> My beloved is gone downe into his garden, to the beds of spices, to feede in the gardens, and to gather lillies.
> I am my beloveds, & my beloved is mine: he feedeth among the lillies.

The love duet continues as the lover interrupts with praise for his beloved, whom he compares in beauty to Jerusalem. Paradoxically, she is as "terrible as an armie with banners." She is undefiled; among all women (the daughters of her mother), she is supreme (chapter six). Just as abruptly, the lover recalls that he is in his garden:

> I went downe into the garden of nuts to see the fruits of the valley, and to see whether the vine flourished, and the pome-granats budded.

In the seventh chapter, the shepherd compares his "Shulamite" to the growth of the garden. She is like a palm tree; her breasts are like "clusters of grapes." The lover vows to embrace the tree and to partake of the fruit of the vine.

In the final chapter we detect several echoes of earlier verses. Again, for example, we hear that the lover's left hand is beneath his beloved, and that his right arm is about her. Again the friends are warned not to disturb the sleeper. Once more, too, the speaker asks: "Who is this that commeth up from the wildernesse, leaning upon her beloved?" And we encounter yet another reference to the apple tree: "I raised thee up under the apple tree: there thy mother brought thee forth, there she brought thee forth, that bare thee."

The next two lines seem unrelated to the preceding, but since they are of great importance to the allegorical tradition they must be noted:

> Set mee as a seale upon thine heart, as a seale upon thine arme: for love is strong as death . . . .
> Many waters cannot quench love, neither can the floods drowne it: if a man would give all the substance of his house for love, it would utterly be contemned.

Verses eight through nine speak of a concern for a little sister who has no breasts: What shall be done when she is older, and men pursue her? "If she be a wall," we read, "we will build upon her a palace of silver: and if she bee a dore, we will inclose her with boards of Cedar." Presumably, verse ten is in reply to this question, for the speaker claims to be a wall, and to have breasts like towers. As if for this reason, she also claims to have found favor in her lover's eyes.

A switch to narrative brings us to a discussion of a vineyard in Baalhamon, once owned by Solomon. King Solomon had rented the vineyard to tenants for a thousand pieces of silver. The speaker, who seems now to own the vineyard, states (as if in direct address to Solomon) that Solomon must have a thousand, and those who labor in the field two hundred, pieces of silver. In the closing verse of the Song of Songs the anxious Bride implores her lover to make a swift return:

> Thou that dwellest in the gardens, the companions hearken to thy voice: cause me to heare it.
> Make haste, my beloved, and be thou like to a Roe, or to a yong Hart upon the mountaines of spices.

This brief description should suggest some of the difficulties faced by the men who attempted to explicate the Song of Songs, difficulties no doubt compounded by the persistent challenge to justify the Song before its critics. Commentators who set about this Sisyphean task had first to confront the vexed question of how to explain the density of Solomon's language: Why was the Song of Songs so obscure? How were they to explain its disjointed narrative? And what of its shifts in person and tense? Above all, what of its lavish, patently erotic descriptions? For the most part, answers to these basically stylistic questions took the form of allegorical interpretation. Although to some extent allegorical commentary applied to all Scripture, with such works as the Apocalypse and the Song of Songs it was always more important. Allegorical interpretation (a misnomer to be sure, since allegory was itself only one level of a metaphoric understanding of the Bible) proceeded on the assumption that scriptural meanings might legitimately be construed on several levels. Literally, the Song of Songs was composed to be sung at Solomon's wedding, an historical event. Thus, it represented the physical union of Solomon and the daughter of an Egyptian Pharaoh. Since the purpose of the Holy Ghost was never simply to relate the truth of history, but to reveal the mystery of divine love, this actual marriage must be seen on another —the allegorical—level, where the simple historical fact shadowed forth and lyrically expressed the love between Christ and his Spouse, the Church. The subtitle of Richard Sibbes' *Bowels Opened* (1639) is typical of this allegorical view. These sermons on the Canticles unfolded "A Discovery of the Neere and deere Love, Union and Communion betwixt Christ and the Church, and consequently betwixt Him and every beleeving soule." The last phrase points out that ingenious exegesis did not stop with allegory. For the "Church" was itself a complex figure. One must consider the tropological (personal) and anagogical (experiential) meanings of the Song before he could fully comprehend the mystery.

According to this view, only part of the difficulty in reading the Song of Songs could be attributed to shifts in tense, person, and number. Actually, the mystery derived not from a linguistic source at all but from the obscurity of the true subject of the Canticles, from the "parables and darke speeches" which veiled "verye divine heavenlye matter." Thus, commentators believed the Song of Songs to be deliberately obscure. Such an interpretation gained a distinct advantage by imputing wisdom to Scripture's divine author, the Holy Ghost. Its adherents held that the method used by the Holy Ghost served two good purposes, "not onelye that the eyes of the wicked might be stopped from beholding spiritual comfort: but also that the good might know, that whatsoever light they have, they have it from him, ..." [26] Rather than a weakness, this obscurity was a strength. William Gouge, who set out to answer Castalio's attack on the Song, admitted that his adversary was right in one important matter: Solomon's Song was not to be approached "rashly or unadvisedly." Certainly there was ample opportunity here for the sinful mind to discover purely physical (or literal) meanings in the love passages. But this fact should not mislead the righteous. They must see here not the failing of the Holy Ghost but the sad indication of human depravity. When the allegory of the text was properly unfolded by a true and learned interpreter, the proper reader would see in this love lyric "the holy of holies." [27] Such a view, as we can see, did more than exonerate the author of God's Word: it justified the role of commentators on the Song of

Songs. And this justification was a ready tool to poets, whose paraphrases were executed under the same pious design.

So great was the impetus of this allegorical view that certain writers (Beza, for example) were led to deny the literal meaning of the text entirely. Such repudiation of the physically erotic elements in the Song of Songs is indicative of that uneasiness concerning the Canticles felt as far back as the earliest rabbinical writers. This was, nevertheless, an extreme position. Even the Song's most loving exponent, St. Bernard, believed that the Song was actually sung at Solomon's nuptials. For men like Beza, however, assent to this interpretation threatened the serious understanding of the work, which, since its subject matter was "altogether allegoricall and enigmatical," was properly "to bee taken and altogether to be understood in a spirituall sense." Beza insisted that the means of expression—and the means only—involved "things naturall and corporeall." [28]

To one degree or another Beza's view was shared by many, especially by writers with a mystical turn of mind. Commentaries like those of St. John of the Cross were grounded on an even more thoroughgoing denial of the literal meaning of the text. In his explication of *The Spiritual Canticle* (1584), St. John defended in the most vigorous terms what he considered the inscrutable mystery of the Song of Songs. Its obscurity was not merely valuable but necessary. Nor could the reason for this necessity be discovered by learned explorations of the text; on the contrary, it was rooted irrevocably in the limitations of the human understanding. The true subject of the Song of Songs was the wonder of the mystical state, and this no words could ever express. For this reason, it was foolish to approach the figures in the Song of Songs with any pretense at rationality; these figures merely hinted at the ineffable splendors of spiritual marriage. Such an admittedly subjective attitude led St. John to the relativistic view "that everyone may pluck advantage" from the Song of Songs "according to his manner and to the measure of his spirit." The only matter of any consequence was the reader's attitude, for without "the simplicity of the spirit of love and understanding embodied in them," readers might easily mistake the Song of Songs for "nonsense rather than the expression of reason." [29] St. François de Sales writes that when St. Thomas was asked whether he would finish the commentary on the Canticles begun by St. Bernard, he responded in words similar to St. John's: unless he possessed the spirit of Bernard, such a task would be impossible.[30]

Morton Bloomfield is probably right in saying that, while most biblical writers proclaim their interest in the four levels of biblical meaning, in practice they seem reluctant to follow these through.[31] But for many writers of the Renaissance it would be just as true to say that these levels were thought to merge into each other. John Weemes, for example, considered the meaning of Scripture to be divided, first into a simple, then into a compound, sense. His distinction is the one I refer to in speaking of the individual as opposed to the general application of Scripture. Weemes goes on to break these two classes down; the simple sense (despite efforts to fragment it further) "is the sense, which agrees to one onely, and hath but one part (to wit, the literall sense)."[32] The compound sense "is that whereof there are two parts, literall and figurative, to make up one sense, which is fulfilled two manner of wayes, *Historicê* and *Propheticê* in the type, and literally in the thing signified."[33] In other words, the compound sense encompasses the literal meaning; but the converse would not be true. Again, both historical and prophetic meanings may be divided into "proper" and "figurative" classes. This is how Weemes distinguishes the "Historicall" from the "allegoricall" level. For while the historical may be figurative (i.e., refer to the analogy between two objects), the allegorical transcends the simple apprehension of correspondences: "An Allegoricall sense is that sense which the words meane not at the first: but that which the Author intends either in words or matter."[34]

The last quotation lends voice to the typical Renaissance semantic argument which holds that meaning, especially sacred meaning, exists independent of linguistic forms. Allegory transcends history and parable precisely in the way in which it apprehends this "mysticall" meaning beyond form. Allegory does not stop with the simple relation of the truth of history; it fully renders the glory of the future and of all time. Here we come upon what seems, perhaps, a confusing use of language. For while Weemes has already argued that allegory is identical to the "mysticall" meaning of

Scripture, he now insists that the "mysticall" dimension is divided into levels, the allegorical, tropological, and anagogical. His explanation is interesting in that it shows the way in which the commentator could hold the various levels to be, simultaneously, both different and the same: "These are not properly divers senses, but divers applications of one sense to our instruction, faith, and manners." [35] The levels of Scripture, in other words, corresponded in their application to different aspects of the spiritual life. The allegorical implications of allegory were the typological relations between the Old and New Testaments. The tropological understanding of Scripture concerned the relation between biblical metaphor and human conduct. The anagogical level (preeminently the domain of the finest seventeenth-century poets) applied "when things literally expressed, doe signifie something in heavens blisse." [36]

SPIRITUAL MARRIAGE

Clearly, the distinctions among the various levels of biblical interpretation are not easy to pin down, and the same applies to the distinction between the aspects—individual and general—of particular figures which were part of that system of discourse. This point is of great importance when we consider such figures as the "Church," which is the "Bride" represented in the Song of Songs.[37] Both figures are ambiguous, referring alternatively to the Church at large or to the individual soul. The reader must decide whether a writer, in speaking of the Church, refers to the Congregation or to the particular member who is a microcosm of the whole. It may be that the context of the utterance in question allows no decision, or demands a reading in which both interpretations apply. Nevertheless, this ambiguity is an ever-present factor in interpreting many sacred poems, and it is a frequent source of density in so-called "metaphysical" poetry. Donne's sonnet, "Show me deare Christ, thy Spouse," is a case in point. Here the ambiguous meaning of the term "Spouse" is the crux of a paradox in which the form and statement of the poem are mutually exclusive. The poem begins with the speaker's prayer that he be shown the "Spouse." His intensely devout posture asserts what the implied statement of his question denies, namely, that the speaker is himself the Bride of Christ. The conflict in the poem deals with the speaker's vision; one may only be shown what he does not already see, or what he presently sees in an inadequate way.

Critics have argued the relevance of this sonnet to our understanding of Donne's own doubts about the Church of England.[38] Certainly the question concerning the physical location of the Visible Church emerges in the poem. This appears in more than the geographical references, which present little difficulty in themselves. It is the subject of the contrast between "me" and "us." The latter term applies to the Church of England, the former to the speaker who is praying for guidance. But there is no necessary connection between the two. The "us" refers to the physical group where perhaps the Spouse dwells, while the "we" is a group which —when his search is successfully over—the speaker may join. Though not mutually exclusive, the groups are distinct. In any case, the figure of the Church cannot be limited to a single level of meaning. In fact, the question of the whereabouts of the Visible Church is structurally subordinated to a much deeper one, this concerning the condition of the speaker's soul. The sonnet is, after all, the speaker's prayer that he be shown what is already known to be "bright and cleare." And here is the crucial paradox in the poem. For if the "Spouse" is bright and clear, why should her whereabouts be obscured to men? And why to the speaker in particular?

As we reread the poem we see that the question raised is not simply whether one or another of a sect's worldly claims should be honored. There is a contradiction at the very core of the poem. We know that the speaker's soul is "amorous"; he is found in fervent prayer. Once the devotional context of the poem is held in mind, we see that the speaker's questioning is rhetorical. He asks:

> Dwells she with us, or like adventuring knights
> First travaile we to seeke and then make love?
> Betray kind husband thy spouse to our sights,
> And let myne amorous soule court thy mild Dove,
> Who is most trew, and pleasing to thee, then
> When she'is embrac'd and open to most men.

Consider: How does the speaker know Christ as a "kind husband"? The answer to this question would seem to be that he does so in the same way that he knows his soul to be amorous: by experience. Yet this would seem to contradict the implicit statement that the "Spouse" has not been revealed to his sight.

But the meditative tradition which draws so often on the figure of spiritual marriage offers a way out of this apparent dilemma. For the opposite of spiritual marriage is spiritual fornication. And the speaker's wish to court Christ's Spouse certainly does not introduce the figure of harlotry into the poem. Quite the opposite. It points rather to the anxiety of even the most "amorous soule." Miss Gardner offers a rich hint in this direction as she reminds her audience of Donne's allusion to the apocalyptic tradition.[39] All souls must remain in an anxious state, to one degree or another, until the final wedding in the New Jerusalem. Yet the Church of Christ has been from the moment of the Sacrifice "embrac'd and open to most men." It was for this opening, and this embracing, that Christ came into the world. The irony of Donne's sonnet rests partly on the speaker's point of view. More than the "amorous soule" impatient for the end of time, he is one whose mind is jaded by the factions of competing religious claims: as if the Church could sleep a thousand years, and then peep out for one year to take a lover. To conceive of Christ's Church in such a way is to impute arbitrariness rather than mercy to divine love. And if the beauty of divine love were not manifest, why should the speaker's soul be "amorous"? It is because of the perfect love of God that the speaker courts the true Church, as if seeking some visible sign of the body of which he is already an invisible member.

A quite similar conceit is found in Joseph Beaumont's "The True Love-Knott." This poem bears the epigraph taken from the Canticles, "I am my Beloveds, & my Beloved is mine," and begins with a description of the spiritual combat. Two lovers are locked in pitched battle, which both are bound to lose yet neither can but win. This paradox testifies to the very nature of that "Sweet" love which is "Captivitie." The characters in the poem, "Shee" and "Love," complain of their condition. But even before the battle began, Love knew that, whether he won or lost, union would be the triumphant end; he knew that both lovers must lose in order to win. The analogy is clear: Christ knew that he must surrender his life in order to tie the "Love-Knott" with his Bride. The poem ends in paraphrase of the Song of Songs:

> Then this
> The Spouses Song & Triumph is:
> *Not Thou, but I and Thou, are Thine,*
> *Not I, but Thou and I are Mine.*[40]

Here is the paradox of religious experience in which only by losing one's life will it be gained, of that love described by Solomon which is as strong as death.

The connection in Donne's poem between the "amorous soule" and the divine "Spouse" shows how closely the levels of biblical meaning could function. The allegorical understanding of the Song of Songs allowed for treatment of the most sacrosanct subject in language commonly linked with the troubled passions of the individual. Donne's speaker, like Solomon, was a man placed in history to endure the temptations of flesh. Thus the literal meaning of the Song of Songs had its own integrity, and this helped preserve a vitally erotic tradition. It was in this physicality that poets found the most powerful claim of their verse paraphrases over the rival sonnet sequences and *libertin* pastorals. The invitation of the "amorous soule" was—for the pious as well as for the wicked— still to frolic in physical delights. But for men like Gervase Markham, the carpe diem sung by Solomon in his "eight eclogues" had divine sanction:

> Come, come my Love, the best joy of my minde,
> The onlie one is pleasing in mine eies,
> Let us goe forth and frolike with the winde,
> Sport with the ayre, and wanton with the skies,
> Let us ore view the fields, love let us finde,
> Whence all the meadowes beauties doe arise.[41]

The allusive force of the marriage figure as seen in these two poems derives partly from its great flexibility. Its meaning could range in at least two directions, from the human model to the divine, and vice versa. While it was common for treatises on marriage to include references to Solomon's wedding, and to argue from this example the need for a purifying of one's motives to ensure a happy married life, at the same time (and perhaps this is less generally the case) spiritual matters might be treated through reference to conjugal love. The last chapter of Robert Crofts' *The Lover* (1638), for example, is entitled "Of the good use of this Nuptiall Love, and so concluding with a briefe discourse of Divine Love," and begins with the proclamation that no man should demean the love of God by belittling the gift of a wife. If man would exemplify the wisdom of Solomon, he must discern in conjugal affections the benefice of a loving Deity. This does not mean that the two forms of love are not in some sense in competition; heavenly love, if considered superior, must be in some way comparable to the more typical human impulse. It is the comparison which makes selection significant here. But at the same time, certain purposes required emphasis on the comparison, rather than on the choice. The consecrated love of married couples could be seen as a hieroglyphic shadowing forth the Form of its heavenly counterpart. Because of this comparison, Robert Crofts could argue that any denigration of earthly love, per se, was tantamount to blasphemy. Love is a creation of God; it mirrors his magnificence, his productive power. And if properly employed, even the love of the world is a means of spiritual ascent: "So, as wee may make, a very good use of Earthly felicities in this respect, (as men doe of Spectacles;) for by, and through these, our dimme Eyes may see the cleerer into heavenly Excellencies. And consequently, bee the more enamour'd of them, and so stirred up to seek and enjoy them." [42]

Regardless of how arcane its true subject matter was taken to be, language allusive to the Song of Songs was seldom arid or prudish. There is nothing in the Song of Songs, writes Joseph Hall, *"that savours not of extasie, and spirituall ravishment."* [43] Even in devotional treatises (in some cases, especially there), wherever paraphrase of the Canticles is part of the writer's technique, a vividness of erotic detail appears:

> Thus then, THEO: our Saviour shewing the most delightfull bosome of divine love to the devote soule, he drawes her wholy to himselfe, gathers her up, and doth, as it were, fould all her powers, in the bosome of his more then motherly sweetenesse, and then burning with love, he thrusteth, joyneth, presseth, and

glueth her to the lips of his delightes, and to his delicious breastes, kissing her in the holy kisse of his mouth, and making her taste his dugges more sweete then wine.[44]

The repetition here of figures representing erotic love—drawing, thrusting, joining, kissing—suggests a physical, even violent, union of lovers. Similar examples are legion in the literature of the late Renaissance. To mention only one, Crashaw describes the "immortall kisses" of the divine Spouse in singularly passionate language:

> Amorous Languishments, Luminous trances,
>   Sights which are not seen with eyes,
> Spirituall and soule peircing glances.
>   Whose pure and subtle lightning, flies
> Home to the heart, and setts the house on fire;
> And melts it downe in sweet desire:
>   Yet doth not stay
> To aske the windowes leave, to passe that way.
>
> Delicious deaths, soft exhalations
> Of soule; deare, and divine annihilations.[45]

Crashaw is writing in the tradition of the Song of Songs, where he finds his model of the languishing lover. Similarly, the first engraving in the fifth book of Quarles' *Emblemes* (1635) bears the inscription, "I charge you, O daughters of Jerusalem, if ye find my beloved, that ye tell him, that I am sick of love." The emblem depicts the Spouse with her heart pierced by the flaming arrow of love, and is followed by this paraphrase of the Song of Songs:

> I charge you, Virgins, as you hope to heare
>   The heav'nly Musick of your Lovers voice;
> I charge you by the solemne faith ye beare
>   To plighted vowes, and to the loyall choice
> Of your affections; or, if ought more deare
> You hold; by Hymen; by your marriage joyes,
>   I charge you, tell him, that a flaming dart,
>   Shot from his Eye, hath pierc'd my bleeding heart;
> And I am sick of love, and languish in my smart.[46]

It should be clear from this short passage that love, even in its most passionate form, was not intrinsically evil. Love, as William Gouge wrote, was a *"uniting affection."* [47] His argument proceeded in the following way: manifestly, in no case could virtue become vice, for if it did, then it was not virtue. It was equally clear that the love of God was no vice. Thus, the affection of love had absolutely no moral consequences: "Affections are as they are well or ill used." Whether good or evil in its consequences, love remained love. It was for this reason that God commanded His children to love all men, their enemies included. In His divine wisdom, He knew that no man could be identified with a single quality, no matter how repugnant that quality might be. Christ died having eternally conquered sin, yet he loved every sinner who would ever live. Thus, like fire, love was capable of good as well as evil. It offended only when it was not appropriate to its object, when, for example, it was withdrawn from the superior to be attached to the inferior. This argument was a logical development of the view that love tended toward union with the loved. Since the inclination toward one object as against another rested in the will (the ultimate seat of man's eternal destiny), here lay the potentiality of separation from or union with God. Fray Luis de Granada recognized the improper placing of love as the primary hindrance to devotion. Properly in love with God, man is rather "far in love with himselfe, and is a great follower of hys owne will and appetite: whereby it commeth that hee cannot denie himselfe, nor imbrace the Crosse of Christ, nor mortifie hys owne nature, and so hee cannot attaine unto the perfection of the Evangelicall life." [48]

As we can see, sacred poetry did not impute intrinsic evil to the passion of lust, for to do so was to cast doubt upon God's mercy. He created man's affections, and these alone could aim at good as well as evil. The soul, like the body, could and did experience lust. And more important, even the Holy Mother, and God Himself, lusted and satisfied their lust with a "kisse." The question of value entered only with the object toward which the affections were directed. (We will remember that Origen made the same point at the beginning of his *Homilies* on the Song of Songs.[49]) Love of whatever kind—whether active or passive, good or bad—tended toward union with some object outside the self. And the choice of that object rested with the will. It was the Virgin's will which resisted corruption by the flesh. The purity of that will (typified by her virginity), rehearsed in the sermons commemorating her purification and solemnized by the lives of those women who followed her in their renunciation of physical lust, directed her toward union. The "holy flame" of her desire ended in her wedding with God.

The concept of the spirit's lust for union with its Spouse was a familiar motif in the works of Renaissance mysticism. Francis Rous, one of the most unjustly neglected of seventeenth-century English prose writers and heir to the influence of the Counter-Reformation in Spain, wrote a treatise, entitled *The Mysticall Marriage* (1635), based on this single metaphor. This brief discourse falls little short, in quality, of similar works by St. Teresa, St. John of the Cross, Fray Luis de Granada, and Juan de los Angeles; and deserves comparison with St. John's *Spiritual Canticle*. They are alike both in impassioned personal view of biblical metaphor and in cleanness and simplicity of style.

According to Rous, spiritual lust is of two kinds, one positive, the other negative. The spirit lusts, just as does the flesh, but the spirit lusts against the flesh, and for the objects of the spirit.[50] The prayer of the soul is that this lust be—not stopped—prolonged until the Bridegroom enters the chamber of the soul: "Yea tell him resolutely thou wilt not leave him till thou heare a voyce in thy soule, saying: *My welbeloved is mine, and I am my welbeloveds*. To this end bee still gazing on him, and still calling on him; *Kisse me with the kisses of thy mouth*; Yea kisse my soule with such a kisse of thy spirit, that they may be no longer two, but one spirit: . . . ."[51] Since man was breathed from heaven, his original, his essence, and his character "must be divine and heavenly: For to a divine and heavenly essence, can agree no other but a divine and heavenly happinesse." The soul lusts for union with its essence. Indeed, so strong is its desire that Solomon describes it as a form of sickness: "Tel him that thou art sicke of love. . . . It is the right voyce of the spirit, *I found him whom my soule loveth, I held him and would not let him go*."[52]

It would be right enough, though insufficient, to point out that examples of erotic language based on the Song of Songs were justified by their allegorical intentions. Such a view is misleading insofar as it apologizes for the eroticism in the Song of Songs.

Unless we see the full power of the erotic language in the tradition of the Canticles, we miss an important aspect of Renaissance poetic culture. Poets did not, as some critics would have us believe, simply polarize lust and love. The latter word, until placed in a proper context, is too passive to describe the passion sung by Solomon. The Song of Songs dealt in no uncertain terms with the fever-burn of lust:

> Say blessed Poet, with what sacred fire
> Blazes thy soul? this flight of thine is higher
> Then ever fancie yet upon vain wings
> Could fanne to.[53]

In his "Meditation upon the Song of Songs," John Saltmarsh writes that Solomon's soul was one afire, that his passion lifted his soul higher than the "vain wings" of secular poetic fancy. It was quite natural for such passion to generate heat. Clearly Saltmarsh says nothing to suggest the picture of a man in full control of his emotions. Instead, he describes the poet Solomon as "drunk with holinesse . . . ravisht with a holy lust." In examining the nature of this lust we begin to see that recurring pattern of parallelism with secular poetry:

> When to these flames my fainter flames I trust,
> I see thee ravisht with a holy lust:
> There is a *Cupid* more divine I finde
> Then that same wanton wandring boy that's blinde;
> I see there's arrows too, but yet I spie
> That they are pointed with more sanctitie:
> There is a *Venus* too, but not like this;
> One whom the Trinitie will court and kisse:
> There's *Hymens* tapers too, though not the same;
> These lighten with a farre more holy flame.[54]

From one point of view, then, the Song of Songs was an un-interrupted prayer for the satisfaction of a burning lust. As we read in *A Treatise of the Love of God*, this explains why Solomon chose to begin his Song with so obvious a prayer for erotic contact: "Let him deigne me with a Kisse of his mouth." The kiss, writes St. François de Sales, is the most ancient and best figure of "perfect love," and thus is an appropriate beginning for the "Canticle of Canticles." [55] Moreover, this judgment applied no matter what level of Scripture was under consideration. John Dove writes, for example, that

> These wordes are either the prayers of *Salomon* in his owne person, or the meditations of every particular member of Christ, or the longing desire and expectation of the Fathers, which groned under the burden of Ceremonies and carnall Rites, or the allegorie of the Church in general, under both the Law and the Gospell.[56]

Almost any interpretation of the kiss led to the same conclusion; as St. Bernard had written, it was a "token of reconciliation," which should be understood as the mediation between flesh and spirit: "The mouth which kisseth, is the Word which assumeth; The Mouth which is kissed, the Flesh which is assumed; the Kisse it selfe the Person it selfe, which consisteth of both Natures, the Mediator, Jesus Christ." [57] The wedding of the flesh and spirit is the ultimate subject of this "Epithalamion." That consummation, which was to be repeated two more times before time came to an end, was typified appropriately by a kiss.

Henoch Clapham, one of the most spirited and prolific of seventeenth-century commentators, wrote a treatise on the second verse of Solomon's Song, much of which is meant to clarify the meaning of this mystical kiss. Clapham begins by pointing out that in this passage the Church expresses her affection in two ways: first, in prayer; second, in "setting forth the excellencie of her beloveds Love." After further dividing the prayer into two parts, form and matter, he goes on to say of that prayer: "[*Let him kisse mee*] it is as if she said in moe words, *O Father of heaven, vouchsafe to hasten the sending forth of* Messiah, *who hast appointed him to be a light to the Gentiles.*" [58] For Clapham, the invitation represents the cry of the multitude of believers in every dispensation for the coming of Christ. As we know, the Incarnation was construed as the wedding of spirit and flesh, God and man. It was, however, only one of three such celebrations; in the fulness of time, Christ would wed on three different occasions. The first meaning of the kiss was derived from the reference to the physicality of the Incarnation, to the first appearance of the Messiah. Thus, one meaning referred to the past. A second meaning looked to the distant future, to the coming of Christ—not in flesh but in glory. Finally, there was the immediately apprehended relevance of this kiss. Clapham urges his reader to see that Solomon describes not one but many kisses; and the plural form of the word entailed a mystery. For while it was true enough that "no doubt the Gentile Queene, Pharaoh's daughter, had no slender affection for communion with Salomon, the glorious tipe of our Messiah," and that the two historical lovers engaged in many "kisses," the multiplicity here, from a standpoint of the individual soul, referred to the intimate joining of all the faculties of the "soule and body; sense and affections, and all active powers" with the spiritual Bridegroom.

After all, was not the kiss (or spirit of the mouth) in other words the breath? And what does the breath refer to but life? God breathed on dust, and there was life; wherever God breathes, life is quickened in the lifeless. The most powerful example of this breathing was the Virgin Birth. With just such a divine kiss, God quickens the conscience of man. In Mary's womb the Word was quickened. Solomon's kiss was, in the final analysis, an emblem of regeneration, representing the life-giving power of God. In *A Brief Exposition . . . Upon the whole Book of Canticles* (1655), John Cotton describes Solomon's kiss as "a speaking to the heart," an affectionate response to the love revealed in Scripture: just as Christ "kisseth us when he speaketh to our hearts in his Word, we kisse him when we [r]eceive his Word with faith, love, joy, obedience." [59]

Here is the sense of Crashaw's figure, "immortal kisses." They are the kisses which endow the kissed with immortality, the tokens of regeneration. Looked at the other way, because the blessing of the Sacrifice endures forever, the effects of the kisses never end. Which is the same as saying that the kisses continue forever. Crashaw does not by any means present us with a unique poetic example of interest in this figure. The image of the divine kiss had its own importance in the poetry of the seventeenth century. John Davies' "A Desire of the loving Soule, of God, to be kissed with the kisse of Peace" is very close to verse paraphrase of the Song of Songs:

> Kisse me, ô kisse me, with Loves honyed *Kisse*,
>   ô dearest Love, and sweet'st-Heart of my Soule;
> Whose love is like pure Wine that cordiall is;

> & doth sowre cares, with Comforts sweet, controle
> Thy *Name* is like to sweet suffused *Balme;*
> which makes *chast Soules* ev'n sick for love of thee.[60]

The kiss, therefore, is the spiritual analogue to the desired consummation with the physical loved one. And its ramifications include the longing of the soul for spiritual delight, implicitly, for mystical union, and for "sinnes release." In the latter instance, St. François de Sales summed up the complex metaphor of the kiss by saying that the lips of the Spouse are scarlet, for the blood of Christ.[61]

The fact is that the "kisse" was a type of the Crucifixion. In an interesting discussion of the three marriages of Christ, John Dove launches into a lengthy commentary on the divine kiss. Alluding to St. Bernard, Dove addresses himself to the scene of the Passion:

> His hands bored, that hee might give unto us; his side opened, that in all the bowels of his compassion he might love us; his feete fastened to the Crosse, as if he had a disposition to tarrye with us; his bodie racked, and stretched out to the length, that a man might tell all his bones, to bestow himselfe plentifully upon us; his armes expanded to embrace us, his head hanging downe to kisse us; as if he did say, Come kisse me.[62]

From here, Dove proceeds to consider three types of kisses. Mary Magdalene kissed the Saviour to show her humility; Judas betrayed the Saviour with a kiss. But as Scripture copiously demonstrates, the marital kiss is a holy kiss, and it is to this that Christ's Crucifixion (all its implicit humility notwithstanding) must be compared. John Davies' "The longing of the Soule to be with God" closely follows the same interpretation:

> Celestiall *Bridegroome*, kisse thy Spouse, my Soule,
>   With kisses sweet of unconceived *peace;*
> On thy transpierced *palme* her name enrowle,
>   With thy sinne-purging *bloud* my sinnes release.[63]

CHAPTER II

The Enclosed Garden

THE VIRGIN

In discussing the marriage figure and its relation to the Canticles tradition, we touched briefly on the figure of the Virgin. Bonnard's example (see note 8 to Chapter One), where paraphrase of the Song of Songs appears in the form of a Stabat Mater, is typical of the way in which Mary was cast in the role of Solomon's true Bride; similarly, in *The Sarum Missal*, verses from the Canticles heralded the Assumption of the Blessed Virgin as a type of that "spiritual conjunction" described in the Song of Songs. Among the passages drawn from the Canticles for the Vigil of the Assumption, the longest included iv.12: "Hortus conclusus soror mea, sponsa, hortus conclusus, fons signatus." [1] And in the *Pontificale Romanum*, Mary was the prototype of the Bride, whose wedding was celebrated repeatedly through time by the consecration of nuns ("Vultis benedíci, et consecrári, ac Dómino nostro Jesu Christo, summi Dei Fílio, desponsári? . . . Vólumus."), where echoes were heard from Solomon's Song:

Pósuit signum in fáciem meam, ut nullum praeter eum amatórem admíttam. . . .

Desponsári, dilécta, veni, hiems tránsiit, turtur carnit, víneæ floréntes rédolent. . . .

Annulo suo subarrhávit me Dóminus meus Jesus Christus, et tamquam sponsam decorávit me coróna.[2]

Association of the Virgin with the Song of Songs seems to account for her relation to the figure of the lily ("As the lillie among thornes, so is my love among the daughters"), which came to represent the Bride's uniqueness. As we read in Joseph Beaumont, Mary's "Virginity" far outshone the whiteness of the lily:

> Lillies are cleanly, white & sweet,
> And yet they have but dirty feet;
>> Their Roots from Earth
>> Never look forth,
>>> But grow
>>> Below.
> Onely this spotlesse Flowre, which plants her Root
> Deep in the Heavns, did never fowle her foot.

In fact, so important a figure is virginity that Beaumont attributes that quality to both male and female components of the Virgin Birth:

> For there She grew & flourished
> Before old *Time* began to bud:
>> Yea & brought forth
>> A Stem more worth
>>> Then all
>>> The Ball
> Of Heavn & Earth: The *VIRGIN SIRE* alone
> Eternally begat his *VIRGIN SONNE.*[3]

The theme of virginity, so much a part of monastic lore, was a favored motif in the legends of the saints' lives. Even the *Book of Margery Kempe* treats sexual abstinence as almost coincidental with virtue. A single example from *The Flowers of the Lives of the Most Renowned Saincts* (1632) may help show the relevance of this thematic interest to the subject of this study. St. Bridgett, herself the fruit of an illegitimate union, became aware while still a young girl that her physical beauty was the source of her attractiveness to men. She was deeply troubled. Since she "desired JESUS CHRIST FOR HER ONLY DEAR SPOUSE, and to consecrate her virginitie unto him," she prayed fervently that her beauty might be destroyed and her male suitors discouraged. Her prayer was answered when God caused her to lose one of her eyes, "which burst and dropt out of her head like a dissolved pearle." Now even her father (who had urged her to marry) allowed her to enter the nunnery. At this point in the story the Marian theme of miraculous birth begins to emerge. Legend has it that at the moment of Bridgett's receiving "the holy vayse of chastitie" from the bishop, a pillar of fire descended upon her, and at that moment, when she touched the altar, "which albeit it was of drie seasoned wood, yet at her touch, and in testimonie of her chastity, it waxed greene, and flourished afresh." [4] Immediately her eye—and with it her great beauty—was restored. It appeared at once to all that "her deare spouse would not endure, that she who had desired to loose her beautie to preserve her virginitie, should remayne in such deformitie." In the ritual life of the nunnery, no less than in the lives of saints, the figure of virginity lays weight on the exclusiveness of the Bride. Understandably, virginity and marriage would be apposite allegorical figures. As Rous writes in *The Mysticall Marriage*, "There is a law in heaven, that the heavenly Bride may at one time have but one Husband." [5]

The value of chastity reflects a view of history which is at the core of the Canticles tradition. The choice of a love object is made by the individual in time, and the marriage figure dramatizes the union of subject loving with object loved. Now movement between general and particular applications of the marriage figure has a temporal parallel; the ceremony, one might say, looks both ways in time while holding at once that time is an illusion. During the consecration of nuns (and before and after as well) the novitiates by the commitments of their individual wills enact the values of Mary's life. In this way, the figures of marriage and virginity function to express the exclusiveness of the participant in the drama. While it is perfectly clear that individual emulation of Mary presupposes a separation of two beings in time, it is not always so obvious that all such acts of the human will are made in time. The novitiates, like all the saints and the Holy Mother herself, were placed in the flow of human history; before there could be allegory there must be time. This means that every creature and every object must be seen in two temporal dimensions. And as we shall see, this temporal distinction greatly enriched the meaning of such figures as the enclosed garden.

Put another way, the last point means that according to biblical "facts" Solomon's court had an enclosed "pleasaunce," a garden where the King and his entourage in the actual past enjoyed the physical delights of spice trees and fountains. These same "facts" recalled that Solomon's choice (of wisdom over other values) brought with it untold riches. During his reign the Hebrew nation flourished in an unprecedented way; the temple was built with pillars of silver and floors of gold. Legend told how the Queen of Sheba traveled a great distance just to witness the rumored glory of Solomon's court. In a sixteenth-century needlework representing this encounter (fig. 1), we get a picture of Solomon's pleasance. Providing the backdrop of the scene, an enclosed garden, like the lavish vestments of the King and his courtiers, testifies with its turreted wall, its flower beds and fountain, to the fabulous riches of Israel.[6]

As the commentaries tell us, Solomon's pleasure garden bore witness not only to his worldly achievements but to that aspect of his character which held him short of perfection. Solomon was a "type" of Christ, to be sure.[7] But like his father, he was so because of his vices as well as his virtues; in typology, Solomon is both compared with and contrasted to the "true Solomon." As we read the following description of his glory, Solomon represents the highest potentialities, but also the most crushing limitations of the human self:

> He who planted himselfe vineyards, made him orchards of all manner of fruit, who had the gold of Kings and provinces, who had men singers and women singers the delights of the sonnes of men, who had nothing withheld from him of all his heart desired: who was seated in the blissefull *Eden* and *Paradise* of all content,

was still the Preacher who, after he had been

> glutted with all delicious viandes; crammed as it were with the pleasures of the world, wanting no delicie [sic] to relish his tast, no elegancie to delight his eie, no symphony to ravish and surfet his eare: when he had had his full repast in sinne, when he had run through *myriades* of delights, glutting all his five senses,[8]

commented only with bitterness on the very concept of human pleasure. From Origen's time, Ecclesiastes was believed to be the statement of Solomon's self-renunciation, and a full, wise commentary on the natural condition of life. Solomon's writings were of three kinds: moral (Proverbs), natural (Ecclesiastes), and unitive (the Song of Songs).[9] In the Song of Songs, Solomon transcended the limitations of the physical world, and with them, the constrictions of human life. In the last analysis, the Song of Songs treated the subject of unitive love, a form of love only dimly seen in Solomon's historic wedding. Similarly, the virtues of the Messiah were only partially manifest in Solomon. Because of the limitations upon his virtue, he succumbed to physical (the sign of spiritual) fornication; King Solomon's many wives and concubines had their allegorical significance.

But despite its limits, Solomon's virtue was eminently manifest in his love for his Bride. Whether to the Queen of Sheba or the daughter of Pharaoh, his marriage was a type of the union between flesh and spirit, and so his Bride was the proper first recipient of that lavish compliment, "A garden inclosed is my sister, my spouse: a spring shut up, a fountaine sealed." On the historical level, the Song of Songs told the story of this matchless human love, attesting to its color, richness, and passion. Even at this level, however, something of the true meaning of the enclosed garden and its related figures began to appear. For since the garden was enclosed, the spring shut up, the fountain sealed, the proper reader was informed about the qualities of Solomon's Bride, who was spotless, dovelike, virginal. And implicitly, the reader learned, too, of Solomon's discernment in selecting so worthy a Bride.

Nevertheless, that discernment had its limits, and these were of great importance. Solomon's infidelity, for example, was but one manifestation of the way in which even the worthiest man must answer to the limits imposed by the Fall. In just the same way, the virtues of Solomon's Bride foreshadowed the higher perfection of Mary, while reminding of the flaw in her predecessor, Eve. The glory of Solomon's wedding paralleled his triumph in the successful construction of the Temple; the two were similar in that both were temporary. Yet one aspect of the ceremony, the prophetic, was not subject to immediate dissolution. Insofar as it referred to the advent of a new dispensation, Solomon's epithalamion laid claim to temporal transcendence. Seen in a wider historical frame of reference, the nuptials celebrated the first of Christ's three marriages, which would be to the Virgin Mary.[10] At the moment of that union (the Annunciation) history changed forever; Mary became "true" Solomon's eternal Bride.

Of course this marriage paralleled and superseded the literal event described in the Song of Songs. It was, in fact, the very union toward which the desire of these lovers actually aimed, and properly so. For as we may judge from an emblem (fig. 2) in Otto van Veen's popular *Amoris Divini Emblemata* (1660), the Annunciation united the Virgin with the essence of love. The meaning of the emblem is provided in part by a text drawn from St. Augustine: "Ama amorem illius, qui amore tui descendit in uterum Virginis, & ibi amorem suum amori tuo copulavit, humiliando se, sublimando te, conjungendo lumen suæ æternitatis limo tuæ mortalitatis." Because of His strong affection ("for love is strong as death"), God humbled Himself to take on mortality. He entered the flesh in order to save man from it; He descended into the realm of time in order to lift man from it. Further commentary on the engraving is drawn from the sermons of St. Bernard on the Canticles. The two scenes, the Annunciation and the lovers' embrace, complement each other by presenting a dual representation of the union between Spirit and Word. In recognition of the honor bestowed on her, the Bride responds in the language of the Song of Songs: "Dilectus meus mihi, & ego illi. Ille intendit meæ liberationi, ego illius honori; ille saluti meæ, ego illius voluntati: ille mihi, & non alteri, quia una sum columba eius; ego illi, & non alteri: nec enim audio vocem alienorum." [11]

If we consider the icon (our fig. 3) representing the Song of Songs in Robert Whitehall's *Sive Iconum* (1677), the historical meaning of figure 1 should become clear. In this lovely engraving we find Solomon on his throne; above him the "curtains of Solomon" hang in rich folds. In the background, we see a sunken garden set within the palace courtyard, and enclosed with a stone railing. Standing at the entrance to the throne room, magnificently nimbed and bearing a cornucopia of flames, is Love. The halo and the flame bear testimony to the intensity of the feelings expressed in "The *SERAPHICK DIALOGUE*": "*Ego sum dilecti mei, & dilectus est meus.*" This emphasis on mutual belonging is strongly reinforced by the image of the enclosed garden; the Spouse belongs to the Lover exclusively. The accompanying text, however, reveals a paradoxical aspect of this exclusive belonging:

> *Christ* and his *Spouse* pathetically Court
> Each other, with unspeakable *Effort*:
> Their *Dialogues* are all of things above,
> Until at last they both *fall Sick of Love.*
> *Affection* heightned with a strong desire
> Is *restless* 'till it's end it can acquire.[12]

Though they belong to each other, and to each other only, their courtship is "pathetic," carried on with "unspeakable *Effort*." The pathetic aspect is explained by the fact that for a time the lovers reached for each other through the limited affections of Solomon and his Bride. Their effort was "unspeakable," as if spoken only through the mysterious language of the Song of Songs. Thus, Love hands Solomon the Book in which he is to write his Song. The lovers fall *"Sick of Love"* because, regardless of the intensity of their passion, their union must wait for the appointed hour. That hour, in turn, is the "end" toward which their "strong desire" aims. As Henoch Clapham writes, the kiss in the Song of Songs suggests the "means wherby the Virgin should conceive." [13]

The engraving from *Amoris Divini Emblemata*, then, is made up of two scenes, both understood as referring to the same mystery. In the moment she received the divine seed, the Holy Mother was embraced by Love, just as now (in the foreground) the cherubic Spouse is embraced by divine Cupid. Select among all women, Mary was that Venus whom the "Trinitie would court and kisse," the fulfillment, according to Luis de la Puente, of the prophecy of Solomon:

> Then was fullfilled that which her spouse sayed of her: *My sister spouse is a garden inclosed, a garden inclosed, a fountaine sealed up.* He twise calleth her an inclosed garden, for that shee was perfectly chaste both in soule, and in body, confirming it with a perpetuall vowe, which served as a locke for her greater security: adding for gardes, humility, modesty, silence, and abstinence, by reason whereof hee also calleth her a garden: to give us to understand, that her virginity was not barren, but accompanied with many flowers of vertues.[14]

The figure of the enclosed garden, image of the splendor of Solomon's kingdom and of his Bride, referred to the supernatural quality of the Virgin's chastity. Chosen by God, she remained untouched, enclosed, sealed. Though shut from the world in both body and spirit, yet she bore fruit; her garden flourished with the flowers of a new dispensation.

The Annunciation is, of course, a familiar subject in iconography. More often than not, paintings like Roger van der Weyden's "Annunciation" (fig. 4) follow the illustrations in missals and books of hours in showing traces of garden allegory; they remind the viewer that at a particular moment in time God entered a virgin womb. Then too, as in figure 5, a fusion of images associated with the garden sets up an implicit contrast between Eve and the terrestrial Paradise, on the one hand, and Mary and hortus conclusus on the other. These polarities find expression in the illustrated Bibles of the medieval period. In the Morgan Speculum—for that matter in every version of Speculum I have examined—each miniature forms part of a suite of scenes, which in turn reiterate the Christian theme of Fall and Redemption. Thus, around a given text of Scripture a cluster of images appears, representing the limitations of man and the power and mercy of God. Quite naturally, the first scene depicts the Expulsion of Adam and Eve from Paradise; the second shows Adam at his labors in the field. The initial sequence ends with a miniature of Noah's ark; we see the dove returning with the twig of olive in his beak.[15] Hence, the sequence moves from the Fall to its consequences to the promise of the approaching covenant between God and man.

The second sequence is composed of only two scenes: the Annunciation and hortus conclusus. As we can see, neither subject is drawn from Genesis—or even from Exodus, Judges, or Kings. In order to complete his sequence, the artist has gone beyond the Old Testament. In so doing he has achieved an impressive parallelism and contrast. Though directly antithetical to the Fall, these scenes also present a parallel to the return of the dove. The Annunciation is juxtaposed to the Expulsion, while the figure hortus conclusus justifies the appearance of Mary as a subject of the sequence: the answer to man's Fall and Expulsion is God's entrance into the Mary-garden. Not only does this bring Mary into contrast with Eve, but implicitly man's limits are placed in contrast to God's infinite power: man loses, God creates, a Paradise. The second sequence represents, then, not the coming of the Law

as foretold by the dove's return, but the fulfillment (or the beginning of fulfillment) of the plan which would rescind the Law.
It must be remembered that little more than a century later the
Council of Trent would proclaim the Virgin Mother sinless; already, sermons on the Purification of the Virgin recognized Mary's
preparation for Christ's birth as the fulfillment of the Law. In this
context, Mary was the meeting place of two dispensations—in
truth, the garden where the manifold parts of time merged and
disappeared.

Taken together, the two sequences mark the complete cycle of
history from Paradise through wilderness to Paradise. They represent in little the great mystery of the Christian plan of Redemption
by showing how the life of Mary enclosed the mystery of the Incarnation, how in the life of a single human being all history became one moment. Through Mary, the effects of history (the
consequences of the Fall) had begun to be undone.

A single miniature found in an early Psalter offers a truncated
version of the same iconographic idea. This picture is divided into
three parts; the top half is further divided into two scenes.[16] A
thick silver bar separates only the two top quarters of the painting.
The reason for this selective separation is understood once we
have examined the painting in detail. Above at the left Adam and
Eve are set outside the gate of Paradise. The wall of the Garden
of Eden is clearly visible. At the right we find Adam at work in
the field. In other words, the top half of the miniature, like the
first two scenes in Speculum, depicts the Fall of man and its immediate consequences. The wall of the garden and the garden gate
represent the separation of man from the state of innocence; the
primary contrast is between the garden and the field, the one enclosed, the other open to the assault of nature. Adam's spade symbolizes man's newly required toil, with its ultimate futility, man's
natural end in death. Behind the wall, marked by the luxuriance
of the garden where man had lived in complete harmony with
plants and animals no less than with God, man had left a life of
perfect fullness and content. Thrust into the wilderness, he was
doomed to an existence of enmity with nature.

Spanning the bottom half of the painting, signifying the "Action
de graces pour la délivrance accordée à l'Eglise," is the scene of

the Annunciation. (In many treatments in books of hours, the background for the Annunciation is a walled garden, often, as in fig. 5, with some reminder of the Fall.) The juxtaposition of Eden and hortus conclusus, with the interposition of the wilderness, completes the recurring theme of Fall and Redemption. From beneath Eve's feet light radiates upon the scene below; a dove descends in its rays upon Mary. The alcove in which the Holy Mother sits has a tightly shut door, signifying *porta clausa*. Behind Mary, and facing in the opposite direction, sits Joseph.

We begin to see that Adam's labor is in contrast to the passivity of Mary and Joseph. Joseph's inactivity parallels his exclusion as a witness to the Annunciation, further testifying to Mary's virginity and to his own humility. As Adam's toil appropriately foreshadowed the dispensation of Law, under which man's actions were the sole predicate of his salvation, so Mary's passivity represents the proper state of the recipient of Grace. In this context, the light radiating from beneath Eve's feet results from more than a random choice on the artist's part: it is a pictorial reference to God's promise in the third chapter of Genesis. With the Annunciation, the fulfillment of that promise was set in motion. It was within the Virgin that the seed flourished which would crush the head of the serpent. The reemergence of the wall in the lower scene attests to the success of God's plan of salvation, which restored man to the garden. God's love gave to man what he could not earn. While throughout the dispensation of Law the enclosed garden had remained, as Eliot might have put it, a "perpetual possibility" in the mind of God, to whom all time is one, from the human point of view this sequence represents a movement through time. The scene of the Annunciation spans and therefore links the two upper scenes, for, at the moment represented, "possibility" turned actuality.

The association between Mary and the enclosed garden stems in large part from her identification as the Bride of Solomon's Song. This is nowhere better seen than in the block book *Canticum Canticorum* (c. 1465), where the sequence of the Song of Songs is interrupted after the first scene by a cut representing the Assumption of Mary (fig. 6). There is no reason to doubt that the Queen ascending here is the woman previously seen walking with

her Lover toward a plot enclosed by a wattle fence. A scroll establishes the erotic context of this cut: "Osculet me osculo oris sui
quia meliora sunt ubera tua vino." The second scroll serves as a
gloss on the figures represented: "Veni in [h]ortum meum soror
mea sponsa messui mirram meam cum aromatibus meis." Later in
the same work, and on three occasions, the Virgin appears in an
enclosed garden. In figure 7, the "true Solomon" approaches the
garden, which is surrounded by a wattle fence. The house, of
course, represents the Temple. In another case we find the lovers
in the garden, accompanied by the "Daughters of Jerusalem." The
King and his Bride address each other with endearing remarks:
Solomon has descended to the garden of nuts to see if the vine
flourishes; his Bride points to him with pride. Finally, the Virgin
appears, standing in a garden, which is now enclosed by a crenellated wall (fig. 8). In this woodcut, which seems to be intended
as the obverse of such typical representations of the Fall and Expulsion as are found in books of hours or seen in the Kitto Bible
(fig. 9), winged Gabriel holds a large key to the lock of porta
clausa;[17] angels surround the wall holding the shields of the Holy
Roman Empire, while outside the walls the Lover comes praising
his Beloved: "[H]ortus conclusus est soror mea sponsa [h]ortus
conclusus fons singnatus [sic]."

This was one of the most familiar ways in which the Virgin was
known to the Middle Ages. In a typical lyric apostrophe to the
Virgin, Adam of St. Victor describes Mary in language which is
like the combination of particulars depicted in figures 10 and 11:

> She is that sealed fount, ne'er drying,
> That walled garden, fructifying
>   By the good seed in it sown:
> She is that close-fastened portal,
> Shut by God 'gainst every mortal
>   For some secret unknown.[18]

This stanza and figures 10 and 11 are perfect examples of the association of images controlled by a central context or idea. The
names of Mary are not abstractions but pictures, concrete images
each one discrete in itself, but each being part of an integral fusion
of images. This image-cluster carried well into the seventeenth
century, as poets like Dunbar, Quarles, and Watkyns often echo

the Victorines. Indeed, even the Protestant writers like Gervase Markham could not fully suppress a strong Marian overtone:

> O Fountaine of the garden, and her flowers,
> O blessed Well, whence lyving waters flowe,
> And thou sweet spring, head of the dewing showers,
> Which from the tops of *Lebanon* doe goe.
>   O garden fount; ô living waters well,
>   A spring which on Mount *Lebanon* doth dwell.[19]

If it is argued, however, that Markham's Ecclesia (the Bride of his *Poem of Poems*) has been thoroughly protestantized, it must certainly be admitted that the hearts of Catholic poets could not resist the lure of a tradition so closely associated with the names of Mary. We think of Richard Rowlands' "Porta Caeli," "Turris David," "Lilium Convalium," "Fons signatus," and above all, of his "Hortus Conclusus":

> Moste pleasant garden plot, true *Paradise* of praise,
> Erected in the roome, of *Paradise* of iore,
> But yet that garden far, exceeding sundry wayes,
> As perfect second woorkes, exceed things wrought before:
> All closely wall'd about, inviolate it stayes,
> No serpent can get in, nor shal for evermore,
> All goodly flowers and frutes, here in perfection grow,
> Vertue on stockes of grace, hath them engraffed so.[20]

As the enclosed garden, Mary surpassed the original Paradise just as she surpassed the first Mother. No serpent could enter the walled garden of her womb. It remained (and allegorically it still remains) "inviolate." The growth in this "Moste pleasant garden plot" results from God's husbandry; the plants growing there have been "engraffed" by Grace. Here, as in numerous exegetical and iconographic works, the Mary-garden is in contrast to the lost terrestrial Paradise.

For the orthodox, Mary was the portal, sealed throughout the dispensation of Law, opened by the Incarnation to the Gentiles, and therefore (symbolically) to all men. Her active participation in the salvation of the individual soul is a recurring theme in recusant poetry. We might take as one example a poem attributed by E. K. Chambers to Donne, "O Frutefull Garden." The title given to this poem by Chambers aptly fits its subject matter, for the poem is a prayer "To the Blessed Virgin Mary":

O Frutefull garden, and yet never tilde,
Box full of Treasure yet by noe man filde.
O thou which haste, made him that first made thee;
O neare of kinne to all the Trinetie;
O Pallace where the kinge of all, and more;
Went in, and out, yet never opened doore; . . . .

Here are the familiar images alluding to Mary's virginity and its fruits, the traditional praise of that chaste one "Whose flesh is purer, than an others sperrit." To the Virgin the speaker bears his petition:

Reache him our Prayers, and reach us down his merrit;
O bread of lyfe which sweld'ste up without Leaven;
O bridge which joynst togeather earth and heaven;
Whose eyes see me through these walles, and throughe glasse,
And through this fleshe as thorowe Cipres passe.
Behould a little harte made greate by thee
Swellinge, yet shrinkinge at thy majestie.
O dwell in it, for where soe ere thou go'ste
There is the Temple of the Holy Ghoste.[21]

It is not hard to see that the speaker's prayer for the indwelling of the Virgin expresses the soul's desire for inclusion in Christ's Church; and, therefore, in terms of the contrasts working in the poem, the enclosed garden and the Virgin Mary are alternative figures representing the Church. In the final line of the poem this equation is stated through repetition of the theme of the Virgin Birth, introduced earlier. As we read in Henry Hawkins' *Partheneia Sacra* (1633), the wind of the Holy Spirit was all that could penetrate the wall of Mary's garden:

The Virgin *was a* Garden *round beset*
With Rose, *and* Lillie, *and sweet* Violet.
Where fragrant Sents, without distast of Sinne,
Invited GOD *the* Sonne *to enter in.*
But it was clos'd: Alma's *shut up, we know,*
What Gard'ner then might enter in to sow?
Or plant within this Eden? *Or, what birth*
Might be expected from a virgin-earth?
The Holie-Spirit, *like a subtile wind,*

Peercing through al, only a way could find.
As th' Earth brought forth at first, how't is not knowne:
So did this Garden, *which was never sowne.*[22]

The irony in "O Frutefull Garden" would seem to be that the speaker, in praying for the spirit of the Virgin to enter his soul, summons Grace to enter the Mary-garden of the Church; he asks, in short, to be born of the Spirit. In so entering the Church, man imitates Christ; born of the seed of the New Adam, the soul now flourishes in the "Frutefull garden" of Mary's womb. Christ's Church, "the Temple of the Holy Ghoste," is the New Testament answer to the Temple built by Solomon. But the Temple founded on the gospel was built of material which neither moth nor rust could corrupt. The contrast between the two temples is an important theme of *Partheneia Sacra,* and of the tradition of the Song of Songs.

Partheneia Sacra, a charming emblem book attributed to the Jesuit Henry Hawkins, is dedicated to the Virgin. Written "for the entertainement of DEVOUT SOULES, Contrived *AL TO THE HONOUR of the Incomparable Virgin* MARIE *Mother of* GOD; *For the pleasure and devotion especially of the* PARTHENIAN SODALITIE *of her Immaculate* CONCEPTION," *Partheneia Sacra* is squarely in the tradition of the Song of Songs. As such, the work distinguishes the enclosed garden of the Canticles—that "Mysticall GARDEN itself, the Paragon of Gardens" —from all others:

> I Speake not heer of the *Covent-Garden,* the garden of the *Temple,* nor that of the *Charter-house,* or of *Grayes-Inne Walkes,* to be had and enjoyed at home; nor of the *Garden* of *Padua,* or of *Mountpelier,* so illustrious for Simples. I speake not of the Garden of *Hesperides,* where grew the golden Apples, nor yet of *Tempe,* or the *Elizian fields.* I speake not of *Eden,* the Earthlie Paradice, nor of the *Garden* of Gethsemany, watred with Bloud flowing from our Saviour's precious bodie: But I speake of Thee, that GARDEN so knowne by the name of HORTUS CONCLUSUS; wherein are al things mysteriously and spiritually to be found, which even beautifyes the fairest Gardens: being a place, no lesse delicious in winter, then in Summer, in Autume, then in the Spring; and wherin is no season to be seen, but a perpetual Spring; where are al kinds of delights in great abundance, that can possibly be devised; where are faire and goodlie Allies,

streight and even, . . . strewed with the sands and dust of her proper Humilitie; where are Arbours to shadow her from the heats of concupiscence; flowrie Beds to repose in, with heavenlie Contemplations; Mounts to ascend to, with the studie of Perfections: where are hearbs, and Simples, soveraigne medicines of al spiritual maladies, where (I say) are the Flowers of al Vertues: . . . .[23]

Altogether, there are twenty-two emblems in *Partheneia*. If we consider the first of these ("The Garden") as an introductory piece, the remaining twenty-one emblems may be divided into three sequences of seven meditations on the emblems of Mary.[24] Fourteen of these twenty-one figures are literally as well as figuratively included within the garden walls. The engraving (fig. 12) which serves as frontispiece to the work is highly reminiscent of the illumination on the names of Mary seen in figure 11.

In the passage just quoted (from the preparatory section), Hawkins is careful to distinguish the Mary-garden from all other gardens, whether Christian or pagan. Hortus conclusus is singular in that it does not answer to the changes of the season, in that it includes "al things" needful to the healing and comfort of the spiritual body. "The Emblem" for this introductory piece (fig. 13) makes Hawkins' meaning for the figure of the enclosed garden especially clear: Mary's garden bore the medicinal flowers of Grace.

THE GARDEN AND THE TEMPLE

If we turn to Hawkins' "The House," we find an engraving of Gabriel knocking on the shut door of a stone house (fig. 14) with two domes—which fits the subject, identified by the accompanying poem as the Annunciation. Like the garden in figure 8, where the Archangel stands with his key to the locked gate, the house is the dwelling place of the Virgin. Paradoxically, she awaits her Bridegroom by *"keeping closd"* the portal of her house. So similar, in fact, is the meaning of the two figures that Hawkins not only includes the house within the garden (fig. 12) but scarcely distinguishes between them:

> *I have sanctifyed this House, which thou hast built, to put my name eternally therin,* sayd GOD to *Salomon,* not being yet (as I suppose) affected so to that material *house,* as he pretended thereby rather to shew the love he bare to his spiritual *house,* & yet corporal both, of his Incomparable *Mother,* whom he hath so sanctifyed with his eternal predestination before, and enriched so with his personal presence, to put his name eternally in her. For that saying can not so wel be verified of the *house* built by *Salomon,* which was afterwards demolished & razed; but rather of *Marie* heer, who shal be sayd & preached for ever, the *Temple* of GOD, the *holie House,* where al glorie hath entred in, as to a chast Bower, ...[25]

Hawkins tells us that God spoke to Solomon, not about the "material *house,*" but about the "spiritual *house,*" Mary. This statement harks back to a contrast visible in the frontispiece of *Partheneia,* where the house near the center of the garden dominates the small castle seen atop the mountain to the right (fig. 12). In "The Mount" we read that Mary is like "*Mount-Moria,* a certain hil in the Cittie of *Jerusalem.* For as on that *Mount-Moria, Salomon* first founded his Temple, the house of GOD: so in this our *Montain Maria,* was the heavenlie and Celestial Temple of the true *Salomon* raysed indeed." [26]

The contrast between Mary and the Temple of Solomon was a recurring motif in Renaissance painting. In Melchior Broederlam's "Annunciation and Visitation" this comparison is achieved by the typical means of a carefully drawn contrast between Gothic and Romanesque architecture. In his distinguished book, *Early Netherlandish Painting,* Erwin Panofsky discusses this work.[27] Panofsky describes the distinction between the Gothic loggia (where the Virgin sits before her prayerbook) and the Romanesque dome of the Synagogue as the key to the meaning of the painting.

The dome, with its gloomy, slitlike windows, stands for Solomon's Temple, and more generally, for the dispensation of Law. Of the windows in the Gothic porch, Panofsky writes: "The window being the accepted symbol of illuminating grace, and therefore of the 'new light' (*lux nova*) of Christian faith as opposed to the 'darkness' or 'blindness' of Judaism, a triad of windows so prominently, even incongruously, placed upon a cornice and so pointedly opposed to the dark apertures in a building of

different style, can mean only one thing: the Trinity, which as-
sumes the form of physical reality in the very act of Christ's Incarnation." [28] The same contrast between Gothic and Romanesque
architecture may be found in the "Basle Altarpiece," painted by
Konrad Witz (c. 1430), where the scene of the Annunciation is
flanked on one side by the Synagogue and on the other by the
Church.[29]

One of the better known examples of this iconographic idea is
Robert Campin's "The Betrothal of the Virgin." Here, Campin—
the Master of Flemalle and painter of the celebrated "Merode
Altarpiece"—makes emphatic use of the figure of the shattered
wall. The wall in "The Betrothal" is attached to the Gothic narthex
of an unfinished church, which is in contrast to the oriental dome
of the Temple of Israel. Within the Temple, scenes from the Old
Testament (understood as types of the New) are enacted, while
at the right the holy couple arrives at the entrance of the church,
where they are met by a bishop.[30] True to convention, the broken
wall of the church testifies not only to the artist's "realistic" observance of chronology (the plan of Redemption has not yet been
completed) but to the broader theological antithesis between the
dispensations of Law and Grace. Panofsky argues that the absence
of Romanesque architecture in Campin's "Merode Altarpiece" indicates a closely related use of artistic convention. In both examples
the walls of the enclosed gardens and the Church are equated,
while the condition of the wall is determined either explicitly or
implicitly by the scene's temporal relation to the Sacrifice.

Though this is by no means the time or place for an extended
discussion of the iconography of the unfinished wall, that figure
was important to the development of garden allegory. Suffice it
to say that scarcely an event from the life of Christ exists for
which some artist at some time or other has not provided a backdrop of an unfinished enclosure. Figure 15 from the "Hours of the
Virgin" for use at Champagne is a typical example. We think, too,
of the Nativity scenes in such works as the celebrated "Hours of
Isabelle of Brittainy," [31] and in the magnificent "Hours" illuminated by Jean Bourdichon.[32] In the "Kildare Book of Hours," the
Garden of Olives bears a striking resemblance to the garden, completely enclosed, where Christ rises from the grave (fig. 16).[33]

Similar examples from works like the "Heures de Milan" may easily be multiplied.[34] But the meaning of the unfinished wall is probably best demonstrated in a painting which now hangs in the Metropolitan Museum, "The Annunciation" (our fig. 17), attributed by Panofsky to Hubert van Eyck.

In this painting, we find Mary standing in a Gothic archway, the beautifully vested, winged Gabriel kneeling in the foreground. At her right there is a garden overrun by weeds; vines climb its ruined wall. Panofsky explains that the niche in the archway above the Virgin is properly the place for a statue of Christ.[35] Since it is empty, the niche suggests the unfinished work of the Incarnation, and in so doing parallels the crumbling garden wall, which (in turn) represents the breach between God and man caused by the Fall. From the point of view of this painting, that breach is as yet unhealed. The unmended wall, like the garden gone to seed, typifies the hopelessness of man's reliance upon himself, the endless frustrations to which man was doomed under the Law.

A similar technique may be seen in Roger van der Weyden's "Madonna Enthroned," where the Virgin and Child are shown seated within an aedicula, which represents a chapel.[36] This structure clearly projects from wall to lawn; flowers grow on either side. An outstanding feature of the painting, Panofsky notes, is the marked disproportion of the human figures to the archway. This disproportion is comparable to that found in Jan van Eyck's "Madonna in a Church," [37] where the Virgin Mary stands much higher than the naves. In both instances the disproportion is the result not of poor perception or planning but of artistic choice. Thus the chapel in the "Madonna Enthroned" is "a symbolic representation of the Church." [38] This point bears special significance when we realize to what extent garden imagery was employed by Flemish painters. As we have already seen, Gothic architecture signifies the dispensation of Grace, while Romanesque typifies the Law. This contrast gives us an interesting slant on Roger van der Weyden's work, as well as on such miniatures as "Le Paradis Terrestre" in "Très Riches Heures." [39] For in the "Madonna Enthroned" this Gothic chapel is literally within an enclosed garden. We find, then, three iconographic statements of the same religious idea: Mary, garden, and the Church are one.

The frequent appearance in books of hours of the Virgin seated beneath a canopy in a garden, or within a small Gothic structure, represents an elaboration of this allegorical convention (figs. 18 and 19); the miniature of Mary, St. Anne, and the Infant in the "da Costa Hours" (fig. 20) and Robert Campin's "Madonna of Humility" are typical examples.[40] A further possibility of the tradition is expressed in works like Gerard David's "Betrothal of St. Catherine," in which St. Catherine takes Christ's hand in marriage while kneeling before the canopied throne of Mary.[41] As in numerous other examples, the setting for the marriage is a walled garden. At the same time, the canopy over Mary's throne is similar in function to the cape held by angels behind the Virgin in Jan van Eyck's "Madonna at the Fountain." [42] Here, the turfed bench and the fountain (*fons signatus*) remind one that the Virgin was a "garden inclosed, a spring shut up, a fountaine sealed." The repetition of such examples made the cape into a sign of the Virgin's protection of the faithful; both cape and canopy testify to Mary's stature as Holy Church.

We may distinguish, then, two senses in which Mary was the "garden inclosed." She was so, first, in the literal (or historical) sense. As the "Imperial wall" enclosing the blessed Babe,[43] she stood in history as a partition between two dispensations of time. The allegorical meaning of the text from Canticles viii, "I am a wall, and my breasts like towers," was that Mary separated the dispensations of Law and Grace. Her purification ended the former; her womb gave birth to the latter. But the text also meant that Holy Church still flourished in the truth of both Testaments. As the Mother Church, the Virgin still encloses the "Garden of God." This second role was also revealed in the Song of Songs, where it was written that Mary was the Tower of David, built for an armory, bearing the shields of a thousand fighting men.[44] The Church was a wall shielding the Congregation in the same way the Virgin's outspread cape protected her children.[45] In the seventeenth century a closely related iconographic idea finds poetic expression in J. B.'s "Turris Davidica," which identifies the Tower of David with the Holy Church:

> TOWER OF DAVID, as that pious king
>   Did, for his cities strength, this tower erect,

> So spiritual DAVID thee to th' world did bring
> The holy Church (his citie) to protect,

and makes clear that the function of the Tower (see our fig. 21)
is to aid the soul in spiritual combat:

> In DAVID'S tower all warlike armes were layd;
> Thou still art ready, as the Church'es shee[l?]d,
> Our soules against all Hell's assaults to ayd.[46]

Since both Mary's virginity and the garden wall represent the
exclusiveness of the divine Bride, the two figures function in a
parallel manner. The garden wall and the soul of the Holy Mother
specifically excluded any intrusion by sin or the world. Thus the
meaning imputed to the Church walls in Christopher Harvey's
The Synagogue (1639) appropriately compares to that of the fence
surrounding God's "inclosure." [47] Moreover, since the figure of the
Church had a microcosmic as well as macrocosmic application, the
same images (conveying the same meaning) could apply to the
individual soul. In Harvey's adaptation of Benedict von Haefton's
Schola Cordis,[48] after the soul has learned the means by which its
garden was seeded, watered, and cultivated, it is taught that divine
Cupid walks for his own enjoyment among the flowers of his
garden. Now the soul must learn another lesson: how the growth
of the plants within that garden is maintained. The text from
Proverbs, "Keep thy heart with all diligence," along with the poem
and emblem, shows that, although the garden is under the protection of Divinity, still the soul must exert itself in its own defense.
Somewhat petulantly, the speaker, complaining that the garden is
under constant attack from wild beasts, asks whether the Lord will
endure the invasion of his "pleasant garden" by such brutes. Christ
gives this chiding answer:

> What is the matter? why do'st thou complaine?
>   Must I as well maintaine,
> And keep, as make thy fences? wilt thou take
>   No paines for thine own sake?
> Or doth thy self-confounding fancy feare thee,
>   When there's no danger neer thee? [49]

Despite this direct response, the speaker continues to complain:

The world's a wildernesse, wherein I find
    Wild beasts of ev'ry kind,
Foxes, and Wolves, and Dogs, and Boares, and bears . . . .
Besides the light-abhorring Owles and Bats,
And secret corner-creeping Mice and Rats.[50]

LIKE to a garden, that is closed round,
That heart is safely kept, which still is found
Compast with care, and guarded with the feare
Of God, as with a flaming sword, and speare.[51]

Harvey's poem, a dialogue between the soul and Christ, provides us with yet another variation on the traditional theme of the Bride's uniqueness. When she inquires, "Canst thou endure thy pleasant garden should/ Be thus turn'd up as ordinary mould?" she implicitly (and pertinaciously) reminds her Creator that she is unique among all creatures, being neither born of nature nor subject to its laws. She knows that, as in figure 22, outside the walls of this "pleasant garden" all is "wildernesse, or at best . . . a wide field, where all manner of unclean, and wilde beasts live and feed."[52] In the natural world, garden walls protect the plants from destruction by foraging animals and intemperate weather. But in a larger sense these walls are only partially successful. For all that is born of nature is bound to die; even the thickest, highest wall is reduced by time to powder. And while man very often outlives the rose, the stone wall he built to protect the rose would doubtless be left standing long after he has turned to dust. Nothing was more certain than that natural man must suffer the decimation of time. But on the other hand man's soul, made in the likeness of God, was potentially the ground in which the spiritual seed of the Word grew; quickened by Grace, the spiritual Adam (*adamah*, or earth)[53] became the "Paradise" in which God Himself took pleasure. Against the walls of that garden no power, time included, could prevail. As we can see, then, the allegorical use of the garden wall represented the removal of Christ's Church from the physical necessities of the world. It shadowed forth the contrast between the two Adams in man: one born under the Curse and living under the pressures of the moment, only to die at last as had his original predecessor; the second born by the Grace of God, of the spirit, into the prospect of eternal life.[54]

George Herbert provides us with a subtle example of the poetic use of this figure. Though the model for Harvey's *Synagogue*, Herbert's *The Temple*, has no poem on the Church walls per se, it appears that Harvey drew on the idea of Herbert's charming little poem, "Paradise," which reads:

I Blesse thee, Lord, because I	GROW
Among thy trees, which in a	ROW
To thee both fruit and order	OW.
What open force, or hidden	CHARM
Can blast my fruit, or bring me	HARM,
While the inclosure is thine	ARM?
Inclose me still for fear I	START.
Be to me rather sharp and	TART,
Then let me want thy hand &	ART.
When thou dost greater judgements	SPARE,
And with thy knife but prune and	PARE,
Ev'n fruitfull trees more fruitfull	ARE.
Such sharpnes shows the sweetest	FREND:
Such cuttings rather heal then	REND:
And such beginnings touch their	END.[55]

The technical achievement of this poem goes far beyond the witty use of paring rhyme and will not be fully appreciated until Herbert's allusiveness within the wider framework of *The Temple* is seen. To begin, "Paradise" echoes a recurring Herbertian motif of praise. Praise is owed, as we discover in "The Thanksgiving" and "Employment (I)," for the best of all reasons: the very existence of the "inclosure," and the inclusion of the speaker within it, derive from God's mercy. Alone, man cannot flourish, for by nature he is wilderness and weed. "The H. Communion" recalls that time before the Fall when Adam moved from Paradise to earth and back again "As from one room t'another." Partaking of the Eucharist (the very Incarnation of God's loving power) man re-entered the enclosure of Paradise. Thus, in "Grace," the speaker prayerfully confesses his limits, and petitions for the benefit of the Sacrifice:

My stock lies dead, and no increase
Doth my dull husbandrie improve:

> O let thy graces without cease
> Drop from above!

And similarly, in "Paradise" the speaker prays (in Stanza III) for the continued intervention of God's "ARM," for outside that "inclosure" the spiritual plant withers before the assault of nature. Ultimately, this thematic development presents the reader with a contrast between nature and Grace.

In Herbert's poem, God's "ARM" provides the Church with walls just as it encloses Paradise from nature. Through the Eucharist, by God's Grace, the Temple and "Paradise" are one, and so (of necessity) their walls coincide. The speaker offers his praise because he has been made aware of his election to the Paradise of Christ's Church. In the context of the soul's struggle treated in *The Temple*, the speaker has achieved that blessed state of passivity in which he no longer yearns to reward his Saviour for the Sacrifice. Man's restlessness, his struggle to repay ("Love" from the Williams MS), manifests the human will to assert its own claim to salvation; but in any way to offer praise as if it might be needed ("The Crosse") is to arrogate to the self an inappropriate role in the regenerative process. Conversely, to impute to the soul such a lack of worthiness as to approach despair of election is to arrogate to the self the divine prerogative of judgment, and to call in question the sufficiency of Grace. Love has pursued, overpowered, wholly conquered nature, and so, to contemplate a means of repayment is to place in competition with the divine plan of Redemption a "design" of man's own. In reality, the soul must give—not needed, but owed—thanksgiving; the answer to the speaker's question in "The Thanksgiving":

> Shall thy strokes be my stroking? thorns, my flower?
> Thy rod, my posie? crosse, my bower?

is solidly answered by *The Temple* as a whole, and by its epitome, "Paradise," in the affirmative.

Allegorically the contrast between nature and Grace corresponds to that protean opposition between art and nature. Vineyards were not common grounds but lands enclosed from the open wilderness by the art of man's husbandry. In just the same way, the enclosure of the Church in Herbert's "Paradise" and elsewhere represents the triumph of divine art over nature. This comparison explains the discussion of the garden in the fifth chapter of Isaiah found in Nehemiah Rogers' *Strange Vineyard In Palæstina* (1623):

> A Vineyard we know is a place severed and hedged in from the open champaine or common. It doth not of it selfe spring up, or naturally grow; but it is planted by hand and Art, and so it is made a *Vineyard:* And thus the Church is called and separated from the rest of the world both in life and conversation, and is gathered by the word.

This enclosure, as "testimonies" from Deuteronomy, Leviticus, and the Canticles reveal, represents the chosen Bride, whether she be Israel or the Church:

> *Thou art an holy people unto the Lord thy God* (saith *Moses*) *and he hath chosen thee to be a peculiar people unto himselfe above all Nations that are upon the earth.* [Deut. xiv.2] And againe; *I am the Lord your God which have separated you from other people.* [Levit. xx.24] This is that *Solomon* saith, *A garden enclosed is my sister* (whereby he understands the Church) *my spouse: A spring shut up, a fountaine sealed.*

Again, the act of removing or separating the vineyard is one of loving mercy: "Thus we see God hath taken it in out of the vast wildernesse of this wretched world, and hath imparked it with the pales of his mercy, and separated it from all other grounds whatsoever, to be a Vineyard for himselfe." [56]

Man requires mercy because he is, by nature, a "Wild Plant." Born in an unregenerate state, he springs from the "poysonous Roote [of] originall corruption," and this may easily be seen, writes Ralph Austen, in the fruits of man's natural endeavors: "They are but *apples of Sodome, Splendida peccata,* glorious sinnes: for while the *Tree is corrupt,* the *fruit* is so, Math. 7.8." [57] On the individual level, the garden wall separates the wild from the regenerate plants. And this is a way of saying that flesh and spirit are different things, potentially responding to different values, aiming often at different ends. Since the flesh is the incarnation of Adam's seed, it is cursed; and Austen is convinced that unless man is reborn of the seed of the second Adam he must be left outside "the wall of his [God's] Orchard." [58] As John King wrote in a sermon on the last chapter of the Song of Songs, all who lay outside the walls of Solomon's vineyard in Baalhamon are damned:

> For this *vineyard* is planted in *Baal-hamon*, not in the open field, whose portion is the *curse of brambles & briars;* but in a several, peculiar, enclosed peece of ground, it is *hortus conclusus*, as the garden of Eden, and lieth within a hedge or fense, as the mount within railes. And whosoever groweth without it, is *labrusca*, not *uva*, some *sower* or *hedge grape*, not good to eat, or rather the *grape of Sodome* or *cluster of Gomorrhe*, which groweth but to the fire. My meaning is, *extraecclesiam nulla salus, without the Church no salvation.*[59]

When man comes to terms with the injunctions of Scripture ("*Gardens inclosed are, Gods word is so*"),[60] he is blest with the heaven-sent alternative to doubt and anxiety. Where the struggle of Herbert's pilgrim began in complaint:

> My throat, my soul is hoarse;
> My heart is wither'd like a ground
> Which thou dost curse,   ("Longing")

it ends in calm, as the speaker finds himself secure behind an impenetrable wall, protected, as St. John of the Cross writes, by a sense of peace, which the garden wall in the Song of Songs represents:

> By the wall is meant the rampart of peace and virtues and perfections which the soul now has, and by which it is now protected, which is the wall and defence of the garden of its Beloved. Wherefore He speaks of it thus in the Songs: *Hortus conclusus soror mea*. Which signifies: My sister is a garden enclosed. Wherefore, He says, "touch not this wall." [61]

Peace, virtue, perfection. As if the three are equivalent terms, all abstractions representing the proper end of the holy life. The temporal significance of St. John's commentary, and of Herbert's poetry in general, is that protection is given to man in the here and now—at some definite point in time—very often after a long, dark struggle with despair. In the conscience of Herbert's speaker, the Curse is relived; he feels the Fall in the soil of his own nerves and bone fibers. Though elected, he feels despair; he feels, as St.

Teresa often did,[62] like dry and useless ground. But all said and done, Grace, the abiding, "dreadfull Presence of God in the midst of his Church," provides the saints' rest at last; the wall of God's love preserves the garden of the soul:

> What open force, or hidden   CHARM
> Can blast my fruit, or bring me HARM,
> While the inclosure is thine   ARM?

Once secure behind that enclosure, man escapes the extremes of heat and cold which accompany the progress of the seasons. He is no longer killed and quickened, hurled "down to hell/ And up to heaven in an houre," for he has been shut away from the world of change. His prayer voiced in "The Flower" ("O that I once past changing were,/ Fast in thy Paradise, where no flower can wither!") has been heard and answered. Not that human life as Herbert pictures it here is marred by the absence of spring. Throughout his life man is confronted by "Many a spring." Unfortunately, though, where there are many springs there must be many winters; the blaze of summer comes round as surely as the colors of spring. Paradoxically, the value sought by the speaker, and provided by the garden wall, is escape from what the speaker himself knows to be the inescapable processes of nature. Rest, "alone of all his treasure," is God's ultimate gift to the Elect ("The Pulley"). Only by the Grace of God may man transcend the changes of the seasons. "The Flower" conveys the speaker's longing to break through the bounds of human life, to be bound— infolded—only by the Deity. Yet he is aware that not even the saints escape from pain and anxiety. For Herbert, the figures of winter and spring mark the simple division between successive moments of man's life as he is turned from ease to anxiety, from despair and doubt of his relation to God, to certainty of his election. Such intense shades of human emotion, as *The Temple* unfolds them, represent the ambivalent attitude of a speaker who at once glimpses the wonder of Grace while seeing with stark clarity the awful, irrevocable consequences of the Fall:

> These are thy wonders, Lord of love,
> To make us see we are but flowers that glide:
> Which when we once can finde and prove,

> Thou hast a garden for us, where to bide.
> Who would be more,
> Swelling through store,
> Forfeit their Paradise by their pride.

Ironically, the speaker of *The Temple* is both inside and outside of Paradise. He is enclosed in Paradise by virtue of his membership in Christ's Church; his soul is that "living stone" from which the Lord has hewed an "Altar." He is that stubborn ground which God enclosed for his enjoyment from the world. But insofar as he is still a lump of flesh, formless dust more or less resisting the artistry of God's workmanship, man is that very wilderness of self-will into which the Archangel had expelled him. The contrast between dearth and growth is Herbert's way of saying that man cannot fully escape his own nature; even the Elect waver in their knowledge of election, and by doing so, dally with the sin of despair. As we read in such poems as "The Thanksgiving," "The Reprisall," "The Crosse," and "Love" (from the Williams MS), Herbert's speaker seems never to learn how to rest in the love of God.

But even this failure has its relevance to salvation. It is not for man to judge either others or himself: "We say amisse,/ This or that is." There is no logical answer to the problem of pain, no certain antidote on earth against doubt and insecurity. But answer there certainly is to the way in which man should handle the antinomies of existence: "Thy word is all, if we could spell." There is, of course, no verbal panacea to the thrust and fall of human emotions; "The Flower" focuses on the tensions of the speaker as he confronts with clarity and intensity his own instinct to rebel against mortality in the very moment of his recognition that salvation rests upon acceptance of that mortality: "Who would be more,/ Swelling through store,/ Forfeit their Paradise by their pride." On the other hand, those who, like Herbert's speaker, embrace these limitations—even while they fret and complain, even as they express almost with wonder,

> O my onely light,
> It cannot be
> That I am he
> On whom thy tempests fell all night,

their concern with the awful heats and storms that continue to assail the flesh—in that moment enjoy the blessing of a further awareness. The Elect know that while the body may be torn by tempests, already a garden has been prepared for the soul. Indeed, the soul is already fast enclosed in that garden "where no flower can wither." Having submitted to the "word," the soul finds rest in the promises; chastened and subdued by the pruning knife of the heavenly Gardener, the spiritual plant flourishes in "Paradise":

> Such sharpnes shows the sweetest FREND:
> Such cuttings rather heal then   REND:
> And such beginnings touch their   END.

In the Paradise created for the Elect, the seasons and all change had been walled from entry, this just as certainly and eternally as mankind had been excluded from reentry into the Garden of Eden. In the Paradise of the Church, the soul enjoyed eternal Spring. Daniel Price's sermon, *The Spring* (1609), might well serve as a gloss on "The Flower" and "Paradise." Price begins by pointing out how spiritual growth must always be seen in relation to the irrevocable passing of time. Man's hope was in divine intervention: "*God* our father is the husbandman, *Wee* are his husbandry, the *Soule* is the ground, the *Seede* is the word . . . ." [63] The bare branches of the spiritual tree had their prototype in the withering, winter plants of the Hebrew dispensation. Mankind had been summoned to leave the winter of the Law, to enter the garden of eternal Spring:

> It was the springing voyce of the spring, . . . in the Canticles: Arise my love, my faire one, and come away, for behold Winter is past, the raine is gone away, the flowers appeare in the earth, the time of the singing of birdes is come, the voyce of the Turtle is heard in our land, ... [64]

Price goes on to ask: "What is meant by the Dove but the voice of the Church, what by the land of the Spouse, but the life of the blessed?" It must be borne in mind, in this regard, that Jeremiah had called to the earth, "*O Earth, Earth, Earth, heare the voyce of the Lord*," and that John the Baptist had gone into the wilderness for the same reason—to call man from himself: "so may I say to the drie, empty, bare, barren desart, desolate hearts of unfruitfull hearers, O earth, earth, earth, bring foorth fruites worthy amendment of life." [65]

As we can see, the figure of the garden wall functioned as an emblem of divine intervention, pointing up the power of Grace to undo the natural propensities of human will. This interpretation applies to both Catholic and Protestant poets of the late sixteenth and early seventeenth centuries. For the difference between the way a Rowlands and a Herbert use the tradition is one, finally, of emphasis. The question is not which aspect of the garden does the Catholic or Protestant writer use; indeed, as we have seen, the general and particular aspects of the image are present for both Catholic and non-Catholic artists. Herbert's *Temple* is primarily an image for the soul, but it is still the "Paradise" containing the sacraments of which the Congregation as a whole partakes. Nor does the Catholic emphasis on the Marian implications of the garden image preclude such examples of a highly personal kind as are found in the writings of Robert Southwell, St. Teresa, and St. John of the Cross. The figure of the garden wall implies the life-giving separation between nature and Grace, and the fact that this contrast allowed for at least two distinct emphases merely accounts for a certain aspect of the density of the poetry written in this tradition.

CHAPTER III

Shade

"I AM BLACKE, BUT COMELY"

In the context of the Song of Songs, the figures of the wall and the seasons did more than point up a contrast between human and divine powers; they also hinted at the divisions believed to exist among the differing ages of man. The question asked in the Canticles, "Who is she that commeth up out of the desert, abounding in pleasure, leaning upon her welbeloved?" was also answered there. She was the unique Spouse who leaned, wholly dependent, on God's Grace to rescue her from the wilderness, where she once dwelled. It was she, St. Augustine insists, who properly responded to that often-echoed invitation: "Arise my love, my faire one, and come awaie. For behold, the winter now is past; the raine is changed, and gone awaie." [1] As Henry Hoddeson writes in his *Treatise, Concerning the Death and resurrection of our bodies* (1606), spring stood for the temperate weather enjoyed by the soul when in the state of Grace: it was that season entered by the soul after the spiritual death of the body. Spring signified rebirth in Christ, after the cold winter of condemnation. [2] But as we now must see, the figure of spring represented value in yet another context. Just as one might suffer from intense cold, he could languish in extreme heat: in the dead of summer (or in the noon of day) the sun burned at its strongest, destroying the weak or unprotected plant.

When Solomon's Bride complained, "I am blacke, but comely, (O ye daughters of Jerusalem) as the tents of Kedar, as the curtaines of Solomon," she referred, tradition has it, to man's desolate state, but not necessarily to the soul's subjection to spiritual winter. Instead, as the following verse paraphrase by T. S. shows, this passage concerned the Bride's discoloration, and her confession of its true meaning:

> I now deformed am, and black,
> As black as *kedars* tents by name,
> Afflictions great, and sin (alack)
> Hath brought me to confess the same.[3]

This paraphrase (clearly influenced by the rubrics of the King James and other versions) shows how black was believed to represent a natural deformity, which, under the stress of affliction and sin, the Bride confessed. Her affliction, in turn, was either caused by or identified with an excess of heat. Tyndale's gloss on the figure "blacke" speaks of the "brennyng of tribulacioun." [4] Here and elsewhere, we read that the Bride of the Song of Songs was "sunburnt."

According to the commentaries, the Bride's color derived from God's demand for "absolute perfection in the lawe." [5] Throughout the Old Testament dispensation, Israel (the Church) had languished beneath this terrible "*Sunne of Justice*." Extending the metaphor, John Dove described fallen man as "That seede which fell on the stonie ground, where it had not much earth, . . . and when the sunne arose, it was parched." [6] The soil of human nature, as the chronicle of God's chosen people clearly showed, had failed to yield the shoots of spiritual regeneration. The Bride's complaint in Quarles' *Emblemes*, "*Who can indure the fierce rayes of the Sunne of Justice? Who shall not be consumed by his beames?*" [7] expressed the solemn recognition of the futility of man's struggle against nature. The implication of exegesis on Canticles i.6 would seem to be that labor beneath the "*Sunne of Justice*" produced only the outward sign of the Bride's guilt: "they made me the keeper of the vineyards, but mine owne vineyard have I not kept."

As everyone knows, though Adam's first responsibility was to "dress" the Garden, demanding physical labor entered his existence only after the Fall. In Paradise man was not required to gain the necessities of life by the sweat of his brow. Indeed, Adam's spade became a symbol of the Fall; his labor in the field was in marked contrast to the passivity of his prelapsarian state. If passivity is the proper attitude of the Bride (and there is overwhelming evidence to show that it is), then special consideration must be given to the cause of her discoloration, which she lays unequivocally to her debilitating labor beneath the sun:

> Looke not upon me because I am blacke, because the Sunne hath looked upon me: my mothers children were angry with me, they made me the keeper of the vineyards, but mine owne vine-yard have I not kept.

Here the Bride explains that she is black "because" scorched by the sun. At the same time, she appears to suggest extenuation of her guilt—as if it were, at least in part, the effect of a congenital condition, passed through the generations of her mother's (Eve's) sons. Wither's verse paraphrase of the Song of Songs typically emphasizes this supposed contingency:

> And Daughters of *Jerusalem,*
> I pray you doe not me contemne,
>   Because that blacke I now appeare. . . .
>
> Though blacke I am, regard it not:
> It is but *Sunne-burne* I have got;
>   Whereof my *Mothers* Sonnes were cause:
> Their Vineyard-keeper me they made, ...[8]

Regardless of how the blame was distributed (we shall return to this question later), one point remains clear: all such interpretations of the Bride's hue presuppose her exposure to the elements; in order to be burnt, the skin must first be open to the sun. As the commentaries agreed, since all men suffered the consequences of the Fall, all were open to the discoloring effects of the sun of God's justice. John Wall construes the love of Solomon for the Queen of Sheba as a type of Christ's own love for "the blacknesse of our nature." [9] Thus, Solomon's "Aethiopian Queene" represented fallen human nature; the sun was the condition under which the Fall had placed mankind. Considered in this context, the imagery depicting the frequent contrast between the walled garden and the open field was meant to distinguish shaded, fruitful ground from the unproductive earth exposed to the assault (in this case, the blazing heat) of nature.

A sequence of engravings in Joseph Fletcher's *The Historie of the Perfect-Cursed-Blessed Man* (1629) makes use of this motif.

In the first of these (fig. 23) the thick foliage of the trees forms an umbrella over Adam and Eve. About the garden various species of animals, from swan to lion (the latter pictured with his Eden-esque, humanoid face), live in peace. In the center of this fruitful scene, Adam and Eve stand—naked—in relaxed postures, with their arms entwined. The following engraving (fig. 24) presents a bitter contrast. The world is in chaos, the sky black with storm. Earth-quake and fire destroy man's dwelling. Fully robed, man sits in agony, powerless to save himself from the lion, which now devours him. Nor is this the end of his torment, for beast and serpent assail him with impunity. The position occupied by the most prominent tree in figure 23 has been taken by a sparse and wind-whipped tree. Against this landscape of despair man suffers alone; unhappily, the Curse isolated him in the pain of death from the spouse who had been given for his succour. Fletcher explicates the illustration in this long passage:

> 'Cause Man Himselfe from God was now declin'd,
> God made the Creatures all goe-out of *kinde*.
> He curst the *Ground*, or with *sterility*,
> Or else with hurtfull weeds *fertility*:
> Which (once b'ing blest to bring-forth wholsome meat
> Of its accord, without Mans care, or sweat:
> Now) yeelds Him nought, or things that are worth nought
> Till by his pains to goodnes they be brought.
> He's therefore forc't with sorrow and with toile,
> For his reliefe to digge and till the Soile:
> Lest by Life-wasting hunger raw-bon'd Death,
> Through want of *Bread* do bring him to want *breath*.
> The Living-creatures also, once all tame,
> Now refractary, and all wilde became.
> All things b'ing harmless, now all harmfull grew;
> And still than old, more harmfull is the new.
> For Natures selfe, and all that's naturall,
> Unnat'rally prov'd all unnaturall.
> Thus all for Him, and He for his offence
> Became accurst: loe here Sins recompence.[10]

Not only does this sequence illustrate the continuing icono-graphic tradition of Speculum, it suggests the multiple associations —the density—of the contrast between the garden and what we might call the not-garden. Figures 23 and 24 introduce the sections of Fletcher's *Historie* entitled, respectively, "Mans Excellencie By His Generation," and "Mans Miserie By His Degeneration." Figure 24 depicts the degenerate branch of Adam's corrupt root, and the surrounding world is a further projection of that decay. In the engraving of Eden, on the other hand, the peaceful sky (the over-hanging branches of the largest tree in the garden reach above the heads of Adam and Eve) and the luxuriant flora convey a sense of the general harmony of terrestrial Paradise. All particulars of this scene have their contraries in the picture of fallen man. After the Fall, the animals once named by Adam rise up against him. Barren of growth, his land is swept by storms. In every way natural man is exposed to the brunt of nature's hostile force; not only does the fruitless tree now fail to cover his head but in general nature assaults him from all sides. As Fletcher writes, the desolation of the second engraving corresponds to man's imperative to work. For as the picture Bibles impressed upon their users, Adam descended into the world with his spade in hand. Rehearsing the tragedy of this descent (which is finally to the grave), Fletcher touches on its personal implications. The banner of the engraving (taken from Job) reminds us that Adam's toil, in which all men share, shortly ends in death.

Commentaries on the Song of Songs recognized in the Bride's exposure to the weather her condition as heir to the Fall. This blackness, as we read in Francis Thynne's "Art cannot take awaye the vice of nature," cannot be effaced by human effort:

> The healthfull bathe which daielie wee doe see
> to cure the sores and fleshe of lothsome skinn,
> cann never make the Negro white to bee,
> or clense the harlot from her loathed sinne,
> ffor such defaults as nature dothe committ
> in the outward shape which she doth us impart,
> or such defaults as growe by minde or witt
> cannot be cured by anie outward art;
>> ffor though a time wee bridle natures strength,
>> She will break forth, and houlde her course at length.[11]

For Thynne, the protean distinction between art and nature pro-vided only one more example of man's inability to cope with his intrinsic discoloration. Nature in man was as unchangeable as the color of the Negro's skin. A "born Moor," man must wait on a power transcending nature in order to change.

The point is that art was a distinctly human enterprise, and the futility of human effort in general had been clearly demonstrated. Under the dispensation of Law, man had failed to meet the opportunity extended to restore himself in God's eyes. It is important for us to see that (at least in one sense) this failure was a necessary one. Though cast into nature, man was also a part of nature. In no case could he, of himself, alter himself. Indeed, the self was made up of the very cells of the body, over which man's control was severely limited. As William Gouge puts it, "sinne is in us as the spots are in the Leopard, not by accident, but by nature, which no art can cure, no water wash off, because they are not in the skinne, but in the fleshe & bones, in the sinowes & in the most inner parts." [12] According to this strongly pessimistic conception of man, the Old Testament rehearsed the saga of man's futile struggle against himself. It was the record of a world in which even the most worthy, the types of Christ, fell victims to human instinct. In the last analysis all men, the saints included, fell short of the glory of God. Unhappily, even "regenerate man falleth many times, and falleth grievously and fearefully, loseth of his hold, and of the bewty God hath given him." [13] Still, no matter how dim this view of human nature might appear, it was balanced by an almost equally optimistic faith in God's mercy. Gouge himself would admit that, once regenerated, the soul could not return to its originally blackened state. By God's Grace, man had been freed from the congenital aspect of sin. But in spite of this beneficence, man's nature perpetually inclined him toward the condition of his birth. Thus, in all Christians, there remained a mixture of holiness with sin, a mingling of spiritual colors, so "that there is no part white but it is blackish also." And as if these shades of gray were rooted in the bone marrow, these colors were mixed, "not as chaffe is mingled with corne, but as wine is mingled with water." [14]

When we have explained the meaning of the figure "blacke," we have but scratched the surface of a mystery. For the Bride complained, "I am blacke, but comely . . . as the tents of Kedar, as the curtaines of Solomon." Explanations of this paradox make up some of the most interesting parts of commentary on the Canticles. Typically, Thomas Adams writes that the Bride was "black indeed by her own misery" just as "Every soul is black by nature." True, in part this color referred to original sin. But this is by no means the whole story: "We have all a natural corruption, that deprives us of all habitual goodness. We are born Moors, and have increased his [Adam's] swarthiness by the continual tanning of unceased sins." [15] By acts of his own willfulness man adds to the corruption of his inherited estate. This quotation and others like it echo St. Bernard's assertion that the Bride was "Black by nature, beautiful by Grace." [16] Her physical deformity, a consequence of the Fall and of her own continued apostasy, was no ultimate justification of despair. Rather, it merely provided opportunity for the exercise of the power of divine love, in which man's hope rested. Thomas Adams goes on to write that the misery of the Bride's black estate was the necessary prelude to the bestowal of "her Saviour's mercy," which would make her (and had made her) "white and fair." [17]

Thynne's obvious little poem may remind us of the impressive and difficult poems of Lord Herbert of Cherbury on "Black Beauty." The significance of Cherbury's use of black is suggested by the title of what is perhaps his most enigmatic poem, "Sonnet of Black Beauty." One need only compare this poem with those by John Collop and others to be sure that it is not merely a traditional panegyric on the ugly or discolored mistress. On the contrary, Herbert's intention is wholly different, for not only does he impute intrinsic beauty to black but black becomes, through his handling of it, a rhetorical device employed to lend to his description of a woman's loveliness an allegorical dimension. But this remark requires explanation.

The "Sonnet of Black Beauty" is the last of a sequence of poems written as compliments to the spectacular beauty of Mrs. Diana Cecyll.[18] The sequence ("To Mrs. Diana Cecyll," "To her Eyes," "To her Hair," "Sonnet of Black Beauty") moves toward increasing abstraction, from praise of Mrs. Cecyll's physical to praise of her spiritual beauty; and, finally, Herbert describes her beauty in quasi-mystical terms. At first, her hair and eyes (unlike those beams and streams admired by "vulgar Poets") are rather black than pale, and then that blackness is an image of the Creator ("To her Eyes"). Next, in "To her Hair," the beauty's blackness becomes an emblem of transcendence ("because past black, there is not found/ A fix'd or horizontal bound . . ."), and, at last, in "Sonnet of Black Beauty," the poet pays the supreme compliment. As the paragon of Black Beauty, Mrs. Cecyll is like Solomon's dark Bride, whose blackness shadowed forth the mysterious power of her beauty.

Unlike all colors, "black" is not subdued by darkness. Similarly, Solomon's Bride and Mrs. Cecyll are unlike all other beauties. Again, in the power of blackness to resist the passage of the sun (and, therefore, of time) is "a spark/ Of light inaccessible." By the time the sequence ends, Black Beauty has become a symbol of the enduring in a world of change:

> And like an object equal to the view,
>   Art neither chang'd with day, nor hid with night;
>   When all these colours which the world call bright,
> And which old Poetry doth so persue,
>
> Are with the night so perished and gone,
>   That of their being their remains no mark,
> Thou still abidest so intirely one,
>   That we may know thy blackness is a spark
> Of light inaccessible, and alone
>   Our darkness which can make us think it dark.

Part of the difficulty in reading this poem stems, I believe, from the ambiguity of the figure of day. Then too, a play on the word "Art" is not only possible but likely; and this would fit nicely with the "blacke, but comely" motif. For Herbert is saying that "Art" did not change the color of this "Beauty." As day and night pass (as life passes), the condemnation of man is changed by absolutely nothing in this world. Indeed, all else changes but the very limitations of human nature, and the mercy of divine love. Thus, the Bride is "blacke, but comely," black by nature, beautiful by Grace.[19] Only a profitable awareness of man's natural corruption allows him to partake of God's mercy; only as he remains in the "dark," blind to the light of God's Word, does he pass from his day on earth into the endless night of Judgment. In other words, man's stubbornness, and that alone, precludes the vision of God's mercy implied by the limits of human nature.

THE SUN

Joseph Beaumont's *Psyche* (1648) offers a detailed anatomy of the nature of the burning sun as it functions allegorically in human events. In this very long Spenserian poem, the dominant interest (namely, the onslaught and defeat of lust) is treated in terms of two figures: the garden and shade. The heroine of the poem, Psyche, enters a certain garden in search of Paradise. We learn that she has been spurred on in her search by the hope that her desires will find fulfillment in the state of pleasure. Pleasure, she believes, if pursued to its ultimate end will lead at last to the garden of perfect bliss. Beaumont summons the reader's associations of traditional garden allegory, which were nourished by such works as the *Roman de la Rose*, by poems in which gardens function as mirrors of man's mistaken view of love. In Beaumont, as in his predecessors, there is an implied connection between religious and erotic experience; so in *Psyche*, as in such works as William Nevill's *Castell of Pleasure*, the bewildering scene of the garden is the externalization of the soul's confusion over the nature of love; pleasure in love is neither what it appears nor what the creature has been led to expect.

Thus, with Charis in close pursuit, Psyche soon learns that "pleasures paths" are "pathlesse." Like the deceived Guyon, she is lost. She finds herself on a path that is no path; in other words, her aims have not been toward proper ends. As she goes "loosely tripping on," it is as if she is without a will of her own. When at last she enters the "pleasant Grove" of the senses, the trees salute her and offer her their sweets. A wonderful sound of music meets her ear. Presently, Psyche is so anxious for full participation in sensual pleasure that she is forced to sit down in order to gather her thoughts. By now even the simple choice between the alternative means of perceiving sensual enjoyment has become a source of anxiety. Psyche realizes that, if only for this reason, the pursuit of pleasure necessarily involves anxiety.

At this moment a boar attacks, but Psyche is rescued by a "lusty gallant, *Aphrodisius* hight," who summarily deceives her by feigning sympathy. Assuring her of his virtuous calling (in the form of his gentle training as a scholar in Greece), he offers jewels as tokens of his sincerity, and suggests that their sanctified desires require immediate consummation in the lover's embrace. In Heaven's eyes, he argues, they were doubtless married already. *Syneisesis* (Conscience) tries to arouse Psyche to defend herself, ominously warning that the garden grows "thick with Charms" calculated to subdue the will. But the warning is in vain, and it remains for Charis to intervene to protect the maiden's virginity. Finally cognizant of her great danger and fortunate escape, Psyche prays for forgiveness. At once Phalyx invites Psyche to visit another garden, which only with great reluctance does she agree to do. It is clear from the description of this garden, however, that it is not actually the garden but her view of it which has changed:

> For now those flattering Beauties which of late
> Had made that Place a Temple to Delight,
> Were all unmask'd; and *Melancholy* sate
> Shrowding her hideous selfe in mid-day night.
> The heavy nodding Trees all languished,
> And every sleepy Bough hung down its Head.[20]

On a tree hangs Aphrodisius' periwig; now his bald head and black horns are visible. We begin to see that the garden is the externalization of desire—of Aphrodisius himself. The extreme difference between the once luscious grove and the now rotting garden is a commentary on the elusiveness of the pleasure toward which desire supposedly aims (a commentary not unlike the sentiment of many of Keats' lyrics):

> Two Rows of Roses on those Lipps did grow,
> To sweeten every word that passed by:
> But now scorch'd black as Hel's own mouth, they show
> What kind of Breath is wont through them to flie; . . . .[21]

Desire's cheeks, once hills of spices, are now quite sunken, and Desire is pictured as a decaying satyr, as well as an odoriferous garden. We see in this context the figure of passion's heat not as a life force but as a scorching, destructive power. Sexual pleasure when pursued as an end in itself does not heat but overheats.

Profoundly moved by her new awareness, Psyche bids farewell to this garden, reconsecrating herself to Christ, "Whose *Paradise* shall be [henceforth] the onely Grove." [22]

Again at home, now wrapped in prayer, Psyche is conveyed in her imagination into a garden surpassing all others, one whose lilies "scornd comparison with Northerne Snow." Flowing with streams of milk, the garden surrounds a castle made of "Virgin-christall." She is told this place is chastity. She sees the exalted Joseph, and next, Susanna, to whom she tells her sad history. Later, when Psyche is beset by two "lusty" Elders, the garden which had once appeared so beautiful to her eyes is described in terms of intense heat:

> *Cancer* then scorch'd the World, when tender she
> Into her Garden went, there is a spring
> Almost as clear as her own Chastity
> To coole her selfe: But they straight issuing
> > Out of their ambush, in their Clothes expresse. [sic]
> > More shame than did *Susanna's* Nakednesse.
>
> We too are hot, cry they; but none but thou
> Can quench the furie of our mighty Flames:
> Thou art the Fountain where all Sweets do flow,
> And We must bathe and coole Us in thy streams:
> > Yield, as thou lov'st thy Life; else We will swear
> > That in Adulterie We caught thee heer.[23]

Now, as if her newfound will to die rather than be seduced has saved her, Psyche learns that all danger has passed; before her stands the second Joseph, a carpenter "of Heroik Worth, and Poverty." She is told to look on Mary: "Behold Her face, and read all Paradise." "Loves Mystery" is revealed in the polarizing of two gardens, for as we read in the sixth canto, a description of Eden,

> No Weed presum'd to show its roytish face
> In this Inclosure: Nettles, Thistles, Brakes,
> Thorns, Bryars, Cockle, Hemlock, rampant Grass . . . ,[24]

these having been eliminated by "a Wall/ High built with Beauty." Clearly, "this Inclosure" is the adumbration of that walled garden of Jerusalem which the poet will soon describe, with its crystal river and its "multiplying Tree." Hanging from this paradisian tree is "blessed Fruit," the twelve fruits of Virtue. Humbled by this new vision of love, Psyche addresses the tree: "O noble *Tree!* whose very Shaddow is/ Th' eternal Roof of sure substantial Blisse." [25]

Doubtless *Psyche* is not a poem that will be of any great interest to the wider reading public. But the works of the Spenserians may serve as a gloss on the imagery of their more popular contemporaries. The juxtaposition of the figures of heat and the garden might be used, by lyric as well as romance or epic poets, to suggest the choice (with its concomitant anxiety) forever confronting man. Here was the crux of the human drama, after all: placed on earth without his consent, endowed with a will of his own, man was required—though not compelled—to do God's will. And all poets knew that the prototype of his failure to comply with God's will—the flame of conscience[26]—had been described in several closely related texts of Scripture. For George Abbot, Jonah iv.8,

> And it came to passe when the Sunne did arise, that God prepared a vehement East wind; and the Sunne beat upon the head of Jonah, and hee fainted, and wished himselfe to die, and said, It is better for me to die, then to live,[27]

concerned the same "fire," or "heat of the Sunne," which caused "the spouse in the Canticles [to] say of her selfe, *I am blacke, for the Sunne hath looked upon me.*" We may remember that only after the shadow of the gourd (provided by God) had been removed did Jonah suffer from the heat.[28] The gourd's shadow allegorically referred to God's mercy, extended to both Nineveh and Jonah, neither of whom saw fit to follow God's bidding. Nevertheless, both were spared the full weight of His wrath. The emerging polarity between the sun's heat and shade clearly reflects the distinction between what man deserves and what God gives him. This contrast, it was believed, both accentuated and resolved the paradox of the Bride who was comely, though black. In the fifth chapter of the Song of Songs, as Fray Luis de Granada writes, the reader encounters certain testimony to the Bride's transfiguration: though once black, now she was white. This dramatic change, happening in time, was accomplished by the Sacrifice:

Now what is more filthie, then a man conceaved in synne? and what is more cleane, and bewtifull, than our Saviour Christ conceved of the holie Ghoste. *My welbe loved is whyte, and well coulored* (saieth the spowse) *and chosen out emonge thousandes.* This most sweete and lovinge Lord then, that was so faier, and so cleane, was content to receave into him selfe, all the spottes and filthynes of our soules (to witt, the paines which our synnes deserved) and that he might leave our soules cleane and free from them, he himselfe remained (as yee see him upon the crosse) all bespotted and defyled with the same.[29]

The role of the Sacrifice in this context will be understood once we consider the constancy of divine justice, the fact of which, as we shall see in the next chapter, has an important temporal corollary. Now it is sufficient to recognize that, since from man's point of view the heat of condemnation had indeed diminished, some form of umbrella (umbra) between man and the sun must have been interposed. (For *"Who can indure the fierce rayes of the Sunne of Justice? Who shall not be consumed by his beames?"*) Again, the *"Sunne of* [God's] *Justice"* could not be seen to vacillate in intensity without imputing arbitrariness to divine will. And just such a shade, the allegory of the Song of Songs continued, was described in the second chapter:

> As the apple tree among the trees of the wood, so is my beloved among the sonnes. I sate downe under his shadow with great delight, and his fruit was sweete to my taste.

In the shade of this tree the once-scorched Bride at last found respite from the devastating "sun of God's wrath." As we may judge from the following verse paraphrase by William Loe, this apple tree was considered as a type of the Bridegroom:

> O thou my deare, that one I love
> Thou art the tree of life;
> Thy shade let sheeld me from all harms
> And I will be thy wife.[30]

Thus, the Bride addresses the apple tree as her protector and Spouse.

This connection—a stereotype for centuries in the sermons on the Canticles—was a central part of the elaborate allegory of the garden. The Bride rested, after the persecutions and afflictions of her natural state, in "the shadow of Christ." [31] The meaning of this metaphor did not puzzle biblical scholars: Christ's Sacrifice protected the Bride "from the scorching heat of the wrath of God, the curse of the Lawe, death and condemnation." [32] In the last chapter of the Canticles one reads that man was born beneath a tree, where he was reared by his mother, Eve. As Luis de Granada and others wrote, this tree was none other than the interdicted Tree of Paradise. Not only was man raised there, his flesh was the very branching (or rather, withering) of its root. In this single metaphor the symmetry of God's plan of Redemption was manifest: man lost his favored position "beneath the tree," and beneath a tree it was regained, "namely beneath the tree of the Cross." The apple tree in the Song of Songs represented the Grace bestowed by the Passion; St. John of the Cross interprets Christ's words in the verse under consideration:

> And thus He speaks with her and tells her how by means of the Tree of the Cross she was betrothed to Him; how He gave her herein the favour of His mercy, being pleased to die for her and making her beauteous after this manner. For He restored and redeemed her by the same means whereby human nature had been ruined, namely, by means of the Tree of Paradise, in our first mother, who was Eve. Thus the Spouse says:
> Beneath the apple-tree,
> . . . Meaning by the apple-tree the Tree of the Cross whereon the Son of God redeemed human nature, and in consequence was betrothed to it, and consequently to every soul, giving to each soul in token thereof grace and pledges through the merits of His Passion.[33]

With this exegetical tradition in mind, we might place the stanza quoted moments ago in context to see how completely the allegorization of the Song of Songs determined the poet's choice of language:

> I now deformed am, and black,
> As black as *kedars* tents by name,
> Afflictions great, and sin (alack)
> Hath brought me to confess the same.
>
> Yet daughters of *Jerusalem*,
> Like to the curtains bright and fair,
> Which once surrounded *Solomon*,
> I comely am through Christ as they're.[34]

Just as divine intervention was required to separate the garden
from the wilderness, so the Bride depended on the "true Solomon"
for her fairness. It was the shade of Christ's Sacrifice which determined the extent of productive spiritual ground. Ultimately, the
shade of the apple tree coincided with the boundaries of the garden
wall. Outside that shade (which was itself a wall), writes William
Gouge, no growth could be sustained: "For hee onely it is that
with his sweet shadow fenceth us from the burning wrath of
God." [35] The above paraphrase is the verse analogue to the commentary of Thomas Wilcox, where the Bride herself explains her
beauty:

> but I am like to them that dwell under Solomons Tapistry, (that
> is to say) moste faire and comely for those that dwell in Kinges
> houses and specially those that are continuallye in the places of
> most costly furniture and rich hanging are not only verie faire,
> as whose beautie the sun or sharpe weather doth seldome touche,
> but also are comely, because of beeing continually in the Kinges
> presence. [36]

It is in this context that we should understand the seven meditations of William Prynne on the figure of the garden. For here the
observation of the physical fact of the garden is only the prelude
to the allegorical understanding of the figure:

> Gardens are fraught with Arbors, *Trees, whose shade*
> *Cooles and repels Heate, stormes* which would invade,
> And scorch us sore: Christ hath *a shade most sweete*
> *Against all scalding Heates, all stormes we meete,*
> *Yea from his Fathers burning Wrath and Rage,*
> *Which none but he can quench, coole, or asswage:*
> O then in all such scorching Flames still fly
> To Christs sweete shade, for ease and remedy. [37]

Prynne sees in the garden shade a perfect picture of Christ's love,
which is the soul's rest from both storm and heat. As he writes
elsewhere, the souls of the saints are "*Sinne-burnt,*" and they "*can
gaine/ No rest but in his shade.*" [38] In this shade, which is the
"Christian Paradise," the soul finds "blest" repose:

> *Here may they find, blest rest, repose, and ease,*
> *When nought else can them comfort or appease.*
> O let our soules for ever dwell and rest
> In its refreshing shade, which makes them blest. [39]

THE TREE

Legend surrounds the multifaceted figure of the Christ-Tree. For centuries men believed that Adam returned to the Garden of Eden to steal the seed of the Tree of Life, and thereby set into motion the idyll of the wood whose issue would eventually be fashioned as the Cross. Closely related to this idea was the belief, celebrated in medieval hymns, that the Cross and the Tree of Knowledge were the same:

> Outraged He, and deeply grieving
>   That the first man Adam fell,
> When he took the fruit forbidden,
>   Which to taste was death and hell,
> Mark'd e'en then a Tree the mischief
>   Of the first tree to dispel.
>
> This alone was found befitting
>   Our salvation's well-laid plan,
> By a better craft to baffle
>   Him whose craft had ruin'd man,
> And to find the healing medicine
>   Where our foe the hurt began.[40]

The legendary history of the sacred wood received considerable impetus from various iconographic sources, and in such works as Donne's "Hymne to God, My God," we read that the Cross and the Forbidden Tree "stood in one place." The parallel between these two trees, which clearly emphasizes the symmetry of God's redemptive plan, provides the major theme of Joseph Beaumont's interesting poem, "The Gardin."

Rich in its development of imagery, "The Gardin" deserves more attention than it ordinarily receives. Much of the poem's complexity is owing to Beaumont's sensitive manipulation of the tree image. The first three stanzas present the speaker's complaint over "a bitter Loss." This loss, directly linked to the opening statement of the poem ("The Gardins quit with me"), confronts the speaker with a mystery:

> The Gardins quit with me: as yesterday
> I walked in that, to day that walks in me;
>   Through all my memorie

It sweetly wanders, & has found a way
To make me honestly possess
What still Anothers is.[41]

The garden has departed, yet it "walks" through the memory; it is both gone, yet owned, while at the same time belonging to another. Again, this owning of another's possession bears no trace of dishonesty. In the second stanza, we find that this possession (while on the face of it distinct from the speaker's loss) has at once a "dainty sence" and the power to "gall" the "Minde." The reference to gall provides a delicate foreshadowing of "remembrance":

Yet this Gains dainty sence doth gall my Minde
With the remembrance of a bitter Loss.
Alas, how odd & cross
Are earths Delights, in which the Soule can finde
No Honey, but withall some Sting
To check the pleasing thing!   (ll. 7–12)

We soon discover that the loss which galls the mind is the memory of the Fall. Moreover, the figure of "gall," in conjunction with the image of the Cross and the idea of remembrance, suggests that existence imposes on the speaker (fallen man) a species of deserved crucifixion (the play on words is highly reminiscent of Herbert's "The Crosse"): "Alas, how odd & cross/ Are earths Delights, in which the Soule can finde/ No Honey, but withall some Sting . . . ." The passage of time offers the speaker no adequate check to the pang of memory—his awareness of loss:

For now I'm hanted with the thought of that
Heavn-planted Gardin, where felicitie
Flourishd on every Tree.
Lost, lost it is; for at the guarded gate
A flaming Sword forbiddeth Sin
(That's I,) to enter in.   (ll. 13–18)

Regretting the entrance of sin into the world, the speaker (recognizing that he and sin are one) in effect regrets his birth. This places him dangerously near despair. So profound is his sense of guilt that he feels as if his entire being has been shot through by the Curse. And of course in one sense it has:

> I feel that through my soule he death hath shott;
> And thou, alas, hast locked up Lifes Tree.
> 　　　O Miserable Me. 　　　　　　　(ll. 25–27)

This shot, this wound, has left the speaker with only the awareness of death: "The Gardins quit with me." Guilt so penetrates his being with the sense of spiritual death that the actual perception of the physical garden is affected. In this way, the sense of spiritual loss is compounded by a further loss. Still, the loss of the physical garden seems simply to derive from what Ralph Austen called "the spiritual use of a garden." [42] The speaker's will has engaged the apprehended sense and applied it in the appropriate way. The garden is "used" as a guide to the contemplation of the Fall and the Passion. Thus, awareness of the speaker's loss is but a prelude to the recognition of God's mercy:

> What help were left, had JESUS'S Pity not
> Shewd me another Tree, which can
> 　　　Enliven dying Man. 　　　　　　(ll. 28–30)

The antidote to the "dread" of the Curse which makes man's physical existence a kind of prolonged death is found in this medicinal Tree. In effect, the scene of Crucifixion presents man with "as good/ A Paradise" as he had lost:

> That Tree, made Fertile by his own dear blood;
> And by his Death with quickning virtue fraught.
> 　　　I now dread not the thought
> Of barracado'd Eden, since as good
> 　　　A Paradise I planted see
> 　　　　　On open Calvarie. 　　　　(ll. 31–36)

In short, the speaker's dread is dispelled by the remembrance now not of Adam's loss but of his gain. In Christ, the barricades of God's garden were lifted. And though the garden was planted and kept by him, through Grace it still belonged to the devout soul. The speaker, who began his meditation in sorrow, ends it in joy. For he has reestablished his understanding of the "way" in which the garden has "found" him. We shall shortly see the iconic significance of this search and discovery.

Examples like "The Gardin" reflect continuing interest in the legendary history of the Cross, which was a very popular subject during the Middle Ages. Many of the frescoes on the domes of churches are dedicated to this medieval romance.[43] Enriched by strains of folklore and commentary on the Apocryphal books, the legend of the sacred wood found a place in Jacobus de Voragine's *Legenda Aurea*, which was translated into English and published by Caxton in 1483. According to this popular work (and in line with the rendition in the "Gospell of Nychodemus"), the wood had turned up at various times in history: "it was founden of Seth in paradyse terrestre, . . . it was founden of Salamon in the mounte of lybane and of the quene of Saba, in the temple of Salamon," and so on. The legendary history of the Cross harked back to the time when Adam, sensing the imminence of death, sent his son Seth to the gate of Eden "for to gete the oyle of mercy." Some men believed that the Archangel Michael refused to release the balm; others held that the angel "broughte hym a braunch, and commaunded hym to plante it in the mounte of lybanye." [44] Both before and after the Crucifixion, the power of the wood was "declard . . . by many myracles," [45] which became, in other contexts, the subjects of numerous graphic treatments.

There is a block book printed by Veldener which is a series of woodcuts depicting scenes from "The Invencion of the holy crosse" in the *Legenda*. In this sequence, Seth is given three "graynes of the fruyt of the tree of mercy." [46] Shown the kernels, Adam laughed and immediately died. We see the three trees which supposedly sprang from Adam's mouth, where Seth had placed the seeds.[47] In succeeding woodcuts, the history unfolds: Moses discovered the rods and kept them with him during the wandering of Israel; it was with one of these that he brought water from the rock. Later, the rods were planted, and then forgotten for many years. At the direction of an angel, King David brought the rods to Jerusalem. On the way, the miraculous powers of the wood were revealed: when three Negroes (encountered on the road) were struck by the rods, their skin turned white. In Jerusalem, the rods, left overnight in a cistern within sight of the Tower of David, grew into trees, finally entwining themselves into a single tree. Witness to this, David ordered the tree enclosed by a stone wall. This verse describes the scene depicted in the wood block:

> King David here his garden all
> Has well secured by a wall;
> And plainly I to you declare,
> He in this place knelt down in prayer.[48]

In the shadow of this tree, we go on to read, David composed his magnificent Psalms.

A good part of this history is based on Apocryphal writings about Solomon. In time, Solomon decided to have the tree cut down and used in the building of the Temple. Workmen soon discovered, however, that the wood could not be fitted to any place in the Temple. Thrown aside momentarily, it was placed across a streambed and used as a bridge.[49] The Queen of Sheba, recognizing the virtue of the wood, refused to step on it; preferring to cross the streambed on foot, she prophesied that on this wood the Saviour of mankind would die. At the Queen's insistence, Solomon had the wood plated with precious metal and placed over the door of the Temple, where it remained until Abias, Solomon's great-grandson, stripped it of its gold and silver covering. At that time the Jews buried it deep in the ground. Much later, in seeking a place to cleanse their beasts of sacrifice, the Jews dug a pool at the same site. Called Bethesda, visited daily by an angel, the pool was discovered to flow with healing waters. As the time of Christ's Passion neared, the wood floated from the water's depths to the surface, where it was found by men seeking staves for the Cross. Here is the proper context of Crashaw's "Hymn of the Holy Crosse":

> Tall TREE of life! thy truth makes good
> What was till now ne're understood,
>   Though the prophetick king
>   Struck lowd his faithfull string,
> It was thy wood he meant should make the THRONE
> For a more then SALOMON.[50]

As has often been remarked, the different versions of the legend of the Cross frequently alluded to the mystical language of such secret societies as the Masons; the very numbering of the leaves in the Veldener block book (there are 33) suggested the mysteries of the Rosicrucians.[51] In the history of the Cross, initiates to the secrets of freemasonry traced the revelation of the mysteries of Egypt and of the universe itself. There is, of course, no need for us fully to explore this wealth of meaning in order to see the relevance of the legendary history of the Cross to the traditions of the enclosed garden. According to the rendition found in Veldener's *History of the Cross*, the Queen of Sheba's journey from Egypt was a type of Christ dispensation to the Gentiles. That the Queen of Sheba sensed the true value of the sacred wood only heightened the irony of the allegorical scheme. The many tests imposed upon Solomon by the Queen were meant to test his wisdom.[52] Contemporary readers would know that his wisdom, however, must be balanced against the superior, divine wisdom of the "true Solomon." The seed of the marriage between Solomon and the Egyptian Queen did not bear the fruit of reconciliation; from their union stemmed—not the House of David—but the royal house of Abyssinia. Again, the significance of this would have been understood: the Queen of Sheba implicitly recognized that the time of perfect union was not yet arrived. But when she recognized the magical qualities of the wood, she referred to a seed (which was never to fit perfectly in the Tabernacle) not her own. Through that seed came the lineage of Christ, who was the "rod out of the stem of Jesse." Thus still another image of the Tree became a part of the iconography of the enclosed garden.

The connection between the Tree of Jesse and the Song of Songs adds a new dimension to the allegorical understanding of the figure of shade. As has already been suggested, the correspondence between the Tree of Jesse and the apple tree overlay an already established connection between the latter and both trees in the Garden of Eden. All four of these, in turn, were believed related to the tree envisioned in the Apocalypse:

> In the middest of the street of it, and of either side of the river, was there the tree of life, which bare twelve manner of fruits, and yeelded her fruit every moneth: and the leaves of the tree were for the healing of the nations.
>
> .   .   .   .   .
>
> Blessed are they that do his commandements, that they may have right to the tree of life, and may enter in thorow the gates into the citie (Rev. xxii.2, 14).

Indeed, rendering of the figure of the apple tree's shade involved the juxtaposition of several biblical texts, from which emerged no less than four manifestations (or types) of a single, fruit-bearing tree. Despite the variety of its manifestations, however, there was really only one Tree, the Christ-Tree, to which the prophets referred:

> In all the Scripture I read but of one Flowre that is praysed, and that Rose from the roote of *Jesse*, sprung in the Vallyes, and grew among thornes, and flourished in the Winter, and withered in the Spring, and was the most fragrant flower that ever grew. It was the Lilly among Thornes: A flower not easily to bee gathered: for we must undergo much labour and smart if wee will enjoy it: the Head thereof is crowned with Thornes, the Heart is pierced with a Speare. the hands and feete strucke through with Nailes: It is a Lilly among thorns.[53]

The scripture in Isaiah, "And there shall come a rod out of the stem of Jesse" (as we all know), prophesied the advent of the Messiah. By the tenth century this text had given rise to a complex literary and iconographic tradition, which was closely related to (if not an adjunct of) the allegory of the enclosed garden. The Tree of Jesse began to appear in hymns to the Virgin, as in this example from John Audelay, early in the medieval period:

> There is a flower sprung of a tree,
> The root thereof is called Jesse:
>   A flower of price;
> There is none such in Paradise![54]

As the rod out of the Stem of Jesse, the Virgin was an important figure in this tradition. For again, "This blissful flower/ sprang never, but in Mary's bower." The image of the Tree of Jesse in bloom brought the Passion and the Annunciation into a close, temporal relation:

> When Gabriel this maid met,
> With *Ave Maria* he her gret;
> Between them two this flower was set,
> And there kept was, no man shall wit,
>   Till on a day
> In Bedlem it gan spread and spray.[55]

The songwriter is depicting the lily of the Annunciation—set between the angel and the Holy Mother—as a blossom opening on Golgotha. Audelay's hymn has its iconic analogue in "the north aisle of St Michael's church in the North gate, Oxford," where in a "fragment of old glass" we find the ultimate thematic statement of the convergence of these two moments in history.[56] Here Christ is revealed, crucified within the petals of a lily: Strabo had written, "Therefore roses and lilies for our church, one for the martyr's blood, the other for the symbol of his hand." [57]

At about the same time, artists began to show interest in the Tree of Jesse. Jan Mostaert's painting, "Stem of Jesse," is typical of this iconographic tradition. Here, as frequently in books of hours, we find Jesse lying in a small enclosed garden.[58] From his chest grows the tree of his descendants. In its topmost branches we see the Madonna and Child. Nearby (and this figure is very common in paintings of this kind) the peacock perches on the garden wall, reminding the viewer of the gift of immortality. Perhaps the most splendid Jesse Tree of all is the one painted on the ceiling of St. Michael's Church at Hildesheim,[59] which covers 2,500 square feet. Its side panels contain eighty-two separate representations. Above Jesse is David, above him Solomon, and so on through the lineage of Christ. Near the bottom of the fresco run the four rivers of Eden, a graphic analogue to the theme of Beaumont's poem: the flourishing of this Tree and Paradise are one and the same thing.

The Tree of Jesse was an especially popular subject in books of hours. In the "Hours of the Virgin" for use at Evreux (c. 1500), a miniature, similar in idea to the Mostaert painting, illustrates the Tree of Jesse, enclosed by a wall (fig. 25). Within the boughs of the Tree is the scene of the Annunciation. In this instance, the Tree resembles a vine, heavy with its clusters of grapes, the descendants of Jesse. Just so in the "Hours of Isabelle of Brittainy," where, instead of Jesse's descendants, we have on the branches of the Tree eleven representations of King David, in each of which he plays a different musical instrument (see also our fig. 26).[60] In the center of the painting is the ultimate issue of the House of David, and the most important figure in all of garden allegory—

the Infant Jesus in the Virgin's arms: "And there shall come a rod out of the Stem of Jesse."

As we might expect, emblem writers of the Stuart period were quick to see the allusive possibilities of the Tree of Jesse, a figure which immediately invoked an allegorical framework of meaning and allowed also for the personal significance essential to the emblem. In one of the more complex examples from Wither (our fig. 27), the Tree of Jesse, though subordinated in its placement by the artist, provides the key to Wither's poem. Dominating the illustration is the figure of the heavenly graft; we see God's hand planting one twig upon another. In the background, two Old Testament scenes transpire: on Mt. Sinai Moses receives the Tablets of Law; nearer to us a priest draws the veil of *Sancta Sanctorum*, revealing the Ark of the Covenant. At the left we see between the branches of the Tree of Jesse the crucified Christ. The speaker applies the emblem to his own estate:

> T'is true, a *wither'd-branch* I am, and seeme
> To some, as voyd of *Hopes*, as of esteeme;
> For, in their judgements, I appeare to be
> A saplesse *Bough*, quite broken from the Tree,
> (Ev'n such as that, in this our *Emblem*, here)
> And, yet, I neither feele *Despaire*, nor *Feare*,
> For, I have seene (e're now) a little *Spray*,
> (Rent from her *Stemme*) lye trodden by the way,
> Three moneths together; which, when *Spring* drew on,
> To take an unexpected Root begun;
> (Yea, grew to bee a Tree) and, growing, stood,
> When those great *Groves*, were fell'd for firing-wood . . . .

Perhaps Wither alludes to the legend of the Cross which frequently depicts the wood cast off as useless, only to spring back to life again, both at Bethesda and at Lebanon. Then too, the echo of the day-year polarity might explain the figure of "Three moneths." Christ's death and transfiguration was accomplished in three days, yet as the text makes clear, he was the abandoned, withered twig, cast under foot and left to die. In spite of its momentary weakness, unless this twig "afford them shade" all men would shrivel. In this twig the speaker places his hope; in effect,

then, his hope is in the Resurrection, which had been foreshadowed
in the Old Testament:

> . . . For, I, who by *Faith's* eyes have seene,
> Old *Aarons* wither'd *Rodd* grow fresh and greene;
> And also viewed (by the selfe-same *Eyes*)
> *Him*, whom that *Rodd*, most rightly typifies,
> *Fall* by a shamefull *Death*, and rise, in spight
> Of *Death*, and *Shame*, unto the glorioust *height*.
>   Ev'n I, beleeve my *Hope* shall bee possest,
>   And, therefore, (ev'n in *Death*) in *Hope* I'le rest.[61]

Those eyes, the eyes of Faith, are the ones which recognize in the
emblem the typological truth of Scripture. It is through this understanding that the soul may see itself grafted into the once withered
—but now triumphant—root of Adam. This new burgeoning plant,
the ultimate issue of the Tree of Jesse, provides the only shade
sufficient to heal the "sinne-burnt" soul. It was in the shade of this
Tree that the Bride of the Song of Songs found the antidote to her
disfiguration.

In spite of the fact that painters often confuse the numbering of
the branches of the Tree of Jesse, the twelve branches of the vine
in figure 25 are of particular interest. An illumination in the
"Psalter and Hours of the Virgin" (13th century) at the Morgan
Library will demonstrate this point. A miniature of the Crucifixion
(fig. 28), the picture reveals, in addition to the staves of the Cross,
a tree with twelve leafy branches—a clear reference to Christ's
lineage in the House of David. Again, in "An Exposition of the
Song of Songs" (c. 1450), a series of miniatures on the Passion
conveys the same idea. This exquisitely illuminated manuscript is
probably the most explicit iconographic statement of the allegorization of the Song of Songs. Of greatest concern to us here are three
miniatures, all of which show Christ in the same outstretched position. The first two are quite typical scenes of the Crucifixion. But
in the third, though Christ is still seen with his arms outstretched
and his head bowed, we see no Cross. Instead, Christ is shown
crucified in the boughs of a fruit tree.[62] The Tree has blossomed
fully and is heavy with fruit. Under its branches on the ground
sits the Bride of Solomon's Song; still eating one apple, she reaches

for another. The multiplicity of fruit (the apples lie all around her) testifies to the sufficiency of Grace, to the fulness of the "Shadow of Christ." It is with this allegorical context in mind that Edward Taylor writes in his "Meditation. Cant. 2.3. As the apple tree among the trees of the wood, so is my beloved among the sons":

> Lord shake their bower and let these apples fall
> Into my Wicker basket and it fill.
> Then I shall have rich spirituall food for all
> Occasions as they essences do still
> And I shall feed on their rich grace my fare
> As they drop from thy Apple tree most rare.[63]

Whether in poetry or painting, the fruit of the apple tree of the Song of Songs symbolizes the Eucharist. The Bride fills her wicker basket with a love that knows no bounds. The tree is heavy with fruit, the ground covered with it. In the succeeding miniature in "An Exposition of the Song of Songs," we find Christ, now robed and standing, with his Bride.[64] Over them stretch the branches of the Tree of Jesse, the Tree of Life, where the Bridegroom purchased the love of his Bride. In this context her modest gratitude, paraphrased by William Baldwin, makes perfect sense: "*I am scarce a flower,/ Where thou art very frute.*" [65]

We are now in a position to recognize the sacramental meaning of the Tree of Jesse and its related figures. This Tree is the embodiment of God's mercy, without which the human soul in general would have perished in the heat. Accordingly, Thomas Page writes, the Tree of Jesse enclosed the soul "in mercies shade":

> Poore naked man! naked alas,
> Who onely cloth'd with fig-leaves was!
> But *Jesse's* branch our souls arraid,
> And wrapt our sinnes in mercies shade:
> Since when is ceast that fatall strife
> Of *tree* of *Knowledge* and of *Life*.[66]

As Page would have it, man had been left naked by his sin. Clothed only by the inadequate fig leaf sewn by his own hand, naked he remained in the sight of God. But having drawn within the shade of the Tree of Jesse, the new Adam found respite from the "strife" imposed on him by the Fall. What had looked like two separate entities, the Tree of Knowledge and the Tree of Life—God and man, life and death—by Grace had become one.

REPOSE

Implicit in the contrast between shade and its absence is that touch-stone of the nature-Grace motif, the contrast between labor and repose. The Bride's torment began "because," in her occupation as the keeper of another's vine, she was exposed to the sun. Brought within the shade of the Christ Tree, not only was she now pro-tected from the heat of that sun but she was blest with the comfort of repose. Indeed stillness was more than her natural response to this shade; it was the sine qua non of her inclusion in it. For effort implied the efficacy of human action, while such figures as the withered plant left no doubt that such action must be ineffectual. If she were to enjoy the delights of the apple tree, the Bride must be wholly engulfed and protected by a shadow. As St. Teresa writes in her *Conceptions of the Love of God* (1571–73), an exe-gesis of "certain words of the Songs of Solomon," the soul in this state of enjoyment is inactive: "A person in this state has no need, for any purpose, to move her hand, or to rise (I mean by this to practise meditation), for the Lord is giving her the fruit from the apple-tree with which she compares her Beloved: He picks it and cooks it and almost eats it for her." [67] It is as if "this Divine apple-tree bows its branches" for the Bride. As we can see, the motions of the Tree (rather than of the soul) provide the defining char-acteristic of this intimate relation. The Saviour gives, the soul re-ceives, the fruit of Sacrifice.

St. Teresa's description of the soul's passivity provides the sub-stance of her meditation on the text, "I sat down under the shadow of him whom I desired and his fruit is sweet to my palate." This text, a source of the iconic density in the use of the figure of repose in many seventeenth-century poems, demonstrates the way in which language—apparently abstract to the uninitiated reader—might have quite rich visual associations for its contemporary audience. In Herman Hugo's *A Collection of Religious Emblems*

(1624), for example, the same text, *"Sub umbra illius quem desideraveram, sedi,"* is represented by an engraving (fig. 29) of winged Cupid, crowned by thorns, his hands and feet pierced by nails. This engraving is almost identical to the one described in "An Exposition of the Song of Solomon." As if this were not sufficient proof of a continuing tradition, the very same emblem (though much inferior in execution) became the subject of one of Hugo's poems in *Pia Desideria* (1628).

Hugo's poem is a good example of the way in which biblical commentary operates in verse paraphrase. The poem deals with the fatigue of a soul too long upon its pilgrimage of life. The speaker (the soul-Bride depicted in the engraving) is aware that in her travels "to an unknown Clime" she has "consumed" an excess of time. As time passes, of course, so do the potentialities of life. For this reason, the soul feels parched, as if annihilated by a terrible heat. Yet her reflection, rather than unfolding some overlooked and hopeful possibility of experience, merely reminds her that life's goal is farther removed than ever. Overcome, she weeps:

> Oh! who will shade me from this *scorching heat!*
> See on my head how the fierce Sun-beams beat!
> While by their fervor parch'd, the burning Sand
> Scalds my gall'd feet, and forces me to stand.[68]

As in the commentaries, the heat of the soul's affliction manifests her inappropriate spiritual state. By wasting time she has consumed her life, estranged herself from her desired country. Now, desperate for shade, she is caught in the burning sand of spiritual wilderness. Even so, as discouragement nears despair, she hears the voice of God:

> Whither your hast designs, *says he,* I know;
> Know *what* you want, and *how* you want it too.
> I know you seek *Jerusalem* above,
> Thither your life and your endeavours move:
> But with the tedious *Pilgrimage* dismay'd,
> Implore refreshment from the *Apple's* shade.
> See, see, I come to bring your pains relief!
> Beneath *my shadow* ease your weary grief.
> Behold my arms stretch'd on the fatal *Tree,*
> With these extended boughs I'll cover thee.
> Behold my *bleeding feet,* my *gaping side,*

> In these free Coverts thou thy self maist hide.
> This shade will grant thee thy desir'd repose,
> *This Tree alone for that kind purpose grows.*   (ll. 20–33)

Presently it appears that the "cooling shade" of the apple tree "invites repose," this repose, in turn, being visibly manifest in the engraving, where the Bride reclines beneath the tree. Beginning with the complaint of an overheated soul, the poem ends in celebration of the Passion:

> Now, now, *my Love,* I thy resemblance know,
> My cool, kind, shady residence below.
> As the large Apple spreads its loaden boughs,
> From whose rare Fruit a pleasing Liquor flows: . . . .
>
> (ll. 50–53)

As the source of the soul's "cooling shade," the Saviour is the Tree, the fruit of the Tree, and the liquor pressed in "the winefat" of the Tree. The quotation attached to the poem provides the context in which both engraving and poem should be understood: *"The Tree of Life, to wit, the* Apple, *is the* holy Cross; *its* Fruit *is* Christ, *its* shadow *the* refreshment *and* defence *of mankind."*

As we read in Quarles' *Emblemes* (1635), the Bride's sickness impels her toward the sole antidote: the fruit of the apple tree. Here the language of Solomon's Song recalls the intensity of her distress, as she pleads: "Stay me with Flowers; Comfort me with Apples, for I am sick of love" (fig. 30). Unable to cope with the terrible heat of her lovesickness, she seeks refreshment from the apple tree:

> O fetch me Apples from Loves fruitfull Grove,
> To coole my palat, and renew my sent,
> For I am sick, for I am sick of Love:
> These, will revive my dry, my wasted pow'rs,
> And they, will sweeten my unsav'ry houres;
> Refresh me then with Fruit, and comfort me with Flow'rs.[69]

Until she finds that "covert in the heat," the soul-Bride remains in a state of confusion. Again, in Quarles' analogue to Hugo's emblem, "I sat under the shadoue of him whom I have desired" (pp. 236 ff.; our fig. 31), the soul swelters before God's "eye of vengeance":

I know not where to go, nor where to stay:
    The eye of vengeance burnes; her flames invade
    My sweltring Soule: My soule has oft assaid
But she can find no shrowd, but she can feele no Shade.
                      (Stanza II)

In this instance, we find that the soul has searched through many shades in her effort to escape the heat. But Mirth, Sleep, even Death—all were simply aspects of God's burning eye:

I sought the Shades of Mirth, to weare away
    My slow-pac'd houres of soule-consuming griefe;
I search'd the Shades of Sleepe, to ease my day
    Of griping sorrowes with a nights repriefe;
I sought the Shades of Death; thought, there, t'allay
    My finall torments with a full reliefe;
        But Mirth, nor Sleepe, nor Death can hide my howres
        In the false Shades of their deceitfull Bowres;
The first distracts, the next disturbes, the last devoures.
                      (Stanza III)

Perhaps Quarles' contrast between kinds of shade refers to the traditional belief, traceable to Origen, that all men were born under the shadow (or Curse) of death. But as Quarles' emblem appears to suggest, this shadow by no means saved man from the inexorable heat of God's Law. Made in the image of God, the soul could never die. It could, however (and this was a potentiality too horrible to either ponder or forget), be hurled into everlasting torment. Indeed, eternal damnation was the appropriate payment of a debt already owed. For again, the blazing heat of God's sun was justice incarnate. It was only God's mercy which spared man from this catastrophe; only divinity could shade man from His uncompromising eyes.

As if recognizing for the first time the true nature of this heat, the soul cries out in near despair:

Where shall I turn? To whom shall I apply me?
    Are there no Streames where a faint soule may wade?
Thy Godhead, JESUS, are the flames that fry me;
    Has thy All-glorious Deity nev'r a Shade,
Where I may sit, and vengeance never eye me, . . . ?
    Is there no Covert that will give Protection
T'a fainting soule, the subject of thy wraths reflexion?
                      (Stanza IV)

Then quite suddenly, as in the model poem from Hugo, she looks up to discover herself beneath a tree. Quickly, the Bride unravels the mystery of the Incarnation:

> See, here's a Shadow found; The humane nature
>   Is made th'Umbrella to the Deity,
> To catch the Sun-beames of thy just Creator;
>   Beneath this Covert thou maist safely lie:
>   Permit thine eyes to climbe this fruitfull Tree,
>   As quick *Zacheus* did, and thou shalt see
> A Cloud of dying flesh betwixt those Beames and thee.
>
> (Stanza V)

The quotation attached to the poem points up the deep irony of God's redemptive plan. Having suffered from the heat of the sun, the Bride finds her repose in that self-same sun. For finally, it is the eye of vengeance which offers the glance of redeeming love:

> Ah, treach'rous soule, would not thy Pleasures give
> That Lord which made thee living, leave to live?
> See, what thy sinnes have done: Thy sinnes have made
> The Sun of Glory now become thy Shade. (p. 239)

The same paradox lies at the bottom of Crashaw's "In the Glorious Epiphanie of our Lord God, A Hymn." Sung as an antiphon between the Three Magi, this poem unfolds the paradox of Christ's simultaneous role as both sun and shade:

> (*Cho.*) We (Pretious ones!) in you have won
> A gentler MORN, a juster sun.
> (1.) His superficiall Beames sun-burn't our skin;
>   (2.) But left within
> (3.) The night & winter still of death & sin.

Not only is the morning of the Nativity seen as the advent of a "gentler" day, but the figure of the sun-burnt Bride is in contrast to the inner darkness of man. Christ comes as a "juster sun," as the "sun" bearing a new Covenant. Ironically, this justice is like the soft darts of love: "Thy self our sun, though thine own shade." We go on to read that as Christ bowed his head on the Cross it was as if a furiously burning lamp had gone into eclipse:

> [1.] Time has a day in store
> When this so proudly poor
> And self-oppressed spark, that has so long
> By the love-sick world bin made
> Not so much their sun as SHADE,
> Weary of this Glorious wrong
> From them & from himself shall flee
> For shelter to the shadow of thy TREE; . . . .[70]

The figure of the eclipse governs Crashaw's language treating the paradox of salvation. This gift was given by the exercise of contrary powers: "A mutuall trade/ 'Twixt sun & SHADE."

Perhaps this allegorical context lends a greater depth of meaning than might ordinarily appear at once to Quarles' use of the figure of Zacheus. "Zacheus" is the title image of two poems in Quarles' *Divine Fancies* (1632). In both of these Zacheus, with his short stature (reminiscent of human failing), represents the soul of man. In "On Zacheus" (I), this identity is established through antithetical comparison of Zacheus with Christ:

> Thy paynes in going up, receiv'd the Crowne
> Of all thy labour, at thy comming downe:
> Thy Statures lownesse gave thee faire occasion
> To mount that *Tree*; that Tree, to find *Salvation*:
> But was't the *Tree, Zacheus?* No, t'was *Hee,*
> Whose bleeding Body dy'd upon the *Tree.*[71]

The irony in the poem derives from Quarles' play on the words "mount" and "Tree." This allows him to juxtapose three ascents upon three trees: Christ's upon the Cross, Zacheus' into the sycamore, the soul's (in imitation of Christ) into the Tree of Life. The distinction here between the definite article and the demonstrative adjective ("the *Tree*" is different from "that Tree") ambiguously refers to the sycamore tree and to the Cross. But if Zacheus climbed "the *Tree*," he climbed—mounted—the Tree of Christ. Understandably, then, in "On Zacheus" (II), the speaker sees Zacheus' ascent into the sycamore as the climb up Jacob's Ladder: "Well climb'd, *Zacheus*; 'Twas a step well given;/ From hence toth' *Tree*; & from the *Tree* to *Heaven!*"[72]

Zacheus climbs the Tree in order to "see" Christ, and in so doing succeeds in the *Imitatio Christi*. He who properly grasps the sig-

nificance of "the *Tree*" knows from experience that the instant of
Christ's death was the moment of his union with mankind:

> This was our Saviour's nuptial day,
> The bitter Cross his marriage bed,
> Where he his patient head down lay,
> His loving Spouse the Church to wed: . . . .[73]
>
> (Watkyns, *Flamma Sine Fumo*)

Not only did Christ's outstretched arms beckon the Spouse to his
embrace, but the Cross was the bed on which their mutual love
was consummated. As in Herbert's "Even-song," we learn that
because of the Incarnation God had taken on a species of blindness. No longer was man banished from his Creator's sight; no
longer need he struggle to be worthy. The gift of love had been
given, and any attempt to repay it became like "balls of wilde-fire
to" the "troubled minde." [74] God had closed His eyes; He had, as
it were, enclosed man within a box. For Quarles, divine love was
a "garden inclosed" where the Bride rested as on a bed, free at
last from the "sowltrie weather" of the Law.[75]

This is the meaning of that delicious passivity described by St.
Teresa. The soul's struggle, futile from the start, has been relin-
quished. Effort, exertion, toil—these recall man's hopeless condition under the Law. On the other hand, as Richard Baxter knew,
this repose is not the same as immobility, for if it were, man, who
had been made in God's image, would be little more than a stone:

> This Rest containeth A Sweet and constant Action of all the
> Powers of the Soul and Body in this fruition of God. It is not the
> Rest of a stone, which ceaseth from all motion, when it attains
> the Center. The Senses themselves (as I judg) are not only Pas-
> sive in receiving their object, but partly Passive, and partly
> Active.[76]

The soul and even the body are aware of "a Sweet and constant
Action" as they receive "their object." It is the act of receiving
that is implied by the lusciousness of the many descriptions of the
mystical shade. The soul passively receives the fruit—passively because that is the appropriate attitude of the recipient of Grace.
And yet the soul receives the fruit of this shade with joy; even in
repose there is a sense of "delight." The apple tree, writes Presby-
terian Alexander Grosse, is a symbol of the Sacrifice partly because

it excels "the trees of the Forrest in comfortablenesse of shadow, sweetnesse of smell, pleasantnesse and plenty of fruit . . . ." [77] The Bride sits down under that shadow "with great delight," to receive the fruit—so sweet to the taste—the fruit being freely given in an act of self-immolation.

Again, the erotic associations of the Song of Songs may be seen. The shade, figure of the Passion and so of spiritual marriage, was the place of the lovers' union. As the soul draws under the shade of the tree, it experiences the pleasures best visualized by a marriage bed; the sweet taste of the Eucharist embodied the union of the soul and Christ. The second chapter of the Song of Songs openly celebrates this extreme of delight:

> Hee brought me to the banketting house, and his banner over mee, was love.
> Stay me with flagons, comfort me with apples, for I am sicke of love.
> His left hand is under my head, and his right hand doeth imbrace me (Cant. ii. 4–6). [78]

Or as Sandys writes in paraphrase:

> He brought me to his Magazines,
> Replenisht with refreshing wines:
> And over me, a tender Maid,
> The Ensignes of his love display'd.
> With Flagons ô re[v?]ive my Powers,
> And strew my Bed with Fruits and Flowres,
> Whose taste and smell may cordiall prove,
> For, ah, my Soul is sick with Love . . . . [79]

Prepare the bed, the Bride urges, for like Solomon she has been made drunk by wine. The difference is that she has partaken of the "newe wine of the kingdome." As one reads in the Song of Songs, the Bridegroom, in the words of Robert Crofts in *The Lover* (1638), ". . . invites us to come into his faire garden, to eate, drinke, with them to bee merry, and to enjoy his presence forever, *Cant, 5.*" [80]

In *Canticum Canticorum* we find the iconographic equivalent of these passages. Our figure 32 shows the Bride and Bridegroom with their goblet of wine, while an angel kneels to fill his flagon. We need turn only one page to witness the logical development of this scene of celebration. In figure 33 the wedded couple approach the marriage bed, which has been prepared with a blanket of flowers. The meaning of this woodcut derives from the juxtaposition of still another passage in the Song of Songs (i.16): "Behold, thou art faire, my beloved; yea pleasant: also our bedde is greene." With this text in mind, Luis de la Puente writes:

> *O JESUS of Nazareth, how florishing art thou on this Crosse! thou hast continuallie blossomed all thy life, but much more at the end therof, now maist thou very well saye unto thy spouse the Church:* Lectulus noster floridus: *Our bed is covered with flowers, for that the bed of the Crosse, is replenished with the sweetnes of flowers that thou dost budd forth upon the same; Admitt me (deare Lord) into this thy bed . . . .*[81]

Plants which once perished in the stark heat of the sun now spring from the shaded, regenerate earth. As we see in Sandys' paraphrase, the Bridegroom has sent forth his invitation:

> Come, my Delight, our pregnant Bed
> Is with green buds and violets spred,[82]

and his Spouse has answered.

The figure, as we can see, may be taken in either one or both of two ways. The bed is the garden bed, the bed of flowers, thus, the flourishing ground of the new dispensation. In this sense the figure functions as an emblem of the Church.[83] On the other hand, the bed is the couch where Bride and Bridegroom join in the delights of marriage. Covered with flowers, reminders of the productivity of this love ("Also our fruitful bed is green"),[84] the bed represents the blest state of the regenerate soul. If this is so, it follows that the color green exactly parallels the figure of shade: shade was the love gift, green the emblem of its divine effect.

Put another way, the flourishing of the Christ-Tree brought God's Paradise—a bed of green—into being, or (more accurately) made that bed a human possibility a second time. The Church, shaded by Grace, now yielded forth the buds of regenerate souls, which were the spears of green in God's garden; the soul, shaded from the Sun of the Law, burgeoned within the borders of Christ's Church, the New Jerusalem. Whichever way one viewed it, the green quality of this shade represented the creative power of God's love, which allowed the once withered soul of man to flourish; which turned mankind's cursed ground (*adamah*) into a garden:

> My soul within the bed of heaven doth grow,
> Where Christ hath set it in his own dear wound,
> That with all grace above it might abound,
> And spread his loaden branches here below.
> Why should not then my love still overflow,
> And flourish on so good a ground?[85]

The answer to Alabaster's rhetorical question was given, of course, in the imagery of the poem: the soul grows "within" heaven's garden "bed." Set in that enclosure by the heavenly gardener, the spiritual plant was eternally protected by his extended, "loaden" branches.

It is no wonder, then, that Zacheus climbs this tree. Wise men, like the monk pictured in figure 34, will do the same. The contrasts in this miniature from the Morgan "Psalter and Hours of the Virgin" (c. 1275) depict the artist's allegorical intent. Retreating from the dualism of human life, the darker aspect of which is represented on the right-hand side of the painting (the black rat, the open jaws and fierce eye of a beast), the monk gathers fruit from the tree of the cloister garden. In climbing this tree, he manifests his emergence from the base interests of the world, making it possible for his soul (the Bride of Christ) to ascend by the Grace of God from the narrow limits of the flesh; prayer is the active aspect of the soul's rest. But in order to achieve that delightful passivity desired by St. Teresa, the soul must be "carried out of itself, and . . . so completely absorbed that its faculties are incapable of action."[86] The soul's aim is to transcend the exertions even of the will and understanding. To be made one with the beloved is the desire which draws the soul toward the "shadoue" of the apple tree:

> When that my soul my magique would aspire,
> *Prometheus* like fetch down Celestial fire;
> *Paul* like to *Paradise* rap'd by th' part divine,
> Sure lust doth me unto this tree recline; . . . .[87]

(Collop, "The Fruit of Paradise")

Ultimately, the passive enjoyment of the shade of this tree represents the mystical union between the soul and her Spouse, and so, the highest stage of the Christian life. The soul longs to transcend all taint of labor, by spiritual endeavor to pass to spiritual union, to surrender its understanding[88] in order to be joined with the object which (the soul now knows) can never in this life be wholly understood. The soul relives, on this highest of all possible human levels, the life of Christ, and the flourishing of the "bed of green" beneath this shade reflects the success of the soul's imitation.[89]

CHAPTER IV

Time

TIME IN THE GARDEN

It was the distinction of the Song of Songs that it embodied at its highest level the mystery of "spiritual conjunction." When one recognized this fact, he knew one thing beyond any doubt: that mystery was nothing short of the mystery of life. For mystical union as described by Solomon took place in history, like any other event, and yet that union was somehow separated from time. Solomon's bed, the mystical bed of the Cross, though incarnate in time, transcended the physicality implied by time's very existence. In one sense, this simply means that the Song of Songs was a "history," a record of past events, which is easy enough: the Canticles rehearsed the story of the wandering of Israel, and further, of the Fall and Expulsion. But the Song of Songs was more than a history, for unlike most histories, this narrative described the trinity of past, present, and future. Moreover, it revealed the triune quality of every human event, which was seen as recapitulative, adumbrative, and immediate. There was then a sense in which no event would stay put in time. The Song of Songs was a "history" of the present and future as well as of the past. It did not stop with the life of Christ, though that life was the final answer to man's Fall and Israel's wandering. Though salvation was assured before time began, though Christ descended into his robe of flesh to accomplish that salvation, the final union between God and man lay in the future (just how far no man with certainty could say). God's plan of Redemption was, nevertheless, a fact of experience in the here and now, and would be so as long as men were born and lived and died, so long as time lasted.

In the seventeenth century, the idea of time was very closely linked to the garden image. The transitoriness of the garden forms reminded of man's impending death (Herbert's "Life"); and, allegorically, the wall, the fountain, and the tree's shade revealed the true meaning of the Incarnation. Artists and poets alike recognized this fact, and by manipulating these figures invested their works with rich associations of the role of time in human events. Erwin Panofsky has shown how painters of the Flemish School, who were so attracted to the figure of the garden, were intensely concerned with the problem of time. Strict observance of historical sequence seemed to them as important as fidelity to physical form.[1] Thus, while adhering to a "realistic" setting, paintings like Campin's "Merode Altarpiece" perpetuate the use of hortus conclusus. Again, paintings which reveal a lapse of order in the walled garden (the Van Eyck "Annunciation," for example) point up not only certain theological ideas but the immense difficulty of the problem of time. With the Creation of Eden, the garden was sown; at the Fall, from man's point of view, it went to seed. The Incarnation restored the garden, yet it would not flourish in its full perfection until time had ended. Paradoxically, with all this ebb and flow (the idolatry and wandering of the Church), it was necessary to see that from God's point of view the garden remained unchanged.

To look at it another way, Christians believed that at given times unique men, in spite of the Curse, became while in the flow of history like flowers set in the Bridegroom's garden, "past" all change, "Fast" in the Paradise of God. If so, they must have partaken in some mysterious way of an experience transcending time. To the question, How may one sense with St. Teresa the flavor and fragrance of flowers and fruit growing only in another world? the answer given was "Taste and see." The mystic neither offered nor asked for a rational explanation of what he considered wholly imponderable. At the roots of the mystical experience one finds almost always an anxious concern with time, which is stilled only by complete submission to the mysterious—experience. An even more baffling aspect of the problem arose from the fact that even the saint knew how limited the most elevated experience had to be, for experience and duration were inseparable. Time was the demon tyrannizing over the most divine of moments, forcing the individual back from Paradise into the wilderness of this world.

With men of the seventeenth century, the idea of time was almost an obsession.[2] Time confounded them with its austere detachment, and with what seemed like power to deliver or remove the precious. Difficulties aside, however, one thing was certain: all men were born and must die in time, that is, *in*—as if inside of —time. One might even think (with the emblem writer) of man's flesh as a "glass," and of every breath as a grain of sand, each grain having been counted and placed in the hourglass before birth; and life would then be seen as a helpless waiting upon that final grain (whose number no man knew) to fall.

If the tone of the last paragraph seems overly dramatic, it is purposely so. For in the seventeenth century the idea of time was (in the most literal sense of the term) dramatically conceived. Time was a figure whom a person might actually meet. Indeed, his stern, awful voice was known to all. Nor are we now talking about the figure of Time, with his wisp of hair in front and bald pate behind, as he was known in various literary and pictorial sources. Encounters with Time in this form were frequent enough, and they had their own importance for literature. But there was a more literal dramatic level involved in this (as we might call it) "masque of time." The setting of the drama we are to consider was always the same: whether with its graveled walks or its pleached alleys, with or without its fruit trees or playing fountain, that setting was the walled Tudor or Stuart garden. The precipitating action might be a solitary walk or a moment of quiet repose; the players were Everyman and Time.

The disguise in which Time most frequently appeared was that of a loquacious sundial. As the masque unfolded, Time was always the aggressor, prodding the passerby for response, only to force upon him a sad reflection:

Diall (*loq.*) Staie, Passenger
Tell me my name
Thy nature.
Pass. (*resp*) Thy name is die
All. I am mortall
Creature.
Diall (*loq.*) Since my name
And thy nature
Soe agree
Think on thy selfe
When thou looks
Upon me.[3]

In this anonymous example, the *contemptus mundi* motif, typical of such inscriptions, is amplified perhaps with special force. The passerby knows his name: given to him by Innocent III, it is the human condition. Man's answer to Time's query must be that he is "mortall Creature," living only to die. The dial has initiated the exchange for the sole purpose of bringing him to this recognition. It is as if he would say to man, "Rehearse to me this moment exactly the way in which I define your limits. Admit to me that even now you are wholly in my grasp." Thus, Time's injunction, "Think on thy selfe," means "Think on your limits when you look on me." For since Time is the very measure of life (and so of the occasion of this meeting), Time implies the fulness of that measure, or death. The seeming circularity of this inscription derives from the assumed identity between Time and mortality. Because of this, the object of man's introspection and the occasion of that introspection are the same—metaphorically, Time itself. The sundial, in turn, is little more than a reminder of human limitation. The name of man and the nature of Time are alternative means of reminding of the irrevocable passage of life, to which mankind is thrall. Thus, the dial is a friend, sternly warning man that he too is a form of clock, measuring out the mysterious quantity of life.

During the sixteenth and early seventeenth centuries, the "art of dialling" gained wide popularity. So popular were sundials, in fact, that certain seventeenth-century gardens were designed like giant dials, the numerals and mottoes shaped from planted box or yew. Perhaps the most interesting of all such remaining dials is the huge floral dial at Broughton Castle, Banbury. Made of clipped shrubbery, it stands over six feet tall. The Roman numerals and motto are formed by carefully planted flowers. The motto is actually a brief prayer: "Give light to them that sit in darkness, and guide our feet into the way of peace." [4] The magnificent, multiplex "sundial of 1630," erected by John Mylne at Drummond Castle, stands at the center of a garden which is laid out like a St. Andrew's Cross.[5] And in the lovely, enclosed rose garden of Broughton Castle, a sundial is the centerpiece, standing atop two circular, turfed steps. Its inscription is eminently typical:

> I tell men hourlie how the shadowes fly,
> For men are shadowes and a shadow I.[6]

The message of dial inscriptions was almost uniformly the same: time was short, eternity long; life uncertain, death sure:

> These shades do fleet.
>   From day to day:
> And so this life
>   Passeth Awaie.[7]

Man must be reminded that his existence was of no more substance than the shadow crossing the dial's face. Indeed, life's movements were less certain than the progress of that thin, dark finger. For while its progress continued, man's life (if God willed) would expire. Whether in the cloister or the gentleman's garden, the sundial warned that the Dance of Death waited for no man. When his glass had run out, payment of his due in full would be exacted. Man's influence on the reckoning that would most certainly be met could be exerted only during his brief pilgrimage on earth. While the finger moved, counting the hours of man's life, man had to choose his eternal destiny.

Such encounters may be found in more serious forms of Jacobean poetry. Aurelian Townshend's "A Dialogue Betwixt Time and a Pilgrime," a poem admired by T. S. Eliot, presents a brief encounter between the spiritual pilgrim and Time, during which the pilgrim poses a series of existential questions. These Time answers succinctly: having asked where he is, the pilgrim is told "In love." As if mistaking the meaning of this, the pilgrim answers, "His Lordship lies above." Time agrees with this, adding only that "His Lordship" is not only above but below, "and round about" where all the flowers of spring suggest the ubiquitous force of love and life. But even here, says the "Aged man," "Time fals as fast a mowing." In other words, Time directs the pilgrim's attention to the immediate situation of their encounter; at the time of their meeting, Time had been mowing the field in the early spring. The pilgrim begins to grasp the meaning of the experience:

> If thou art Time, these Flow'rs have Lives
>   And then I fear,
> Under some Lilly she I love
>   May now be growing there.[8]

He has by no means, however, grasped its full significance. Time's warning, and the subject of this discourse, does not concern the pilgrim's earthly love object. It is this shallow interpretation of the encounter which points up his urgent need of Time's counsel. Careful not to contradict the pilgrim openly, Time accomplishes his intent by sharply focusing attention on the pilgrim himself. For in this momentary self-awareness the true dimensions of the experience are realized: "in some Thistle or some spyre of grasse,/ My syth thy stalk before hers come may passe." This new meaning induces anxiety in the pilgrim, who now would know what the future holds in store. Only now is he prepared for the awful truth that no matter how powerful he appears from the pilgrim's point of view, actually Time is powerless: *Che sera, sera.*

When touched by the hand of genius, this traditional encounter with Time could yield an emotional revelation of considerable wit and depth. George Herbert must have had this tradition in mind when he wrote "Time": in this "Meeting with Time," however, Herbert reverses the role of the speaker by making him the aggressor. Not only does the speaker fail to submit himself to the usual image of Time's majestic power, he belittles the very image of that power:

> Meeting with Time, Slack thing, said I,
> Thy sithe is dull; whet it for shame.
> No marvell Sir, he did replie,
> If it at length deserve some blame:
>   But where one man would have me grinde it,
>   Twentie for one too sharp do finde it.[9]

The speaker is in no mood to accept even this weak rejoinder; though he admits that perhaps in the past certain men loved life beyond all other values (and to these Time's "sithe a hatchet was"), he interposes the statement that "Christs coming" reduced Time's power, making that hatchet "but a pruning-knife." Now, no longer under Time's dominion, man is in his debt, for by Time's "cutting" man "grows better." In Herbert's poem, Time must do God's bidding; he has been reduced from "An executioner at best" to a "gard'ner." Where once he brought death and damnation to man, he now brings the moment of translation. Ironically, now man complains that Time tarries unconscionably; his scythe is dull ("Life is very long"):

And this is that makes life so long,
While it detains us from our God.
Ev'n pleasures here increase the wrong,
And length of dayes lengthen the rod.
    Who wants the place, where God doth dwell,
    Partakes already half of hell.

The last stanza points up the extremity of Herbert's reversal of roles:

Of what strange length must that needs be,
Which ev'n eternitie excludes!
Thus farre Time heard me patiently:
Then chafing said, This man deludes:
    What do I here before his doore?
    He doth not crave lesse time, but more.

Time sees that the speaker's true intent has been to escape from time completely, to have "more" time than a single life can give him, to break beyond the limits of human nature. In a note to the poem (p. 520), F. E. Hutchinson provides the relevant context:

And sware by him that liveth for ever and ever, who created heaven, and the things that therein are, and the earth, and the things that therein are, and the sea, and the things which are therein, that there should bee time no longer (Rev. x.6).

Only if Time sharpens his scythe, leveling the grass of flesh, may man gain the timelessness he craves. Anything short of this is that duration which is like a chastening rod.

Inscriptions on sundials might be considered of minute importance were it not for the fact that they had a direct impact on more significant literary forms, on emblem books, for example. The sundial was a favorite image of that most popular of seventeenth-century emblem writers, Francis Quarles. In Book III of *Emblemes*, divine Cupid and his Spouse are found in an enclosed garden (our fig. 35). The Spouse, covering her eyes from the dazzling light of love, points to a prominently stationed sundial. Two other figures—an hourglass and the distant spire of a grandiose sundial—reinforce the theme of the engraving, which is taken from Job: "Are not my dayes few? Cease then, and let me alone that I may bewayle me a little." The poem itself owes much to that venerable tradition described by Martz in *The Poetry of Meditation*,[10] the meditation on death:

> Read on this diall, how the shades devoure
> My short-liv'd winters day; How'r eats up howre;
> Alas, the total's but from eight to foure.

> Behold these Lillies (which thy hands have made
> Faire copies of my life, and open laid
> To view) how soone they droop, how soone they fade![11]

In this example we find Time as the monster—devouring, leveling, destroying. Most horrible of the tolls he exacts is all chance of man's salvation. The Spouse, recognizing the pathetic truth presented by the situation, addresses her attention to the lilies. The flowers, the creatures around her, indeed, her own body—all are clocks, reminding her of the inexorable passing of time and life.

Conceived in this way, the analogy between various timepieces and man's life could be a powerful poetic device. As several critics have recently noted in connection with Spenser, the calendar was no exception. Just as hours may be thought of as the days of life, the year could be seen as the full measure given to man on earth. Time, like the seasons' round, was the all-consuming fact of life, for only within time could man choose his fate. Once time had passed, so had his chances for Redemption. As we see in *The Shepheardes Calender*, here was one formula for tragedy in the Renaissance.[12]

SPIRITUAL AUTOBIOGRAPHY

Colin's tragedy, which is vividly conveyed in the December Eclogue ("'The fragrant flowres that in my garden grewe/ Bene withered . . . ./ Theyr rootes bene dryed up for lacke of dewe . . .")[13] is that, though given time and experience, he fails to learn—to grow spiritually. He and the setting, whether he sees it or not, are the same. The underlying contrast in the December Eclogue—between wilderness and garden—was a traditional device of spiritual autobiography, a literary kind which had great impact on seventeenth-century poetry.

In this context the calendar provided a convenient structure for juxtaposing biographical fact and spiritual truth.[14] For instance, in Vaughan's "Regeneration," the apparent springtime of youth proves to be illusory, for man is born into the wilderness of nature, where, until he is redeemed by Grace, he struggles along a treacherous path, exposed to the raw blast of winter. Underlying the development of Herbert's *Temple*, in just the same way, is the movement of the pilgrim through the Christian year, and so (since "one day is with the Lord as a thousand years, and a thousand years as one day") through life. To the Christian the seasons' round, often represented by a contrast between spring garden and winter wilderness, is a natural figure of man's spiritual life. If man, who is born into the winter of the flesh, dies in the same condition, the year of his life—for all practical purposes, all of time—has been a waste: "Whatsoever a man soweth, that shall he also reape."

In Herbert's *Temple*, man's confrontation with Time is virtually an epitome of the Christian life; if properly redeemed, time is merely a hindrance to longed-for delights ("Time"). If not, the year of man's life ends where it began, in the winter of spiritual death. Time, went the monotonous theme of dial inscriptions, presented man with a distinct imperative:

> As Time and Howres paseth awaye
> So doeth the life of man decaye
> As Time can be redeemed with no cost
> Bestow it well and let no howre be lost,[15]

and this imperative was no less well understood by the writer of spiritual autobiography, who knew that man, like the object of his contemplation, was a creature whose true meaning was not bound by his physical existence. Like the Word, man's existence must be understood, and to be understood, it must be construed —seen in its relation to the timeless. Like Scripture, the physical body potentially revealed the spiritual truth of the Incarnation.

This sacramental interpretation of human events explains the currency in spiritual autobiography of garden figures, which function in much the same way as the timepieces with which they were associated. Springtime in the garden carried multiple meanings referring to the physical and spiritual worlds. Ambiguity of this kind was, of course, a commonplace of spiritual autobiography. Illustrations for March from devotional calendars in books of hours suggest man's calling as spiritual gardener (fig. 36 is typical); spring is the time of life for planting the seeds which will be reaped eternally.[16]

But where the expectation of the palatable effects of spring conflicted with a literal application of the figure, the pilgrim confronted an occasion for despair. Why? Because physical suffering was a sign of potential afflictions of the soul. In Anne Collins' *Divine Songs and Meditacions* (1653), for example, this passage,

> The Winter of my infancy being over-past
> then supposed, suddenly the Spring would hast
> Which useth every thing to cheare
> [W?]ith invitacion to recreacion
> [T?]his time of yeare,[17]

appears at first glance to be a reiteration of the autobiographical motif (seen most prominently in the author's prosy "Discourse") of physical affliction. Apparently, Anne Collins was a woman who because of illness was forced from early childhood to lead a retired life. In the above passage, the word "over-past" suggests that this particular winter has been a lingering one. It may be that childhood has extended past its normal time boundary. The point of view, at least, appears to be that of a speaker still burdened by winter; the qualities of spring are only those that are "supposed" to follow. Here again is the device, used by poets like Spenser and Vaughan, of the illusory springtime. In this case the discrepancy is between the actual and the expected: Spring as a promise, not kept.

In the second stanza, which is a description of spring as it would be known, the question is raised concerning the sense in which one may describe a spring not seen:

> But in my Spring it was not so, but contrary
> For no delightfull flowers grew to please the eye,
> No hopefull bud, nor fruitfull bough,
> No moderat showers which causeth flowers
> To spring and grow.   (p. 57)

Apparently the "it" refers to the promised and hoped-for condition of spring. We are now clearly dealing with two possibilities: it is not simply that winter has failed to pass but that the speaker's

spring seemed like an extension of winter's dearth. Thus the springtime of promise is distinct in kind from the winter of biographical
youth; the poem is moving toward religious metaphor:

> My Aprill was exceedingly dry, therefore unkind;
> Whence tis that small utility I look to find,
> For when that Aprill is so dry,
> (As hath been spoken) it doth betoken
> Much scarcity.

> Thus is my Spring now almost past in heavinesse
> The Sky of pleasure's over-cast with sad distresse
> For by a comfortlesse Eclips,
> Disconsolacion and sore vexacion,
> My blossom nips.   (p. 57)

Similarly, in the early stanzas of Vaughan's masterful "Regeneration," the sky is cloudy, the way bare of flowers, the sun eclipsed.
The soul's blossom has been nipped in the bud.

As in Anne Collins' poem, so in "Regeneration" the speaker begins his life with an illusory experience of spring:

> A Ward, and still in bonds, one day
>   I stole abroad,
> It was high-spring, and all the way
>   *Primros'd*, and hung with shade;
>   Yet, was it frost within,
>   And surly winds
> Blasted my infant buds, and sinne
>   Like Clouds ecclips'd my mind.[18]

Not only is spring an illusion but the actual condition of life is
hostile to growth. Winter blasts the "infant buds" of spiritual
growth, for by nature "A Ward, and still in bonds," the soul begins its pilgrimage in winter, regardless of how attractive the en-
virons of youth may appear. In Vaughan's poem, the title is illuminated by the juxtaposition of the illusory "high-spring" with a
"new spring":

> Here, I repos'd; but scarse well set,
>   A grove descryed
> Of stately height, whose branches met
>   And mixt on every side;
>   I entred, and once in
>   (Amaz'd to see't,)

> Found all was chang'd, and a new spring
>> Did all my senses greet.   (ll. 33–40)

And in both poems, the winter of body and soul is in contrast to the enclosed garden where no storm may enter. Again, both poems seem to allude to the allegorical tradition of the Song of Songs. This is made clear in the case of Anne Collins' "Song," in the last stanza, which is squarely in the tradition of the Canticles:

> Yet as a garden is my mind enclosed fast
> Being to safety so confind from storm and blast
> Apt to produce a fruit most rare,
> That is not common with every woman
> That fruitfull are.   (p. 57)

Despite the speaker's claim that her spring has been but the extension of winter, she now states that her "mind" is an enclosed garden, completely sheltered from storms. This seems to be contradictory. But again, the paradox is traditional. Anne Collins is writing of the root to which the sap secretly withdraws, thus sustaining the spiritual plant through the physical torments of this world. There is no guarantee that the pious life will be pleasant; indeed, the martyrs often found it otherwise. It was from a spiritual winter that the Bride of Christ was called: "Rise up, my Love, my faire one, and come away. For loe, the winter is past, . . . the time of the singing of birds is come . . ." (Cant. ii.10–12). In the garden of eternal spring, it was not surprising that "a fruit most rare" would flourish. For already the models of that flourishing garden had been elevated in the lives of Mary and Christ. The implication here is that most women bear children, the "common" fruit of womanhood. By her denial of the body and of the world, the speaker conveys with the image of the enclosed garden the figure of "heavenly blis," which marks exactly that departure from the bounds of time. While the Christian calendar measures time on the one hand, it unfolds the timeless on the other.

And if there is any doubt that the garden in Vaughan's poem is that enclosure of the Song of Songs, the quotation attached to the poem should remove it:

> Cant. Cap. 5. ver. 17.
> *Arise O North, and come thou South-wind,*
> *and blow upon my garden, that the spices*
> *thereof may flow out.*

Ross Garner has argued that this quotation from the Song of Songs provides the key to the last half of Vaughan's poem.[19] The poem itself represents the three stages—purgative, illuminative, and unitive—of the mystical life. Though Garner's analysis of the poem leaves little to add, if we are to take his comment on the quotation from the Canticles seriously, some adjustment may be needed. If the poem is in the tradition of spiritual autobiography, why should the passage from the Song of Songs be read, as he suggests, as the prayer of the Church? It is the speaker who has entered the sacred grove, and his prayer is the subject of the last stanza. We have seen that from the beginning commentators held that the figure of the enclosed garden could be interpreted as either the Church in general or the individual soul. While writers like the Victorines emphasized the ecclesiastical, those cited by Garner, such as St. Teresa and St. John of the Cross, emphasized the personal aspect of the metaphor. St. Teresa wrote: ". . . it used to give me great delight to think of my soul as a garden and of the Lord as walking in it. I would beg Him to increase the fragrance of the little buds of virtue." [20] Similarly her pupil St. John had said: "This garden is the soul; for, just as the soul called herself above a vineyard . . . so here she calls herself a garden, because there are planted within her, and are born and grow, the flowers of perfections and virtues . . . ." [21]

This may seem like a moot point. But if it is accepted, another more serious difficulty arises: Why must the closed flowers be symbols of the souls who have not availed themselves of Grace? For that matter, how would it be possible to dwell in God's garden without having benefited from the gift of the Sacrifice? And is it necessary, even when we read "Regeneration" in the context of spiritual autobiography, to agree that the term "sleeping" has always a pejorative meaning? Let us take a look at Stanza IX:

> It was a banke of flowers, where I descried
> (Though 'twas mid-day,)
> Some fast asleepe, other broad-eyed
> And taking in the Ray,
> Here musing long, I heard
> A rushing wind
> Which still increas'd, but whence it stirr'd
> No where I could not find.

It could be that this stanza simply reiterates the theme of the second half of the poem, namely, of the mysterious quality of this grove. First, there is the mystery of the Sacrament of Baptism, which is closely linked to the Sacrament of the Eucharist. The fact that the flowers sleep at noon further evokes a sense of mystery: not only are the flowers *able* to sleep at noon but since they do sleep at that time, perhaps the noon here is eternal. Indeed, Garner himself has argued that the last section of the poem deals with that union between the soul and God which transcends all the dark nights of the soul. Night cannot fall in the enclosed garden because the sun, who is the Son, has eternally risen.

Garner is correct in pointing out the importance of the figure of light in Vaughan's poem. But how does that figure relate to that of shade? In Stanza I, "high-spring" was "hung with shade," and in the grove the speaker finds "dumbe shades." Again, seeking the source of the rushing wind, the speaker turns about, dispatching to each shade "an Eye." If we compare the last section of the poem with the first, it becomes clear that shade, like light in other Vaughan poems, expresses a definite value in the poem. But light and sun are not quite the same thing, at least not as far as theology is concerned. For while the outer world appears to have shade, it also appears to have the growth of spring. As the poem unfolds, we learn that this is not the case. Shade, in the tradition of the Song of Songs, implies an escape from the circumstances of the Law, and from the condition of nature. So that while the "unthrift Sunne" shoots the coin of God's realm ("vitall gold/ A thousand peeces") into the grove, we twice read of the shade found beneath the trees. Just as the scales, then, imply the justice of the Law, the shade of the enclosed garden implies an escape from that justice into the dispensation of Grace. Moreover, as the speaker ascends in perfection, becoming more and more aware of the divine mysteries, more and more passive, he becomes more and more able to see that he need not seek. Ironically, what he finally achieves in his communion with God is a union which has its closest analogy in the physical springtime of nature and of man's life. By dying to this world, the speaker is born again forever in the grove of God.

The movement in Vaughan's poem, which is the equivalent of the passing of time in the speaker's life, is just the opposite of that

found in Spenser's *Calender*. It is the history of one who has passed
from winter into spring, from death unto life, from the illusion
into the essence of spring. This is the meaning of that mysterious
denouement of colloquy in the poem. The speaker has struggled
along life's pathway, struggled upward, has seen his deeds weighed
and found wanting in the balance of God's justice. But all the
while he has been moving in time, moving physically, as if his
effort will lead to the soul's rest. At last, however, he settles upon
an experience which ends all need for effort. Whereas for Colin
nothing of any final importance changes, this pilgrim finds on the
contrary, at his entrance into the garden, that "all [is] chang'd."
He is greeted by a "new spring," and as Ross Garner has shown,
he begins the new life of the redeemed spirit. Released from the
winter (or illusory spring) of nature (and the Law), he has
transcended the limits of human life. While no mere phantom, the
garden into which the soul has entered is mysterious, not to be
fully comprehended by the mind. Ultimately, the garden represents
the mystical union between the soul and God. The utterance of
the wind, "where it please," simply means that though the "how"
may elude man's understanding, the experience of this union is not
bound by time or space, for it represents the reach of the human
spirit, quickened by Grace, which passes understanding, the reach
of the apparently time-bound beyond time.[22]

"WHOLSOME HOURS"

As we can see, the idea of an encounter with Time was a flexible
one indeed. It might be construed as a confrontation with a physical
object (the sundial) or as the expanded experience of the whole
of an age or life. But regardless of how it was treated, the encounter
with Time carried with it an implied imperative that time be spent
properly. Time was given, but it was not man's to do with as he
pleased. Like his body, time was a gift from the Creator, and for
its use man would certainly be called to account. Doubtless the
activity most appropriate to the divinely ordained end of man was
meditation. Meditation, the means by which the spiritual pilgrim
approached Paradise, was the Alpha and Omega of the spiritual

life; it was the method of Purgation, the path to the Unitive Way: as we read in Nicholas Breton's *The Pilgrimage to Paradise* (1592), "tis a walke, of onely vertues will,/ And to be founde, but by the spirits skill." [23]

Of the formal meditative tradition, I need say little. Louis Martz' seminal study has admirably demonstrated the relevance of that tradition (especially as it stemmed from Ignatius Loyola) to the structure of seventeenth-century poetry.[24] Our present concern must be with the role of the garden (whether literal or figurative) in the meditative life. The historical garden cannot be ignored, partly because it played an important role in the "masque of time." As we shall see, the physical garden became an emblem of meditation; its very shape and substance were understood allegorically, and this understanding had much to do with the burgeoning interest during the sixteenth and seventeenth centuries in gardening as an avocation. Though present space prohibits a thorough discussion of that interest, some sense of the backgrounds of Tudor and Stuart gardening will be of help in understanding how the garden image functions in the poetry of the time.

The spectacular interest in gardening during the Renaissance represents the final development of the formal garden, which was originally modeled after the enclosed garden of the monastery.[25] During the Middle Ages the Benedictines reintroduced the love of gardens into Western Europe, and in so doing, with their cloistered gardens revealed the almost universal medieval taste for allegory. At the very center of the ecclesiastical world, one side of the garden touched the entrance to the church. There, blossoms were picked from the flower beds to be sprinkled for Mass. On the other sides were the refectory, the dormitory, and the chapter house. It is in a setting very much like this that we must picture Friar Lawrence—and perhaps even the speaker of Herbert's "Life" —gathering posies; in a garden shut from the world by high walls devoted men wandered through the ages at their prayers until, at last, as G. G. Coulton puts it, monachism, with its cloistered garden, came to represent "the extreme ideal of 'otherworldliness' in the Church." [26] The garden became an important emblem of the meditative life. In other words, as Guillaume Durand writes, the equation of garden and Celestial City worked both ways: "The diversity of the dwellings and offices around the cloisters signifie[d] the diversity of the dwellings and recompenses in the heavenly kingdom." [27]

The implications of Durand's statement are of considerable importance to our study. The comparison between the physical garden and the Celestial City had an immediate personal significance, according to which the cloister represented "the contemplation into which the soul withdraws itself and hides, after being separated from the crowd of carnal thoughts, and where it reflects upon the only real blessings—symbolizing contempt for oneself, contempt for the world, love for one's neighbour, and love of God." [28] As Nicholas Breton writes in "The City of God," the New Jerusalem is not built of metal and stone but of the flowers of virtue, blooming because nourished by "the Well of Life" (the truth of Scripture) springing in the garden's midst.

Implicit in the monastic life was the undoubted value of solitude, and here again the garden was a crucial figure. According to E. Allison Peers, St. John of the Cross, apparently unsuited to the strict pattern of meditation advocated by St. Ignatius, "introduced and encouraged the habit of solitary meditation in the friary gardens" in Spain.[29] St. François de Sales believed that every day one should seek, with Sta. Caterina da Siena, that "holy spiritual solitude" found in gardens, where one was to "gather a little devotional bouquet" and enjoy the profits of meditation upon it.[30] As Martz has shown, George Herbert's "Life" owes much to this tradition.[31] In this short poem, Time emerges as a beckoning, advising figure. Indeed, "Times gentle admonition" is that "time" properly be spent, for only then will the pilgrim's life be "without complaints or grief." Solitude, meditation, the garden—these three go hand in hand. Thus in Marvell's "The Garden," "Fair quiet" and "Innocence" are incompatible with "busie Companies of Men"; these sacred qualities flourish only in the solitude of the garden:

> Your sacred Plants, if here below,
> Only among the Plants will grow.
> Society is all but rude,
> To this delicious Solitude.[32]

Herbert's "Life" (p. 94) is typical of the meditation on a posy, and of the strong emphasis of such meditations on the theme of time, which always functions as a stern reminder of human limitation. Such poems bear close resemblance to the monastic ethic of contemptus mundi, which is closely related to the ideal of solitude. The link in Herbert's poem between the image of the fading flower and death is familiar enough—known even to the sonnet sequences. But here the emphasis is very different from the imperative to seize the moment in a fury of pleasure. Now, the fading flower is the image of beckoning, admonishing Time: "By noon" the flowers "most cunningly did steal away" suggests the masterful elusiveness of time which no man is prepared to match. Even as the flowers appeared fresh and new while the speaker placed them in his bouquet, "the day ran by," and with it his life. The flowers wither before the day is half spent. Even more solemn is the fact that they wither inside the speaker's hand. Not *in* the palm, nor *on* the hand, but *in* the hand. As if no matter how tightly man takes hold of them, he is powerless to resist the swift corruption imposed by time. The second stanza is a moving statement of the speaker's application of present experience to his own "Life," what Martz has called the "analysis" of the situation. The pathos derives from the direct, simple, swift acknowledgment of a new insight:

> My hand was next to them, and then my heart:
> I took, without more thinking, in good part
> Times gentle admonition:
> Who did so sweetly deaths sad taste convey,
> Making my minde to smell my fatall day;
> Yet sugring the suspicion.   (ll. 7–12)

It is as if during this brief meditation the speaker has suddenly or in a new and powerful way been confronted with the meaning of life. Or as if not until now has he fully understood the demand implied by the passage of time. Life is short—over even in the moment it seems grasped most securely. Since no man can know or change the length of his life, it is therefore of no consequence. He can, however, alter the quality of his life regardless of its length. Indeed, for this he is fully responsible:

> Farewell deare flowers, sweetly your time ye spent,
> Fit, while ye liv'd for smell or ornament,
> And after death for cures.
> I follow straight without complaints or grief,
> Since if my sent be good, I care not if
> It be as short as yours.   (ll. 13–18)

Figure 1. "Solomon and Sheba." Needlework. Reproduced by permission of the Henry E. Huntington Library and Art Gallery.

Figure 2. Otto van Veen, *Amoris Divini Emblemata* (Antwerp, 1660), p. 119. Reproduced by permission of the Henry E. Huntington Library and Art Gallery.

Figure 3. Robert Whitehall, *Sive Iconum* (Oxford, 1677), icon 141. Reproduced by permission of the Henry E. Huntington Library and Art Gallery.

Figure 4. Roger van der Weyden, "The Annunciation." The Metropolitan Museum of Art, Gift of J. Pierpont Morgan, 1917. Reproduced by permission.

Figure 5. Hours of the Virgin [nine large miniatures cut from books of hours . . . .
Paris, 16th century], HN 129342, leaf 2. Reproduced by permission of the Henry E.
Huntington Library and Art Gallery.

Figure 6. *Canticum Canticorum* (Netherlands, c. 1465), p. 2, bottom. Reproduced by permission of the Pierpont Morgan Library.

Figure 7. *Canticum Canticorum* (Netherlands, c. 1465), p. 4, top. Reproduced by permission of the Pierpont Morgan Library.

Figure 8. *Canticum Canticorum* (Netherlands, c. 1465), p. 3, bottom. Reproduced by permission of the Pierpont Morgan Library.

Figure 9. The Huntington Kitto Bible (1836), Vol. II, fol. 248. Reproduced by permission of the Henry E. Huntington Library and Art Gallery.

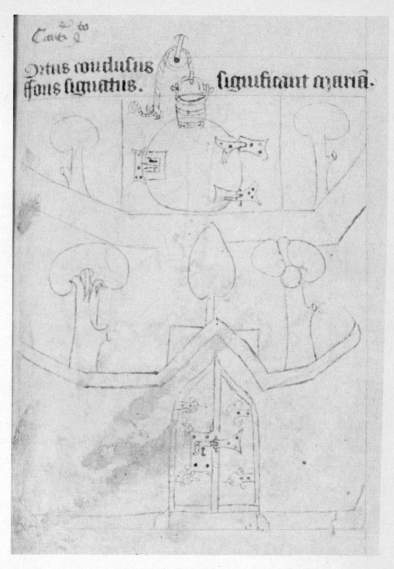

Figure 10. "Speculum humanae salvationis" (England, c. 1390), Morgan MS M.766, fol. 25. Reproduced by permission of the Pierpont Morgan Library.

Figure 11. *Hours of the Virgin* (Paris, 1511), sig. N6ᵛ. Reproduced by permission of the Henry E. Huntington Library and Art Gallery.

Figure 12 (*at right*). Henry Hawkins, *Partheneia Sacra* (Rouen, 1633), frontispiece. Reproduced by permission of the Henry E. Huntington Library and Art Gallery.

Figure 13. Henry Hawkins,
Partheneia Sacra (Rouen,
1633), p. 13. Reproduced by
permission of the Henry
E. Huntington Library
and Art Gallery.

Figure 14. Henry Hawkins,
Partheneia Sacra (Rouen,
1633), p. 172. Reproduced by
permission of the Henry E.
Huntington   Library
and Art Gallery.

Figure 15 (*at right*). "Hours of the Virgin" (Champagne, c. 1430), Morgan MS M.157,
fol. 119ᵛ. Reproduced by permission of the Pierpont Morgan Library.

Figure 17. Hubert van Eyck (?), attributed by the Metropolitan Museum of Art to Jan van Eyck, "The Annunciation." The Metropolitan Museum of Art, The Michael Friedsam Collection, 1931. Reproduced by permission.

Figure 16 (*at left*). "The Kildare Book of Hours" (Paris, c. 1415–20), Morgan MS M.105, fol. 20. Reproduced by permission of the Pierpont Morgan Library.

Figure 18. "The Kildare Book of Hours" (Paris, c. 1415–20), Morgan MS M.105, fol. 85. Reproduced by permission of the Pierpont Morgan Library.

Figure 19. "Hours of the Virgin" (Bruges, 1531), Morgan MS M.451, fol. 66ᵛ. Reproduced by permission of the Pierpont Morgan Library.

Figure 20. "Hours of the Virgin" (Bruges, c. 1520), Morgan MS M.399, fol. 322ᵛ. Reproduced by permission of the Pierpont Morgan Library.

Figure 21. *Canticum Canticorum* (Netherlands, c. 1465), p. 8, top. Reproduced by permission of the Pierpont Morgan Library.

Figure 22. *Antheologia* (1655), frontispiece. Reproduced by permission of the Henry E. Huntington Library and Art Gallery.

Figure 23. Joseph Fletcher, *The Historie of the Perfect-Cursed-Blessed Man* (1629), p. 4. Reproduced by permission of the Henry E. Huntington Library and Art Gallery.

Figure 24. Joseph Fletcher, *The Historie of the Perfect-Cursed-Blessed Man* (1629), p. 20. Reproduced by permission of the Henry E. Huntington Library and Art Gallery.

Figure 25. "Hours of the Virgin" (France, c. 1490–1510), Morgan MS M.175, fol. 21. Reproduced by permission of the Pierpont Morgan Library.

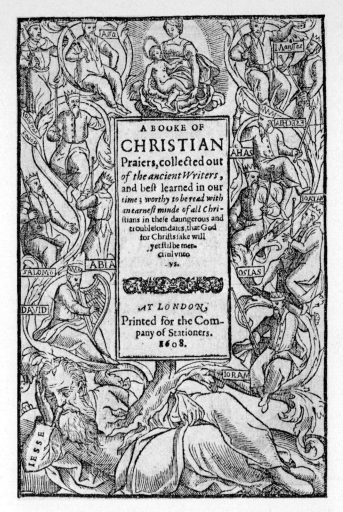

Figure 26. *A Booke of Christian Praiers* (1608), from the title page. Reproduced by permission of the Henry E. Huntington Library and Art Gallery.

Figure 27. George Wither, *A Collection of Emblemes, Ancient and Modern* (1635), p. 217. Reproduced by permission of the Henry E. Huntington Library and Art Gallery.

Figure 28. "Psalter and Hours of the Virgin" (Amiens, c. 1275), Morgan MS M.729, fol. 345ᵛ. Reproduced by permission of the Pierpont Morgan Library.

Sub vmbra illius quem desideraueram, sedi.
Cantic. 2.

Figure 29. Herman Hugo, *A Collection of Religious Emblems* (Antwerp, 1624), p. 29. Reproduced by permission of the Henry E. Huntington Library and Art Gallery.

Stay me with Flowers; Comfort me with Apples, for I am sick of loue. Cant: 2.5.
Will: Marshall sculpsit.

Figure 30. Francis Quarles, *Emblemes* (1635), p. 248. Reproduced by permission of the Henry E. Huntington Library and Art Gallery.

I sat vnder the shadoue of him whom I haue desired. Cane: 2. Will sin son Sculp

Figure 31. Francis Quarles, *Emblemes* (1635), p. 236. Reproduced by permission of the Henry E. Huntington Library and Art Gallery.

Figure 32. *Canticum Canticorum* (Netherlands, c. 1465), p. 6, bottom. Reproduced by permission of the Pierpont Morgan Library.

Figure 33. *Canticum Canticorum* (Netherlands, c. 1465), p. 8, bottom. Reproduced by permission of the Pierpont Morgan Library.

Figure 34. "Psalter and Hours of the Virgin" (Amiens, c. 1275), Morgan MS M.729, fol. 354ᵛ. Reproduced by permission of the Pierpont Morgan Library.

Figure 35. Francis Quarles, *Emblemes* (1635), p. 172. Reproduced by permission of the Henry E. Huntington Library and Art Gallery.

Are not my dayes few? Cease then, and let me alone that I may bewayle me a little.

Iob . 10 . 20 .

will: simpson: sculpsit

Figure 36. "Hours of the Virgin" (Paris, c. 15th century), Morgan MS M.197, fol. 2. Reproduced by permission of the Pierpont Morgan Library.

Figure 37. Otto van Veen, *Amorum Emblemata* (Antwerp, 1608),
p. 79. Reproduced by permission of the Henry E. Huntington Library
and Art Gallery.

Figure 38. Joseph Fletcher, *The Historie of the Perfect-Cursed-Blessed Man* (1629), sig. D4ᵛ. Reproduced by permission of the Henry E. Huntington Library and Art Gallery.

Figure 40. "The Kildare Book of Hours" (Paris, c. 1415–20), Morgan MS M.105, fol. 64. Reproduced by permission of the Pierpont Morgan Library.

Figure 39 (*at left*). The Huntington Kitto Bible (1836), Vol. II, fol. 250. Reproduced by permission of the Henry E. Huntington Library and Art Gallery.

St. AVGVSTINES
Confessions translated:
and
With some marginall notes
illustrated.
By
William Watts, Rector
of St. Albanes,
Woodstreete.

Take up and reade. Tale vp and reade.

Nōt in rio tantone; not
ing and in stripe and
Drunkest enuying
notē ciā Rom: 13:
strife and   13:

London printed by Iohn Norton for Iohn Partridge: and
are to be sold at the Sunne in Paules Church yard. 1631
Ro: Vaughan fecit.

Figure 41. *St. Augustines Confessions* (1631),
title page. Reproduced by permission of the
Henry E. Huntington Library and Art Gallery.

That the physical garden summoned up such associations of contemptus mundi and solitude can hardly be doubted. It seems fair to say that these ideas were an inheritance of the religious provenance of the formal garden. The most important parts of the Italian forerunners of the English secular garden were their fountains, which were called "*tempietti*," or "temples." In just the same way religious meanings permeated the English formal garden. The "summerhouse," while falling often enough to sybaritic use, was primarily a place of meditation, designed as something of a garden chapel. Here the Englishman inclined to devotion withdrew from worldly cares to meditate on his surroundings, and on the proper ends of life. Even his efforts at gardening, as the numerous handbooks show, were understood to have religious significance. A man like John Melton believed that when he entered the walled garden he confronted in the here and now manifold signs of his need of and hope for salvation, signs perceived as, through the process of meditation, his experience in the garden is allegorically applied:

> But as I was seriously looking over this Æden of delight, my eyes tooke notice of a withered banke of flowers, hanging downe their weather-beaten heads, that not seven dayes before had flourished in their full prime; intimating unto Man, that the beautie of all Mundane and Earthly pleasures have no perpetuitie.[33]

Though at first construed only in a moral (tropological) sense, the flowers in this garden—more than emblems of mutability—are later recognized as "the true Type of [Christ's] Death and Resurrection; of his Death, in their decay; of his Resurrection, in their growth and flourishing." Every tree reminds the seer of a biblical thought. To John Melton the garden offered more than mere escape from the frustrations of an increasingly complex world. By presenting him with visual reminders of the Passion, the garden offered the perfect image of regeneration, and so the ideal point of departure for the soul's ascent to perfection.

The association of the physical garden with particular biblical texts accounts in large part for the direction of the allegorical application of the object. Just as the verse paraphrases of the Canticles were a form of biblical exegesis, so the meditations on gardens reflect a common interpretation of particular biblical texts. The relevant texts are agreed upon in the majority of handbooks on gardening, and in meditations on the figure or object of the garden. Almost universally cited are the famous passages from the Song of Songs, and these are closely linked to others equally well known from Genesis, Isaiah, Job, and John. It seems that for certain individuals the garden performed a function strikingly similar to that of Biblia pauperum and Speculum. It was a surrogate Bible, the basis of experiences which prompted the immediate apprehension of the truth of Scripture. The obvious analogue here would be the Catholic use of icons. But whereas Protestants denied the efficacy of these images to the soul's benefit, even William Prynne (irrepressible Puritan though he was) insisted on the usefulness of gardens in devotion. In fact, he argued that gardens should take the place of popish pictures:

> If Bibles faile, each Garden will descry
> Them [the truths of Scripture] to us, in a more sweete
>   and lively wise,
> Then all the Pictures Papists can devise.[34]

Not only did the garden present the truth of Scripture to the seer, it confronted him with a picture of his Saviour: the garden, as Prynne writes, "paints" before his eyes the figure of Christ.[35]

As Prynne and others insist, the garden reminds the seer of Christ partly because the Saviour was very fond of gardens:

> Christ, here on earth did *Gardens* highly grace
> *Resorting oft unto them, in which place*
> *He was betray'd, entomb'd, rais'd up, and then*
> *First there appear'd to* Mary Magdalen.
> Each Garden then we see, should still present
> Christ to our sight, minds, thoughts, with sweete Content.[36]

Catholic poets were especially fond of the same examples. In "The Gardener," for instance, Rowland Watkyns draws on the irony of Christ's encounter with Mary Magdalene ("She, supposing him to be a gardener . . . ," John xx.15). As Watkyns gives a poetic account of that first Easter morning, he describes the monstrous irony of Mary's mistake: she passes Christ, not because he is not, but because he is, the gardener. Blinded by her own very human grief, she fails to see that Christ is the paragon of gardeners, and that so he remains:

He is the Gardener still, and knoweth how
To make the Lilies and the Roses grow.
He knows the time to set, when to remove
His living plants to make them better prove.
He hath his pruning knife, when we grow wild,
To tame our nature, and make us more mild:
He curbs his dearest children: when 'tis need,
He cuts his choycest Vine, and makes it bleed.
He weeds the poisonous herbs, which clog the ground.
He knows the rotten hearts, he knows the sound.

If all this sounds Protestant enough, let it be said that this passage treats of Christ's dressing of the many hearts that make up the Congregation of the Church, and that the poem ends with an echo from Victorine lyrics:

The blessed Virgin was the pleasant bower,
This Gardener lodg'd in his appointed hour:
Before his birth his Garden was the womb,
In death he in a Garden chose his Tomb.[37]

Jesuit Henry Hawkins' method as seen in *Partheneia Sacra* (1633) reflects a similar concern (traced by many to the Council of Trent) for the participation of the senses in the processes of devotion. According to St. Ignatius, the senses were to become fixed upon some physical token of a divine mystery. This focus (coincident with Martz' "composition") was accomplished by Hawkins' "Devise," the graphic representation of the "Symbol" which is to be considered. The first of these is that of the enclosed garden (our fig. 13). The mind is to "dallie" with this figure in the manner of the author's "Character." This is the *imprese*, which the mind is to observe without being taxed. At this point there is no attempt to decipher the figure's meaning. Rather the attention is centered, the mind prepared for the next step, which is the consideration of the "Motto" or "The Moral" (part two of the "Devise"), where the mind looks in a superficial manner upon the motto: *"There is no rule without exception."* Some application to the *"Paragon"* (the Virgin) is made, though this is of a brief, relaxed kind. The mind is to see a relation between the motto and the emblem; the exception in human activities is in that area where human meets divine. Thus the Church has always been considered a sanctuary from civil demands. The mind is still in the physical realm, still thinking rationally, still unmoved. The mind continues to maneuver until it returns to glimpse the connection between the motto and the enclosed garden: The Prince "hath then a private Garden of his owne, and keeps the keys himself. Long live the Prince then, to enjoy his Garden; and cursed be he, that shal but with the mouth or hart seeme to violate the sacred closures of his Garden." [38]

"The Essay" ("The Review") is a consideration of the temporal garden. Here the speaker points to the various flowers, animals, and topiary shapes in the garden. Still, he is emotionally unmoved. But at the same time his intelligence is beginning to order his experience; he begins to distinguish the paragon from other possibilities: "Behold, I say the ROSE, dedicated (they say) to that little elf *Cupid;* whose threads are as golden hayres; whose thornes in steed of arrowes . . . ," [39] and so on. It is not that the speaker openly disputes these alternatives. Rather, his mind constructs an orderly arrangement of the alternatives. Not until the end of this section does the speaker finally address the Holy Mother, "the Soveraigne and *Mystical* GARDEN itself, the paragon of Gardens."

In "The Discourse," efforts are made to distinguish between the paragon and all other objects. The speaker is not concerned with the Garden of the Hesperides, nor with Tempe or the "Elizian fields." Neither is the paragon finally compared with Eden, or Gethsemane. His subject, "HORTUS CONCLUSUS," is the touchstone of gardens, including "al things [which] mysteriously and spiritually" beautify gardens. More sacred than all other gardens, as we have read, Mary had been enclosed:

> *The* Virgin *was a* Garden *round beset*
> *With* Rose, *and* Lillie, *and sweet* Violet.
> *Where fragrant Sents, without distast of Sinne,*
> *Invited* GOD *the* Sonne *to enter in.*
> *But it was clos'd:* Alma's shut up, *we know,*
> *What Gard'ner then might enter in to sow?*
> *Or plant within this* Eden? *Or, what birth*
> *Might be expected from a virgin-earth?*
> *The* Holie-Spirit, *like a subtile wind,*
> *Peercing through al, only a way could find.*
> *As th' Earth brought forth at first, how't is not knowne:*
> *So did this* Garden, *which was never sowne.* [40]

Two sections of the meditation, "The Theories" and "The Colloquy," are now left. Returning to the Song of Songs, Hawkins allows us to see the connection between this meditation and the imagery of Henry Vaughan's "Regeneration": "Ponder lastly these words of the *Canticles: Come Southern wind, and blow upon my garden, and the spices shal flow forth.*" Here is the wind which blew upon Mary, dispersing the fragrance of her productive garden. The "Colloquy" may then be seen as the speaker's prayer that he might profitably emulate the Virgin through his meditation: "*O grant me those flowers of thy delicious* Garden, *I beseech thee;* . . . ." [41]

This meditation is indicative of Hawkins' method. The mind, confronting the garden or any particular of the garden in a rigorously disciplined physical apprehension, is slowly lifted to an awareness of its spiritual significance. Thus, in the second sequence, Mary is the "Mystical Rose" which the speaker addresses in prayer: "*Flower of flowers, O* Rose *of roses, O Flower of roses, O* Rose *of flowers!*" [42] Casual observation directs itself toward the emotional frame of mind proper to devotion; in the Apostrophe, the speaker openly announces his dependence on medieval hymnology:

> Salve CHRISTI sacra Parens,
>   Flos de spina, spinâ carens,
>   Flos, Spinati gloria.
> Nos spinetum, nos peccati
>   Spinâ sumus cruentati;
>   Sed tu spinæ nescia. [43]

The marginal notes of the first two emblems (the enclosed garden and the rose) leave little doubt that the emblems must be considered in the context of the Song of Songs. The same is true of the lily and the sunflower; each figure in the garden is one of the "Flowers of al Vertues," the fragrances of which are dispersed by the visitation of the breath of God as it blows over the enclosed garden. In the "Theories" of the first emblem, Hawkins lists all of the flowers, and each becomes an emblem for contemplation. The image of the wind blowing over the garden links, for example, the first appearance of the lily with the later emblem. The lily represents the Virgin's humility:

> Which Humilitie of hers sent forth such an odour unto God,
> as allured and attracted him to her: *When the King was in his
> seaty* [sic], *my Nard gave forth an odour:* to wit, her Humilitie:
> And these are the *Lillies:* Virginitie, Humilitie, and Charitie,
> which cheefly invironed the *Blessed Virgin*, while her litle
> JESUS was hanging at her breast, being *fed among Lillies;* for
> if these be not *Lillies,* what are they? [44]

The lily is always fragrant, for the Virgin

> was *Embalmed* by the *Divinitie*, when the Deitie was lodged in
> her; spiced with *Mirrh*, through the guift of Angelical puritie
> and Virginitie; and enflamed with a sweet Divine love, which
> is as the powder of Cinamon heer understood, hot in smel, and
> tast; hot in smel, and therefore as love, *draw me with the odour
> of the Oyntments*, to wit, with the love of thy heavenlie graces;
> hot in tast, and therefore Divine; because we are bid to *see and
> tast, how sweet our Lord is.* Of which oyntment it is sayd in
> the Canticles: *The odour of thine oyntments, is beyond al
> spices.*[45]

Similarly, in characterizing the fountain of the garden, Hawkins
refers to the fourth chapter of the Song of Songs:

> Behold we now the Incomparable *Fountain* itself of living waters
> of Grace, that flow from thence: to wit, the Signed *Fountain,*
> the most pure *Virgin Mother* of GOD, according to that of the
> *Canticles: The fountain of gardens, the well of living waters
> which flow with violence from Libanus;* and againe: *My sister
> is a signed or sealed Fountain.* . . . because she was likewise an
> *enclosed Garden.*[46]

The duty of the speaker in Hawkins' work is to seek out the
analogy between the emblem and the mystery of the paragon of
gardens, Mary. As we read in the second chapter of the Song of
Solomon, the enclosed garden is an emblem of Mary's love, which
was the antithesis of all terrestrial affection.

Perhaps the best example of the penetration of allegory into the
Stuart concept of the garden is to be found in Ralph Austen's *The
Spiritual Use of a Garden* (1653). This collection of meditations is
attached to Austen's gardening handbook, *A Treatise of Fruit-
Trees* (1657); the two essays might easily be considered companion
pieces, for it appears that Austen wrote his book on horticulture
as the occasion for his extended meditations in *Spiritual Use.* The

relation between the two works may be seen as that between the literal and the allegorical understanding of a text. In the later work, Austen's method is pellucidly allegorical. After leaving no doubt (in his preface) that men may learn from fruit trees, Austen sums up what he intends to do: he will "set downe some Observations" on the spiritual discoveries which may be derived from the contemplations of "diverse SIMILITUDES" among the trees, Scripture, and experience. We know that at least one reader, a divine whose initials are J. F., took Austen quite at his word. In a letter to Austen he wrote: "I seldome came to your garden but what you made your trees *speak* something of Christ and the Gospel." For J. F., the experience of walking in the garden was the gathering of "clusters of gospell grapes"; Austen referred in the same way to "Fruits of the Spirit, Bunches *of Grapes*." Thus man is the harvester, the gardener, gathering the fruits of his "Observations." But at the same time, just as he gathers, he bears fruit: the Christian man is a tree.[47]

The argument of *The Spiritual Use of a Garden* concerns man's summons in his role as a follower of Christ to the proper function of gardener. The earthly garden, subject of *A Treatise of Fruit-Trees*, but the prototype of God's garden, served as a reminder of the union (the "true-loves-knot" to be secured only at the end of time) between the soul and Christ.[48] The garden where that union will take place may be seen only by the Elect. Yet as we read in Henry Lok, in a sense the Christian soul was already planted in that garden:

> Within thy garden Lord I planted was,
>   And watred well with thy most carefull hand,
>   And yet unfrutefull I remain alas,
>   And these thy blessings did not understand:
> In vaine I did employ possessed land,
>   Ten times three yeares thy servants did replant
>   My stocke, and sought to bend my crooked wand,
>   And did supply ech aide I seem'd to want.
> At length my frutes which daily grew more scant,
>   Wild thee resolve to have me weeded out,
>   My soule affections were with folly brant,
>   My roote of faith was shakt with feare and doubt.
>   And lo I pine, sweet Saviour water me,
>   Paul and Appollos worke, else lost will be.[49]

First the soul prays to be removed from the natural wilderness to the heavenly garden; then it prays for the attention of the gardener (in fig. 37 seen as divine Cupid), without whose water there can be no growth.

The image of the graft is familiar enough in the sermons and commentaries of the seventeenth century. We encountered Wither's use of it in the emblem on the Tree of Jesse. Austen's twentieth "Observation" is an extended meditation on the figure of the spiritual graft. The meaning of the figure was clear to Austen: the soul's withered branch was grafted to the root of Christ, in other words married, joined, united. The gardener, in grafting in a shoot, forms from two beings a single organism. The most important distinction to keep in mind, according to Austen, was that between the stock and the graft. The soul of its own power is a withered branch, a dry stick doomed to dust. But when "Ingrafted into Christ," the soul sapped nourishment from the life-giving root, without (in turn) in any way diminishing the life-giving powers of that root. Because in God's garden only perfect flowers grow, this engrafting was a predicate of inclusion within the walls of that garden. No plant grew naturally in this holy plot. No doubt St. Teresa and St. John were right in saying that they bore the flowers and fruit of perfection and Grace for Christ's pleasure. But this was a great paradox, for whatever any man had besides the certainty of death—a withered branch—must have come from God, must have come up from the root: *Our life is hidden in Christ as the root; our graces are all from him, our sap, fruit and all.*" [50]

Emblematic treatments of this idea lent much to the context of such poems as Herbert's "The Flower." In one of George Wither's emblems, for example, we see a large flower and several smaller ones enclosed by a wattle fence. Wither's text is a consideration of the means of sustaining the flower, which has been trimmed and fenced as if by a human gardener. Implicitly, all earthly gardens show the traces of human effort. But the growth of this plant is owing to a force beyond man, for "when the *Gard'ners* worke is done," only the power of the sun can quicken the garden with life. Here, the sun represents God's blessing upon man, for which man owes God his praise:

Let, therefore, those that flourish, like this *Flowre*,
(And, may be wither'd, e're another houre)
Give *God* the praise, for making of their *Seeds*
Bring forth sweet *Flowres*, that, else, had proved Weeds:
And, me despise not, though I thrive not so;
For, *when, God pleaseth, I shall flourish too.*[51]

Recognition of this flower's dependence upon God is the prelude
to the speaker's spiritual application. He now sees that the flower
of his soul is *"new-borne by Grace."* [52] Just as in the natural world
the flower requires human care, the spiritual plant demands attention. There is a sense, as Wither tells us in another place, in which
man must be a proper husbandman. For the soil of his soul is stubborn by nature; it requires the plow and the harrow:

Our *craggie-Nature* must be tilled, thus,
Before it will, for *Herbes of Grace*, be fit.[53]

In the emblem literature of the seventeenth century, the plowing
of the soil represents the humbling of the will: "Our *high-conceit*,
must downe be broke in us." Nature, without effort on man's part
to aid God in the reduction of his will, is wilderness:

Oh *Lord*, thou know'st the nature of my *minde;*
Thou know'st my *bodyes* tempers what they are;
And, by what meanes, they shall be best inclin'de
Such *Fruits* to yeeld, as they were made to beare.
My barren *Soule*, therefore, *manure* thou so;
So *harrow* it; so *emptie* and so *fill;*
So *raise* it *up*, and bring it *downe*, so *low*
As best may lay it *levell* to thy *Will.*[54]

As Martz has shown, meditation, the use of the senses, and the
repetition of spiritual exercises all aimed at one thing: the will.
Man's will was the seat of human nature. If the will could be conquered, man would recover his lost accord with the Creator. This
truth, even villains recognized. It was Iago who so pointedly placed
all blame for man's destiny squarely upon the individual will:

Virtue! a fig! 'tis in ourselves that we are thus or thus. Our
bodies are our gardens, to the which our wills are gardeners; so
that if we will plant nettles or sow lettuce, set hyssop and weed
up thyme, supply it with one gender of herbs or distract it

with many, either to have it sterile with idleness or manured with industry, why, the power and corrigible authority of this lies in our wills (*Othello*, I.iii.321–28, New Cambridge Édition).

Like Adam, man had been given charge over a garden, to dress it and care for it. As John Hagthorpe writes in his *Divine Meditations:*

> Man hath a garden thats not very large,
>   nor very narrow, and it is his charge.
> To dresse the same, to prune and looke unto it,
>   Least weeds (instead of wholesome hearbs) oregrow it.[55]

The task set for man was not an overpowering one; he was called to tend to his soul's need properly, to know himself, and to regulate his will with respect to the will of his Creator. When he failed at this task, his failure was a serious one indeed, for failure brought to ruin land he did not own. In meditation man tended the garden of the soul.

Now the worlds of spiritual autobiography and meditation begin to merge. The pilgrimage to Paradise and the soul's ascent to spiritual union with God are one and the same experience. That is why St. Teresa's *Life* is also a biography of the soul in ascending levels of prayer, and why she says:

> The beginner must think of himself as of one setting out to make a garden in which the Lord is to take His delight, yet in soil most unfruitful and full of weeds. His Majesty uproots the weeds and will set good plants in their stead. Let us suppose that this is already done—that a soul has resolved to practise prayer and has already begun to do so. We have now, by God's help, like good gardeners, to make these plants grow, and to water them carefully, so that they may not perish, but may produce flowers which shall send forth great fragrance to give refreshment to this Lord of ours, so that He may often come into the garden to take His pleasure and have His delight among these virtues.[56]

By becoming the gardener of his soul, man profitably imitates Christ, who is the gardener supreme. It was he who gave man the pattern of submission to God's will when in the Garden of Gethsemane he offered up his prayer: "Not my will but thine be done." As the soul practices prayer, it establishes the proper soil for the flowers of virtue to spring up, for the delight of their original gardener, Christ.

Again, such a use of the garden image presupposes choice, for an unweeded garden is as good as none at all. We are reminded of the long tradition of the *Roman de la Rose*, where man is pictured as confused over the nature of gardens. Poems like the *Roman*, William Nevill's *Castell of Pleasure*, and Spenser's *Faerie Queene* play upon the theme of unwarranted love, of man's mistaken investment in objects not worthy of his highest affection. Not all gardens represent regeneration. In Southwell's "Loves Garden griefe," for example, the analogy between the garden and the soul is made only in order to depict the barrenness of love when unwisely disposed.[57] Here the speaker is enclosed not by a protecting wall but by thorns of grief and stakes of strife. He is canopied by shade, to be sure, but that shade provides no solace. Called sadness (the outward manifestation of conscience), this shade neither cools nor comforts, but only stings. No song of birds breaks the stillness, and the few trees that manage to prolong their existence in this garden are rooted in sorrow.

One thinks of the garden as a place of growth, just as in the natural sense one considers love creative and gratifying. But this apprehension of the natural man is limited, and if pursued leads to disaster. The barren patch, emblem of human love, deprives the speaker of exactly those expected qualities of gardens. Along its paths lurks the specter of death. Grief is the only harvest of a love spent on an object not fully worth man's investment. As Southwell's poem unfolds we find that he has written what is in effect an antigarden poem, a meditation on exactly the opposite qualities from those found in gardens. Rather than a sign of rebirth, every leaf in this garden is a token of death. And properly so. For the arch antigardener rules over this domain—Satan himself.

The immediately preceding poem in *Saint Peters Complaint*, "Lewd love is losse," serves as a companion piece to "Loves Garden griefe." [58] Its title expresses a distrust of the body, which existed in certain quarters during the Renaissance, and manifested itself in a concern for the sin of lust. In Southwell's poem, since lust is directed solely by a human will, its aim must be toward the total destruction of the mind, and the burial of Grace. Hence, allegorically, the stubborn will continues to crucify Christ. Sin, after all, was the cause of the Sacrifice; and of all sins, lust was the most natural. But in spite of the fact that the world militated against it, only Grace, with its "Viceroy" reason, was capable of staving off man's irrational and self-destructive impulse, in other words, the assault of lust. In short, only Grace could save man from himself. Southwell's speaker, cognizant of this, addresses the reader with this warning, which resembles Thenot's ignored advice to Colin's alter ego, Cuddie: "Gleane not in barren soyle these offall eares,/ Sith reape thou mayst whole harvests of delight./ Base joyes with griefes, bad hopes do end in feares." In Southwell's poem the key word is "Grace," the sine qua non of spiritual growth. The soul yearns, as Southwell writes elsewhere, for escape from the barren garden of this world to a garden where the "flowers of grace" are in eternal bloom.

Of course God was the original sower and husbandman. Those Godlike potentialities in man required (if they were to be fulfilled) that man make a clean distinction between the flesh and the spirit. If man's greatest pains were to clothe the perishable earth, whether, as in the gnomic verses, that earth is his own body, or whether it is the soil against which he struggles to sustain his body, he does so at his own risk. No matter how successful he is through his own efforts, he will have missed the imperative fact that God waters only the earth of the spiritual garden. True, His will ordains the natural movements of the universe, sustains all the forms of life, but except for the spirit, all universal forms must perish. Thus, Thomas Adams warns, in his "Divine Herbal":

> I could wilingly step out a little to chide those, that, neglecting God's earth, the soul, fall to trimming with a curious superstition the earth's earth, clay and loam: a body of corruption painted, till it shine like a lily, (like it in whiteness, not in humility, the candour of beauty, for the lily grows low: *lilium convallium*, Cant. ii. 1, a flower of the valleys and bottoms:).

When man aims at a self-imposed, self-created glory, he manages only to put together a makeshift imitation of life whose very corruption presages the destiny of its maker: "a little slime done over with a pasteboard; rottenness hid under golden leaves; stench lapped up in a bundle of silks; and, by reason of poison sucked from sin and hell, worthy of no better attribute than glorious damnation." [59]

When man's will has been properly subdued, we see in the garden the figure of Love, for he has invested his affections in a proper object. With Prynne, he glimpses in the branches of each tree the emblem of the Sacrifice, which was the essential and eternal meaning of the fruitfulness of gardens: "As the apple tree among the trees of the wood, so is my beloved among the sonnes. I sate downe under his shadow with great delight, and his fruit was sweete to my taste." In the second chapter of the Canticles, as construed by the Jesuit Casimire, the believer received instructions on the means of attaining that blessed receptivity, that ineffable passivity of the soul as it enjoys the fruit of the garden:

> The Apple ripe drops from its stalke to thee,
>   From tast of death made free.
> The luscious fruit from the full Figtree shall
>   Into thy bosome fall.
> Meane while, the Vine no pruning knife doth know,
>   The wounded earth no plow.[60]

Now, all is stillness for, Purgation over, the soul draws near its ultimate pleasure in union. A beginner in prayer no longer, the soul is prepared for what Gaspar Loarte described in the last point of his third meditation on the mystery of the Rosary as "the ineffable joye which the blessed Lady received, who was more then al other replenished with the graces and giftes of the holye Ghost, ..." [61]

In the last analysis, here is the goal of meditation on the garden. All else is means; the end is the subduing of man's will in preparation for union with divinity. The salutary effect of gardens on the body and mind are inconsequential when compared to this, the ultimate objective of meditation:

> But this is nought to those Soule-ravishing,
> Sweete, heavenly Meditations which doe spring
> From Gardens, able to rap and inspire
> The *coldest Muse*, with *a Cœlestiall fire;*
> Yea melt the flintiest Heart, and it advance
> Above the Spheares in a delightfull Trance.[62]
>   (Prynne, "Christian Paradise")

From his consideration of the garden's true (allegorical) meaning to the spirit ("Lord, when we walke in Gardens to delight/ Our mindes, or sences, let the sweetest sight/ Of Thee, and these thy Attributes, . . ." [63]), man grasps the analogy between the garden and the ultimate object of meditation:

> Gardens are fraught with Arbors, *Trees, whose shade*
> *Cooles and repels Heate, stormes* which would invade,
> And scorch us sore: Christ hath *a shade most sweete*
> *Against all scalding Heates, all stormes we meete,*
> *Yea from his Fathers burning Wrath and Rage,*
> *Which none but he can quench, coole, or asswage:*
> O then in all such scorching Flames still fly
> To Christs sweete shade, for ease and remedy.[64]

Now time has been properly spent. The soul-Bride, having brought herself to a contained moment, having subdued her nature, now sees a vision of Christ's love in the object before her. Transfixed in the "Soule-ravishing,/ Sweete, heavenly Meditations which doe spring/ From Gardens," the soul is carried finally "Above the Spheares in a delightfull Trance." [65] And on the mundane or literal level, man can say now, with the speaker of the most noted poem in this tradition, Marvell's "The Garden": "How could such sweet and wholsome Hours/ Be reckon'd but with herbs and flow'rs!"

TIMELESSNESS

The concept of timelessness is paradoxical from the start, for above all things adult consciousness is permeated by the sense of duration. Any idea of experience separated from time contradicts the hardest fact of human life. Yet no idea is more firmly rooted in Christian thought than that of experience not bound by time. Consider, for example, the Christian idea of the city called Jerusalem. As we unfold this multifaceted idea we find ourselves directly in the path of allegory, and so, involved with a paradoxical view of time. According to this, there is a sense in which Jerusalem is an ancient city, with walls blanched and crumbling in the wake of time. But for Moses, Jerusalem was a city not yet born. A fortiori, from the place in time where Sebastian Franck and Peter Damian stood, though Jerusalem was founded in the distant past, in the truest sense it had not yet come into being. Again (and now the paradox is complete), the city could be entered at any time, provided that the soul had properly exercised itself in the spiritual ascent.

"And I John saw the holy Citie, new Hierusalem, comming down from God out of heaven, prepared as a bride adorned for her husband," wrote St. John at Patmos.[66] His apocalyptic vision was a source of inspiration to the poet, who caught through St. John's eyes a glimpse of the heavenly city. And as if that glimpse were as well one of the past as of the future, he described not so much a city foursquare as a "garden inclosed":

> There blustring winter never blowes,
>   Nor Sommers parching heate doth harme:
> It never freezeth there, nor snowes,
>   The weather ever temperate warme.
>
> The trees doe blossome, bud and beare,
>   the Birds doe ever chirpe and sing:
> The fruite is mellow all the yeare,
>   they have an everlasting spring.
>
> The pleasant gardens, ever keep
>   Their hearbes and flowers fresh and greene:
> All sorts of dainty plants and fruites,
>   At all times there, are to be seene.
>
> The Lilly white, and ruddy Rose,
>   The Crimson and Carnation flowers:
> Be watred there with honny dewes,
>   And heavenly drops of golden showers.

The comparison is, of course, with the Garden of Eden:

> With fruite more tooth some, eye-some, faire,
>   Then that which grew on *Adams* tree:
> With whose delight assailed were,
>   Wherwith suppris'd were *Eve* and hee.
>
> The smelling odoriferous Balme,
>   Most sweetly there doth sweate and drop:
> The fruitefull and victorious Palme,
>   Layes out her lofty mounting top.
>
> The Ryver wine most perfect flowes,
>   More pleasant then the honny combe:

> Upon whose bankes the Sugar growes,
>   Enclos'd in Reedes of Sinamon.
>
> Her walles of Jasper stones be built,
>   Most rich and fayre that ever was:
> Her streetes and houses pav'd and gilt,
>   with gold more cleare then Cristall glasse.[67]

Jerusalem, this "garden of glory ever greene," provides the value sought by the spiritual pilgrim: escape from the seasons' round, respite from time.

Examples like this are easily multiplied; they were especially common in the longer allegorical poems of the seventeenth century, where their primary aim was to link the Garden of Eden with the New Jerusalem. Thus, in *The Glasse of Time* (1620), Thomas Peyton describes the Garden of Eden in these terms:

> The lofty walls were all of Jasper built,
> Lin'd thick with gould, and covered rich with gui[lt?]
> Like a quadrangle seated on a hill,
> With twelve brave gates the curious eye to fill,
> The sacred luster as the glistring Zoane,
> And every gate fram'd of a severall stone:
> On stately columes reared by that hand,
> Which grav'd, the world and all that in it stand; . . . .[68]

As we can easily see, his description of the New Jerusalem differs but little:

> That sweete Disciple which the Gospell wrate,
> And lent at supper, (when Christ Jesus sate)
> Upon the bosome of his Lord and King,
> He from the heavens this Paradise did bring,
> Perus'd the walls, and view'd the same within,
> Describ'd it largely all our loves to win.
> The christall river with the Tree of Life,
> Gods deerest lamb, and sacred Spouse his wife,
> The various fruits that in the garden growes,
> And all things else which in aboundance flowes:
> Hath rapt my sence to thinke how God at first,
> Fram'd all for *Adam* and his of-spring curst.[69]

The similarity of these descriptions resided in the nature of the objects themselves, at least as they were understood by men like Robert Hill: "This citie is described in the words following; by a resemblance it is called new Jerusalem, because that was a citie that resembled *Paradise* where Adam was." [70] The objects were *described* as similar because they *were* similar. Again, this marked similarity was a key to the paradox of timelessness as the Christian conceived it. For though a New Jerusalem, this city-garden was of ancient origin. In point of fact, it existed "before the beginning of the world." Why, then, was it called the New Jerusalem? The answer was that the city was new in the same sense that the New Testament was new. Only its revelation to man, not its existence, was new. Although on one level Jerusalem came into being through palpable human effort, though its walls were put together by human hands with mud, wood, and straw, in God's mind the city four-square existed and had always existed unchanged. The similarity between the Garden of Eden and Jerusalem pointed up the symmetry of God's redemptive plan; in allegory, symmetry and similarity were only one step short of identity. From the standpoint of imagery, the many are now pushed into the few, and the few into the One. For behind the allegorizing principle, which ostensibly divides the one text into many meanings, is the Platonic vision of the universe which holds that man's limited view of the manifold forms of reality veils the true glimpse of the One Form which embraces them all. The distinction between time and timelessness is simply another way of stating the formula for the division between physical manifestation and Ideal Form.

The idea of time and timelessness has mystified men for centuries. Mystical writings, and quite orthodox works as well (the two are not necessarily incompatible), offered one solution to this mystery. The idea of timelessness referred not to any view of the perpetuation of temporal forms, but to the transcendence of these forms. The "eternal" was not merely a supernatural perpetuation of earthly forms. Rather, it was a realm of being entirely removed from the conditions and laws to which these forms were subordinated. For God, all time is one. Or, to put it another way, for God time does not exist; He knows the beginning and end of man's tragic sojourn on earth. He sees the limits of man's understanding, and the necessary fate of every material creature in the universe. God created the world in exactly the state of flux in which it exists, and He knew its every turn. But He was in no way subject to that flux; despite the fact that His Being and Perfection could be discerned through observation of the creatures, God existed apart from His Creation. Like material forms, time was a divine invention.

I can think of no better way to illustrate this idea than to recall once again that St. Bernard looked upon the Song of Songs as a history.[71] If we allow for a flexible meaning of the term "history," we discover that in this context history must mean prophecy as well. Man thinks of history as the past, or at the most, as the brief duration of the present (Zeno's paradox notwithstanding) plus the past. But in this thinking he merely reveals his limitation. Unhappily, man is in no position to write a history of the future. In spite of this, he does have access to such a history; in the Song of Songs, he had been given a record of the future as well as of the past. God's "history" rendered to man a full report of all that would happen "inside" of time. Not only does the Song of Songs narrate the love song of Christ to an apostate Church, not only does it trace the history of that Church from the Fall to the Incarnation, it also presents the love call and the condition of the Church in those ages between the Resurrection and the Wedding of the Lamb. As we read in Mrs. Sutcliffe's *Meditations Of Man's Mortalitie* (1634), the only cure for the sickness of the Spouse, expressed in the complaint in the Song of Songs, is the Second Coming, described by St. John in the Apocalypse.[72] Fray Luis de Leon believed that the early chapters of the Song of Songs expressed the love of Christ for a young and thoughtless Church, while the later sections dealt with the requited love for the mature Church. Thus, the invitation, "Let him kiss me with the kisses of his mouth," represents the impetuous love call of a young girl, who would pass through "three phases or states: the state of nature, the state of law, and the state of grace."[73] Put another way, the closing chapters of the Song of Songs tell of the soul's search, or journey, which ends only when the soul enters the promised land: "The journey ends with the arrival of the spouse in the promised land, and once she is established there the Bridegroom speaks of her in these words: 'My sister, My spouse, is a garden enclosed, a garden enclosed [sic], a fountain sealed up.' "[74]

Irony pierces the very fabric of this idea. For though such an image of travel implies movement, actually no movement has taken place. Nothing has changed. Man ends where he began—in a garden. The time lapse (apparent rather than real) exists only in man's limited perspective: hence, for those who arrived at a true understanding of Scripture, the close connection between the Song of Songs as history and Revelation as prophecy. The subject of both was the same. John Cotton, whose *Brief Exposition . . . Upon the whole Book of Canticles* appeared in 1655, praised Thomas Brightman for his commentary on both the Canticles and Revelation, and he particularly admired Brightman's recognition of the close relation between the two books. So completely in fact is Cotton committed to an apocalyptic reading of the Song of Songs that he literally identifies its final verse ("Make haste, my beloved, and be thou like to a Roe, or to a yong Hart upon the mountaines of spices") with the prayer of St. John at Patmos: "Come Lord Jesus, come quickly." For Cotton, the last verse of the Song of Songs is "the Prayer of the whole Church, that is, of all the Churches . . . That Christ would hasten his second coming, as swiftly as the swiftest pleasant creatures, the Roe or young Hart, to come and take them up with himself into the highest Heavens, those mountains (as it were) of spices, ..." Accordingly, this prayer is also "a prophecy as well fore-telling what shall be, as desiring what we will should be." [75]

The identification of the garden with the city foursquare, deriving in large part from this exegetical tradition, leads in several directions, all bearing on a seventeenth-century view of time. First, the link tended to lend sanction to the belief that, notwithstanding the descent of the Golden City in St. John's vision, the city-garden existed from the beginning, indeed, "before the beginning of the world." [76] Second, the drawing of the two figures allowed for a rich shifting of contexts, whereby, for example, passages like this one from the Song of Songs:

> I am come into my garden, my sister, my spouse: I have gathered my Myrrhe with my spice; I have eaten my honie combe with my hony, I have drunke my wine with my milke,

could refer to the dawn of the millennium. This explains why Cotton saw in the last verse of the Canticles, by virtue of its expressing "the Prayer of the whole Church, that is, of all the Churches, whenas all things shall have been accomplished, which the Prophets or the Apostles have foretold," a virtual paraphrase of Revelation xxii.20. As the following example from Mason shows, poetic paraphrase of the Song of Songs responded to the same idea:

> Ah my Dear Saviour! pity Me,
>   Preserve Me in thy Heart.
> And Oh make hast, make hast, that we
>   May Meet and never part.[77]

There was a sense, then, in which the Song of Songs was understood as an apocalyptic prayer. As Morton Bloomfield has pointed out in his interesting book on *Piers Plowman*, the historical level of Scripture ended with the apocalyptic vision, and so on that level all Scripture might be read as aiming for the moment described in that vision.[78] The impact of this eschatological view of verse paraphrase was, as we may see in another example from T. S., considerable:

> My soul dear love's impatient of delay
> Make hast, make hast, and do no longer stay
> Be thou for swiftness like the roe or hart
> My only dear who on the mountains art
> Of spicy pleasures and all rare delight
> That ravish will the heart: and dim the sight
> Of all beholders from those glorious hills
> The swetest pleasures evermore distills;
> While I am here below I am opprest,
> Lord Jesus quickly come, to give me rest.[79]

This conception of the Song of Songs as a prayer is interesting especially when we consider that the same text was thought to be a history. Should we take the levels of explication seriously we would see the way in which the theme of time permeates all of garden allegory. We learn how the garden-soul flourishes in prayer at the very moment it seeks inclusion in the garden. Impatient of delay, the soul is not fully satisfied by the promises; complete rest for the soul lies in the future. Yet in God's mind what shall be is no different from what is: the garden of His Church is now and has been and shall ever be *one* unchanged.

Still, the soul prays—and properly so. Its impatience expresses the soul's desire (loved by God) to be joined in that third and final union with Christ.[80] From the human point of view, it seems as if that union remains to take place: for man, time and the timeless were a lifespan (therefore, since allegory presented history in wider historical or narrower personal terms, centuries) apart. In iconography, this paradox is vividly presented in such works as Jan van Eyck's "Madonna of Chancellor Rolin," where we find the artist's patron kneeling before the Virgin and Child. Panofsky explains that artistic conventions preclude natural man from this sacred presence, which is to be shared only by the angels and saints. The explanation of the patron's appearance in this holy company may lie in that interesting contrast between Gothic and Romanesque architecture. In this instance, Romanesque prevails, but the context does not allow for the imputations implied in Broederlam's "Annunciation and Visitation." Instead, the Romanesque features serve to distinguish "this throne room" from any "of this earth." Panofsky describes the setting of the work: "The beautiful garden seen through a triad of openings, with a cluster of lilies in the center and abounding in roses and irises, brings to mind both the *hortus conclusus* and the Garden of Paradise. The glittering Meuse suggests the 'pure river of water, clear as crystal' that runs through the New Jerusalem." [81]

The bases of the columns and the spandrels of the arcade provide the Gothic counterpart to the Romanesque workings. Here, in these subdued parts of the painting, van Eyck reveals the temporal aspect of his meaning: "examples of sin taken from the Old Testament (the Expulsion from Paradise, the story of Cain and Abel, and the Drunkenness of Noah)" are juxtaposed to one example of virtue (the justice of Trajan) drawn from classical rather than Christian history. Panofsky's analysis, concerned primarily with the technique of architectural contrast rather than with history, does not touch upon a further, even more important, expression of the historic motif in the painting. Yet certainly the most prominent subject of the work looks backward rather than forward in time. No doubt the setting suggests the Celestial City of the Apocalypse, but the Christ represented here is not the One who ascended in glory. He is, rather, the Babe in his Mother's arms. The meaning of this seems inescapable: the Incarnation brought an end to Time's absolute dominion over man. Time which, along with death, had entered the world at the Fall,[82] no longer existed. So that now from the human point of view man is seen partaking (though in the future) of an event which transpired in the distant past. This is only to say that he has passed from the temporal into the timeless.

Closely related in technique to the "Madonna of Chancellor Rolin" is the miniature, "le paradys terrestre," found in "Très Riches Heures du Duc de Berry." [83] This splendid miniature depicts an enclosed garden atop a mountain. Four separate scenes are represented in the painting: the Temptation of Eve, the Temptation of Adam (the Fall), the Curse, and the Expulsion. More interesting than this juxtaposition of temporally removed events, however, is the elaborately beautiful Gothic architecture of the garden gate and of the structure enclosing the "sealed fountain" at the center of the garden. The implication of the architectural motif is that even in the moment when man sinks to his lowest—especially then—God's mercy has already been extended to him. The Church exists, God's Word exists from eternity to eternity. And thus, man's hope has been assured.

Such examples as this present us with the iconographic idea which we might refer to as the "congruity of time." They are predicated on the juxtaposition of divine and human points of view, of the time-bound with the timeless. They are graphic manifestations of that almost ubiquitous medieval and Renaissance idea of timelessness. Indeed, for Louis Richeome, the very purpose of illustration was to unfold such mysteries, to set "before our eyes the holy Images and propheticall Figures of the mysterie that we adore." [84] A "Holy Picture" was, therefore, only another word for "an Allegorie." So such a "Picture" was "otherwise called an Allegorie, that is to say, a mysticall Picture, containing in it selfe a spirituall sense, knowne to spirituall people, hid to the rude." [85] We have already had occasion to consider two of the engravings in Joseph Fletcher's *Historie of the Perfect-Cursed-Blessed Man* (our figs. 23 and 24). We will recall that these illustrations emphasized the traditional contrast between the wilderness of the world and the Garden of Eden. The sharp contrasts point up the vast changes brought about by the Fall, and so by time. Death and decay enter the life of Everyman, not always suddenly, but with the passage of time. Storms gather and vent their rage in time. In short, the contrasts between these two engravings point to the passage of time. One might even say that these contrasts express the theme of change. But if we look carefully at another example from the same work (our fig. 38), we are confronted with a completely different conception of time. For in the same illustration we see depicted scenes of the Garden of Eden—the Temptation and Expulsion—juxtaposed to scenes from the life of Christ: the Crucifixion, Burial, Resurrection, and Ascension. Here the history of the Old Testament is squeezed into a montage of important scenes representing the Fall and Redemption. The idea is an old one, of course; a woodcut found in the Huntington Kitto Bible (fig. 39) is typical of many which depict the figures in the Garden as if in motion (almost as in a cinema sequence) from moment to moment. The viewer witnesses the Creation of Eve, yet the birds at the fountain suggest the time before her birth (Gen. ii.10). The Fall is clearly represented, and yet, implicitly, the garden gate and wall suggest the Expulsion which is to follow. Finally, the identification of the four streams flowing out of Eden with the four Evangelists connotes the coming dispensation of Grace. The temporal meaning of figures 38 and 39 is not hard to discern: taken in at a glance, disparate events, seemingly far removed in time, tend to blend. Space contracts time; the separated are placed near.

The foregoing remarks may help explain the thematic emphasis of Phineas Fletcher's *The Purple Island* (1633), which is on—not the anatomical structure of the human body as some have suggested —but the temporal and eschatological. The poem is a history of the "Isle of Man," which began at the beginning of the world and will continue until its end. The events befalling the island, though they bear the traces of analogy with English history, are meant to remind the reader of the Fall, the wandering, and restoration of man:

> Coëvall with the world in her nativitie:
> Which though it now hath pass'd through many ages,

And still retain'd a naturall proclivitie
To ruine, compast with a thousand rages
   Of foe-mens spite, which still this Island tosses;
Yet ever grows more prosp'rous by her crosses;
With with'ring springing fresh, and rich by often losses.[86]

Fletcher's method is in accord with the Renaissance doctrine of correspondences, according to which the poet might telescope or expand his treatment of any particular in nature. Thus, the island rivers are veins in the body of the commonwealth, while blood vessels are the rivers in the commonwealth of the body. Fletcher's elaborate analogizing is one manifestation of the allegorical nature of his work. For the figure of the "Isle of Man," like the text of Scripture and the life of Everyman, must be understood on several levels. It represents, most obviously, Adam and the human race. But because of that, it must also represent the individual, who is the incarnation of Adam. In a wider sense, the island is the body politic —England—which shows forth all the shortcomings and potentialities of the individual. Finally, the island is the Church of Christ. In time, Adam in both his macrocosmic and microcosmic forms was thrust out of Eden, and in time he wandered and was ultimately redeemed. The sections given over to human anatomy must be seen as Fletcher's anatomy of sin, or of human nature, for the two are the same. Fletcher's interest in anatomy must be considered as an example of the continuing de contemptu mundi tradition, which, with its persistent horror of the human body, would soon find its ultimate expression in the second book of *Gulliver's Travels*. Fletcher uses his anatomy not only to define the nature of sin but to suggest the means by which man must (and would) find Redemption from it.

We are not surprised, then, that Fletcher's poem summons up the old conflict between chastity and fornication. Like the man described by Origen, the island must love something, for that is its nature. The affection of love, moreover, carries the island to be wedded with the object of its love. For Fletcher, only two possibilities exist: the island may love its Creator in a decent affection (symbolized by marriage) or it must wallow in the adulterous love of itself. Spiritual fornication led to the Fall, just as it now perpetuates a gulf between Creator and created. Still, so enamored was the Creator with His island that He left heaven, and followed the steps of Solomon as they are traced in the Song of Songs, to win the island's troth:

> Farre be that boldnesse from thy humble swain,
> Fairest Eclecta, to describe thy beautie,
> And with unable skill thy glory stain,
> Which ever he admires with humble dutie:
> > But who to view such blaze of beautie longs,
> > Go he to Sinah, th' holy groves amongs;
> Where that wise Shepherd chants her in his Song of songs.[87]

The remainder of the poem finds Love locked in pitched battle for the splendid beauty celebrated by Solomon in the Song of Songs. As in *Psyche*, assaults are made on the Bride's virginity. But as time passes, the spiritual combat turns in favor of Continence. Finally, as Fletcher's marginal gloss reminds us, the love that wounded the hearts of both Lover and Beloved is consummated in marriage. It is very clear, as we can see, that Fletcher's history of the island has been a history of apostate man, whether that is viewed as the progress of the Church or of the soul. In effect, it has been a history of Paradise, of the enclosed garden, through the flux of time.

As in spiritual autobiography, so in *The Purple Island* an awareness of time is ever present. Fletcher's poem is, in a sense, a spiritual pilgrimage, and so each of its movements presupposes the existence of time. Man must choose his destiny, but he must choose it in time; and yet that choice confronts him over and over again. Time on the human level seems to run, and so to confront man with an ever-changing set of circumstances. Still, beneath the seemingly different surfaces of objects presented to his view, man always encounters the same choice. In each successive moment he selects from the ever-present alternatives actions (in time) which, because of their consequences, are inextricably bound to the timeless. This is why every human event must be seen against the backdrop of eternity. Every object has its allegorical dimension. Objects, observations—these are only the literal level of human experience, comparable to the literal level of Scripture. Their true meaning lies submerged, gathering existence from outside of history. Thus, to return to the figure with which this chapter began, the sundial—

the emblem of time—presents a surface to the senses, an opportunity for an experience which may function as the prelude to a deeper experience, one which will define the former—and more—illuminate the meaning of human existence. As Francis Quarles writes in *Divine Fancies* (1632):

> Alas, alas; there's nothing can appeare,
> But onely *Types*, and shadow'd *Figures* there:
> This Dyall is the *Scripture;* and the Sun,
> Gods holy *Spirit; Wee*, the Lookers on: . . . .[88]

As might be expected, Quarles' poem ends with a stirring imperative: "Use then the day, for when the day is gon,/ There will be *darkenes*." Again, the day—the literal day—has a deeper meaning. It represents some other, divine, duration. The Incarnation brought the timeless into time, spirit into flesh, God into man. And because of this, the man who looked on the sundial could see it in one or both of two ways: as the natural man (whereupon he would be informed of his mortality) or as the regenerate man. If his perception were quickened by the Holy Ghost, he read the dial in the same way he read the Scriptures; his blindness healed, the experience of seeing was made entirely new. Flesh became Word, temporal was transmuted to timeless in this miracle of spiritual enlightenment. God's redemptive plan was such that time's decay, mortality—all that had been corrupted by the Fall—could be universally and symmetrically reversed. Potentially, man could see through the "shadow'd" figure of the sundial the true image of the timeless.

If we pursue this motif into less obvious sources, we may shed considerable light on such "mystical" poems as Marvell's "Garden," for we apprehend a significant relation between the figure of the sundial and the concept of "annihilation." In John Hall's *Emblems With elegant Figures* [1658], Emblem V of Book II depicts a beautiful young woman removing a portrait of herself from the wall.[89] On the table beside her is a vase of flowers, which represents the transitoriness of beauty and the justification of the young woman's rejection of pride. In Hall's earlier *Poems* (1646) this work was appropriately entitled "Of Beauty," and in *Emblems* the text (taken from the ninetieth Psalm) similarly serves to identify the subject of the poem: "In the morning it flourisheth and groweth up: in the evening it is cut down and withereth." The poem itself presents the speaker's part-by-part denigration of the human body. Even at its most beautiful, the body's value is severely limited. The hue of the loveliest cheek disappears with the coming of evening; the lily is whiter than the whitest hand: "And what's a lip? tis in the test,/ Red clay at best." It was no secret that even the youngest eagle was blest with better eyes. Of all things, beauty seemed to be the least reliable. Yet if this were so, much of man's involvement in physical beauty seemed perverse:

> Is Beauty thus? then who would lie
> Love-sicke and die?
> And's wretched self annihilate
> For knowes not what?
> And with such sweat and care invade
> A very shade? [90]

In this passage Hall's speaker confronts the mysterious quality of love, whether human or divine. Human love is always directed toward physical objects, in which the previously established faults inhere. Yet love is an affection which must be distinguished from those objects. When love is surrendered, it "annihilates" the lover; all lovers, saintly as well as wicked, "languish" with love. Love "annihilates" because it impels the lover toward the love object with the aim of destroying the boundaries between the self and that object. When the affection of love is misdirected, a pathetic, in some cases tragic, event occurs. Man loves blindly, unaware of the true nature of the love object. With great effort ("sweat and care") he pursues the will-of-the-wisp until such time as he places the objects of the universe in proper perspective, then reinvesting his love in appropriate measure. Love properly leads to harmony and repose, but may "invade" the very center of the soul's rest.

Another poem in the same collection employs the figure of annihilation. The text of this poem is taken from St. Augustine ("I will pierce heaven with my mind, and be present with thee in my desires") and is meant as a gloss on the engraving. There, we see divine Cupid aiming an arrow at the suspended and flaming heart of Love. Another arrow crumples from the impact of contact with the winged vessel. Near divine Cupid sits the Spouse in her familiar position of repose. Hall's poem deals directly with the subject of love. Its theme is the limitation of "blind flesh" and "Lethargick sense," which (the speaker insists) will in no way impede him from running with full safety along those "paths that lie above the sun." The speaker's address to the "heart," appearing in the third stanza, first hints at the true aim of his meditation, which is to transcend the immediate circumstances of time and body:

> Swell heart into a world and keep
> That humid sea:
> Become, my bosome, one great deep
> That it may lodge in Thee:
> That glorious sun with his Celestiall heat
> will warm't, and mak't evaporate.[91]

The figures of evaporation and expansion govern the further development of the poem. The speaker would have his heart "Swell," not (as in Donne's "Aire and Angels") into a thin substance but into (in the sense of transmutation) a deep sea. Ironically, only by undergoing a process of deepening does the heart's sea become amenable to the evaporating qualities of God's love. When the metamorphosis ("Become, my bosome") is complete, the sea is warmed, and finally evaporated by the sun. The boundaries between human and divine have disappeared:

> Spring-head of life, how am I now
> Intomb'd in Thee?
> How do I since th' art pleas'd to flow,
> Hate a dualitie?
> How I am annihilated? yet by this
> Acknowledge my subsistence is.

The speaker's questions are, of course, manifestly rhetorical. By virtue of his immersion in the "Well of Life," he is "Intomb'd" by dying to this world. When man surrenders the will of *vetus homo*, he is quickened with *vita nova*. At the same time, he then moves into a new sense of harmony with God's will. Because God is "pleas'd" to have His love flow through all His Creation, the speaker properly detests the condition of human life. For now in a moment of transcendence he fully acknowledges both the limitations of the body and the splendor of the divine essence. His contempt of the world, however, is only a reordering of his affections. He has learned the Imitatio Christi, the way of surrender. By this

new discovery of limitation, ironically he also finds a hitherto un-
appreciated potentiality:

> Still may I rise; still further clime
> Till that I lie
> (Having out-run-short-winded time)
> Swath'd in Eternitie.[92]

Time shares with man a quality of limitation. Man, if properly employed, can "rise" above it, literally "out-run" the creature by
becoming one with its Creator. He can, as it were, step outside of
time to be bathed in the timeless. This is what Hall and Marvell
mean by annihilation.

When we ask the question, To what does this annihilation refer?
we suppose that the poet implies something about objects or events.
In one sense, at least, this is so, but in another, not. The understanding of this idea depends on our recalling a point made early
in this chapter: at birth man was immersed *in*, as if inside of, time.
The idea of annihilation here refers to the movement from that
natural state of the time-bound to the unnatural one of the timeless. The spatial analogy holds, since the subject of Hall's poem is
the passage, or ascent, from one condition to another. We must not
allow the prepositions implied by Hall's use of metaphor to be-
cloud our understanding of his meaning. His use of "annihilation"
is close to that use found in mystical writings of the term "spiritual
union." In the writings of St. Teresa, St. John of the Cross, Juliana
of Norwich, and Richard Rolle, movement from the time-bound
to the timeless is a thematic commonplace.

The aim of meditation is the death of the senses as they are
ordinarily known. Pedro de Alcántara held that the commonplace
absorption of the senses was a waste of "pretious time" and one
of the nine most serious impediments to devotion.[93] Once the
mundane attractions of the sensitive life have been overcome, once
these human processes have been properly fastened, let us say, on
the garden, little by little they lose their hold on the will.[94]
Through prayerful attention to the particular meanings of the
garden forms, the soul rises to higher and higher levels of prayer,
until, writes Alonso Roderigues, at last all sense of time and self
vanishes: "This high, and sublime, rich Kind of *Prayer*, doth not
permit to him who prayes, that he consider then, what he is per-

forming; nor, that he make reflection upon what he is doing, or (to speake more properly) what he is, not so much doing, as suffering." [95] Now is the moment of delicious languishment, infinitely serene, infinitely still. In this state, described as a delightful passivity by St. Teresa, the soul (according to Roderigues) is grasped and held by a force outside itself, "inebriated . . . taken, and absorpt in God." Made one with the Creator, man "remembers not himselfe." [96] It would be wrong to think that the soul is wholly inactive, however; the will maintains an ordering function while the other faculties are at rest. It literally alters the course of the affections. Hopefully now the whole being of man is directed toward the love of God. For by the remaining action of the will, which continually strives to bring itself into unremitting accord with the will of God, the distinction between the man meditating and object of his meditation has disappeared. The soul which had begun its meditation on a garden is now become that "bed of green" described in the Canticles, the fruitive couch of time where the Lover and Beloved are joined in timeless union; the seer and the scene, as William Struther writes, have become one:

> It is a fruitefull Meditation, when the heart receiveth such stampe of God, as maketh it to taste how good hee is, and so thirst for more Grace, that wee earnestly seeke up these sweete streames to the fountaine, even God himselfe, where that perfection dwelleth. Such Meditation bringeth out some point of livelie and affectuous knowledge, and with these holy conceptions worketh a greater puritie and holinesse of the mind that conceiveth it: The soule in that case it is not simple active, but passive also: and is changed to the nature of these heavenly things that it conceiveth.[97]

In this context, Hall's description of the soul as an ocean represents the obliteration of the normal processes of perception, the contemplative state.[98] Behind this aim at "annihilation" is an impulse which is perfectly suited to the ambivalent longings that provide the crux of Christian paradox. This aim is the way of mysticism and martyrdom; the two cannot really be separated, for both are expressions of a choice which belittles the body, and therefore time. Consider, for instance, the miniature (fig. 40) representing the martyrdom of St. Quintin. We find him seated

in a wooden structure. A huge spike is being driven into his left
shoulder; another has already pierced his right shoulder. All of
his fingers and toes have been pierced by nails. One may justly
ask, then, what the meaning of the garden wall (seen in the background) might be. For have we not argued that the wall symbolizes God's protective arm? Indeed we have. But God's protection extends to the soul, not necessarily to the body. The light of
His glory permeates the scene, certain assurance that the garden
wall and the green grass represent a love in which St. Quintin
dwells, and against which no power on earth may prevail. Thus,
on St. Quintin's face we see an expression of supreme repose. Garden scenes like this one were frequently the scenes of martyrdom.
For example, in "Le Bréviaire de Phillippe le Bon," St. Stephan is
stoned while kneeling in an enclosed garden.[99] About him the
ground is strewn with apples; his wicker basket stands filled with
fruit, and as he kneels, waiting for the stones to break his body,
light shines on him from above.

Of course, none of this is very surprising. After all, martyrdom
is the ultimate expression of contemptus mundi, the most defini-
tive statement of the soul's withdrawal from the world. In both
examples, the enclosed garden represents the other world, the
world not seen by the natural man, the world where the wall of
God's arm truly protects the spiritual plant against all intruders.
But to gain this world (and this is the theme of Vaughan's "Regeneration") the soul must die to the world of time: "For to me to
live is Christ, and to die is gaine." The difference between mysticism and martyrdom is one only of degree; both are predicated on
an act of the will, which asserts the value of withdrawal from the
present world. By this exertion of will the world of time is "annihilated," and the momentary becomes eternal. When in tune with
God's will, man's heart does not belong to this world: "I am a
stranger even at home, therefore if the doggs of the world bark at
me, I neither care, nor wonder." [100] As Bishop Hall movingly
writes, "If I die; the world shal misse mee but little, I shall misse it
less; . . . ." [101]

In truth, martyrdom is the logical end of the sickness unto death
described in the Song of Songs. This is what Gerson means, writes
St. François de Sales, when he describes that soul, sick with love,

who in her languishing cries out, "ô God thy love is strong as death." [102] Martyrs and mystics alike have been stung with the desire of a love beyond this world; and St. François, writing of this, says: "How delightfull is this love-dart, which wounding us with the incurable wound of heavenly love, makes us for ever pining and sicke with so strong a beating of the heart, that at length we must yeeld to death." [103] St. Francis of Assisi writhed so beneath the wound of the stigmata that at length, "nothing left on him but skinne and bones; he seemed rather to be an Anatomie, or picture of death, then one living and breathing." [104] In the miniature of St. Quintin we find a similar skeletal figure, with a head shaped to suggest the bare skull. And properly so, for St. Quintin has already died to this world; the mere chaff of his flesh only remains for the world to decimate. William Fuller considered the martyrdom of saints to be the final realization of that love described in the Song of Songs. Here at last the erotic longings of the Spouse were consummated:

> Some burned, some strangled, some broyled, some brayned; all (but only S. *John*) murdered. And ever since that is too true . . . . The woes of Saynts having no ease but custome; and that passage of S. *Bernard* is good: the spouse lovingly (sayth hee) inviteth the beloved to her bed; and hee her againe to armes and trouble: *illâ monstrante lectulum, ille vocat ad campum, ad exercitium;* hence it is that in her garden doe grow Roses as well as Lilies, because the Church is both *operibus candida & cruore purpurea* . . . .[105]

In the last analysis, martyrdom is the true end of the Christian life: this is the Imitatio Christi. As a sequence of miniatures in the "Heures de Turin" reveals with crystal clarity, man follows Christ into the Garden of Gethsemane, to the whipping, and finally to the Cross.[106] Beneath each station of the Cross we find the scene of a martyred saint; we see Christ nailed to the Cross while St. Simon Zelotes, his ankles fastened to the branches of two trees, is sawed in two.[107] Between the Crucifixion and the scene of still another martyrdom we find a miniature representation of the Birth of Eve. The implication seems clear enough; as the Roman spear pierces Christ's side, the Church is born, just as Eve came forth from the side of Adam. Through the Sacrifice of the second Adam,

God's plan, with its almost infinite variations on the theme of Imitatio, had now become a reality. Whether in martyrdom or meditation (the figurative dying to this world), the soul claimed the promise of that moment when time was conquered forever. The mystery of time (at last) was no less than the mystery of the Incarnation. In no place was this better seen than in the day— dedicated to meditation—commemorating the fulfillment of the Incarnation. As George Widley writes in *The Doctrine of the Sabbath* (1604), Sundays called man back to his prelapsarian state, to the timeless, changeless garden walked by man before Time had been given his terrible dominion.[108] Sundays were the models of a Paradise free from the ravages of time; they were veritable slices of the timeless placed in time. That is why man ceased his labors on the Sabbath. His struggle, by the Grace of God, was over. He was now to meditate on the love manifest in the Sacrifice. Without a proper understanding of the Sabbath, man was like *"a garden that hath no water*, Isai. I. 31. where every thing dieth." As we read in Herbert's "Sunday," every Sabbath unfolded the mystery of the Incarnation.

In Herbert's poem two figures represent Sunday—the garden and light. On Easter morning, the Saviour enclosed both:

> This day my Saviour rose,
> And did inclose this light for his:
> That, as each beast his manger knows,
> Man might not of his fodder misse.
> Christ hath took in this piece of ground,
> And made a garden there for those
> Who want herbs for their wound. (ll. 36–42)

The debt of the Fall was underwritten by "a friend, and with his bloud." That is why Sunday allows man briefly to glimpse the joys and taste the fruits of Paradise. Yet that allowance works in two ways. For while Sundays allow man respite from his labors, they also serve to remind him of the Fall and of the need for Redemption:

> The brightnesse of that day
> We sullied by our foul offence:
> Wherefore that robe we cast away,
> Having a new at his expence,

> Whose drops of bloud paid the full price,
> That was requir'd to make us gay,
>   And fit for Paradise.   (ll. 50–56)

Sunday was the "Day most calm, most bright,/ The fruit of this, the next worlds bud." It was the "couch" or resting place "of time." It was so by virtue of its being "cares balm," the medicine for man's "wound." Just as the garden of the Church was enclosed by the Sacrifice from the world, Sunday was set off from the days of the week to indicate the advent of the new dispensation. All labor comes to an end because the condemnation of the Law has been set aside. When man is in tune with Sunday he is at one with God's plan, and so, already included in Paradise:

> Sundaies the pillars are,
> On which heav'ns palace arched lies:
> The other dayes fill up the spare
> And hollow room with vanities.
> They are the fruitfull beds and borders
> In Gods rich garden: that is bare,
>   Which parts their ranks and orders.   (ll. 22–28)

Here is the answer to the anxiety expressed in parts of "The Flower," the solution to the question posed in such poems as "The Crosse." The speaker of Herbert's *The Temple* is, from time to time, lashed by doubts, extravagantly given to despair in the face of pain. He cannot believe that he is elected, when to all appearances he yields no bud ("Employment"). Pressed by anxiety, he wonders how the elected flower can be assailed by storm. How is it that the spiritual bud dwells in eternal spring, while the flower is swept away by apparent winter? How, he asks, does man dwell at once both inside and outside of time? The irony of "The Flower" is that, although the speaker expresses the all-too-human longing to be spared the vicissitudes of time ("O that I once past changing were,/ Fast in thy Paradise, where no flower can wither!"), he also learns the wisdom of St. Quintin, namely that such change cannot be avoided, in fact that his salvation is predicated on submission to this very limitation:

> These are thy wonders, Lord of love,
> To make us see we are but flowers that glide:
>   Which when we once can finde and prove,

Thou hast a garden for us, where to bide.
Who would be more,
Swelling through store,
Forfeit their Paradise by their pride.

Ironically, one passes beyond change by accepting change. By seeing the bounds of human potentiality, the soul catches a glimpse of God's redemptive plan. Man learns that God's garden is not of this world. And then he sees the way in which, by virtue of his inclusion in the Church, he is already "Fast in . . . Paradise, where no flower can wither." Thus, in "Paradise" the speaker asks:

What open force, or hidden   CHARM
Can blast my fruit, or bring me HARM,
While the inclosure is thine   ARM?

Secure in the enclosed garden of the Temple, the spiritual plant is not changed but spared, by the pruning knife of the Lord: "Such cuttings rather heal then REND." It is only proper, then, that "such beginnings touch their END." For by Grace, beginning and end are one. The Church is no physical object existing in time. Neither is the soul. Rather, the devout soul, born of the seed of the "second Adam," is given a new destiny, one which transcends the grave. Even now, by virtue of its inclusion in the Church, the soul exists outside of time. As one of the spiritual plants within its walls, the soul flourishes in the garden of the New Jerusalem.

CHAPTER V

Marvell and "The Garden Enclosed"

THE GARDEN.

I.

How vainly men themselves amaze
To win the Palm, the Oke, or Bayes;
And their uncessant Labours see
Crown'd from some single Herb or Tree.
Whose short and narrow verged Shade
Does prudently their Toyles upbraid;
While all Flow'rs and all Trees do close
To weave the Garlands of repose.

II.

Fair quiet, have I found thee here,
10 And Innocence thy Sister dear!
Mistaken long, I sought you then
In busie Companies of Men.
Your sacred Plants, if here below,
Only among the Plants will grow.
Society is all but rude,
To this delicious Solitude.

III.

No white nor red was ever seen
So am'rous as this lovely green.
Fond Lovers, cruel as their Flame,
20 Cut in these Trees their Mistress name.
Little, Alas, they know, or heed,
How far these Beauties Hers exceed!
Fair Trees! where s'eer your barkes I wound,
No Name shall but your own be found.

IV.

When we have run our Passions heat,
Love hither makes his best retreat.
The *Gods,* that mortal Beauty chase,
Still in a Tree did end their race.
Apollo hunted *Daphne* so,
Only that She might Laurel grow.   30
And *Pan* did after *Syrinx* speed,
Not as a Nymph, but for a Reed.

V.

What wond'rous Life in this I lead!
Ripe Apples drop about my head;
The Luscious Clusters of the Vine
Upon my Mouth do crush their Wine;
The Nectaren, and curious Peach,
Into my hands themselves do reach;
Stumbling on Melons, as I pass,
Insnar'd with Flow'rs, I fall on Grass.   40

VI.

Mean while the Mind, from pleasure less,
Withdraws into its happiness:
The Mind, that Ocean where each kind
Does streight its own resemblance find;
Yet it creates, transcending these,
Far other Worlds, and other Seas;
Annihilating all that's made
To a green Thought in a green Shade.

VII.

Here at the Fountains sliding foot,
Or at some Fruit-trees mossy root,   50
Casting the Bodies Vest aside,
My Soul into the boughs does glide:
There like a Bird it sits, and sings,
Then whets, and combs its silver Wings;
And, till prepar'd for longer flight,
Waves in its Plumes the various Light.

VIII.

Such was that happy Garden-state,
While Man there walk'd without a Mate:
After a Place so pure, and sweet,
What other Help could yet be meet!   60
But 'twas beyond a Mortal's share

To wander solitary there:
Two Paradises 'twere in one
To live in Paradise alone.

IX.

How well the skilful Gardner drew
Of flow'rs and herbes this Dial new;
Where from above the milder Sun
Does through a fragrant Zodiack run;
And, as it works, th' industrious Bee
70   Computes its time as well as we.
How could such sweet and wholsome Hours
Be reckon'd but with herbs and flow'rs! [1]

THE REVISION OF "THE GARDEN"

In the preceding chapters we have explored a range of associated meanings potentially conveyed by a particular image-cluster in a particular Jacobean linguistic context. Though I believe the reticulations of such a context to be interesting as objects of our inquiry in their own right, the purpose of this book has been to show how an awareness of the complex associations of a context enriches (and, by implication, necessarily alters) our conception of a work of art, once that work of art has properly been placed within that context. The examples in this book—drawn from what is in effect a sublanguage of English, with its own lexicon, and its own rules for the use of each word—confront us with potentially relevant analogies, whose relevance may only be decided when we engage a particular poem and ask a particular question about its meaning.

I do not mean to say that the relevance of this context necessarily predicates our belief that the author of a poem intended to invoke the full range of possible associated meanings. To be sure, not every garden in seventeenth-century literature conjured fantasies of Solomon's enclosed pleasance, with its luscious, delightful, soul-saving shade; Campion's "There is a garden in her face" is an interesting poem, but the imagery here functions in its own way—one different, I think, from that discussed in this book: if "allegory" is to be a useful term, we must be able to distinguish metaphoric language which is not allegorical.[2] On the other hand, wherever a text is properly construed—even in part—in the context of the Song of Songs, then an aspect of the meaning of that text (and therefore part of its complexity) will be allegorical. This is an important point when we consider by all means the most complex, most subtle lyric written within the tradition of hortus conclusus, Andrew Marvell's "The Garden." For in this incredibly delicate and complex poem a number of relevant contexts converge, and Marvell holds them all in poised balance, echoing the *libertin* pastoral here, parodying it there, alluding to the occult in one moment, turning to the Christian in the next. The poem is shaped as a meditation (and in this way it is wholly different from the several Christian pastorals of Thomas Randolph), and throughout its imagery tantalizingly suggests the lush, garden eroticism of the allegorized Song of Songs.

Marvell's poem has mystified critics, who have in recent years approached the text with an enormous range of methods, running from impressionism (the garden is like a giant fleshly orchid, ready to devour man) to suggestions that "The Garden" ought to be compared with "Ode on a Grecian Urn."[3] It has been described as light and ominous in tone, as disjunct and unified in structure, as Plotinian, Hermetic, Buddhist, libertin and antilibertin in thought. Whether or not we take this range of testimony as an indication of the poem's complexity, or as a sign of the limits of human knowledge, one fact of importance to criticism remains: as each critic approaches the text he asserts, whether implicitly or explicitly, the relevance of a particular context to the act of construing the text. And as the context changes (Plotinus, Randolph, Montaigne, Freud), so does the "meaning" of the text. Of course, we need not argue that critical accord will descend once critics discover the poem's "true" or "total meaning,"[4] as if that essence has hovered for centuries in the pure realm of air, awaiting the incantation of a proper sensibility to summon it into substantial being. But it is proper to suppose that critics have not always recognized the relevant context of "The Garden," nor always fully understood the implications of that context once its relevance has been established.

For example, one aspect of the poem has almost wholly been

ignored: its allegorical meaning. Yet Ruth Wallerstein once stated that "the literature of the *hortus conclusus* . . . contributes the most" to the immediate context of "The Garden."[5] At the same time (as if in answer to William Empson), she insisted that the poem must not be taken as "an allegory of the Fall of Man," for it is, instead, "a lyric study of Marvell's experience." In this chapter I will try to show not only that the context of the Song of Songs is relevant to a proper understanding of "The Garden" but that, because it is, the allegorical dimension of the poem's meaning ought not to be ignored. For the context of the Song of Songs, as Marvell received and used it, was, above all other things, distinctly allegorical.

Much of the critical argument over the poem concerns the passivity of Marvell's speaker, especially as depicted in Stanza V. Radically divided in their explanations of that passivity, the critics see it variously as an expression of Marvell's sexual ambivalence, a reference to the Fall of man, an allusion to the idea of the hermaphroditism of nature. Thus, one critic points to Freud, another to Bonaventure, another to Randolph, still another to Hermes, and so on. But despite this variety, most critics agree on the underlying importance of a single question: In what sense is this "mystical" poem to be construed as sexual? The attractiveness of the Hermetic hypothesis arises from its relevance to this question; but in spite of the now numerous ventures into Hermetic—and, for that matter, Plotinian—writings, the question remains as vexed as before. For even if the speaker is androgynous (indeed, especially if he is), why should the garden pursue him rather than vice versa? Would not androgyny imply an equal balance of give-and-take in love? If so, we are left with the question of why the speaker is (as he most certainly is) the passive recipient of the garden's affection. The question might more properly be put in this way: What is the relation between the speaker's passivity and the imagery which conveys that passivity? And here the context of the Song of Songs sheds light on Marvell's text.

We know that Marvell was familiar with this tradition; echoes from Solomon's Song are heard in "The Nymph Complaining,"[6] and, as Don Cameron Allen has shown, in "Appleton House" Marvell uses the figure of hortus conclusus to intensify his satiric attack on convent life. Thus, as in the Middle Ages, nunnery, cloister, and virginity still represent separation from the world, but now Marvell caustically alters the convention, suggesting that the completely separated life leads to sterility. Professor Allen shows how the theme of sterility refers also to Fairfax, whose withdrawal from public life gave Marvell pause, and perhaps led him to a serious consideration of the values of the contemplative life.[7] At about the same time—as Marvell was writing "The Garden" and serving as tutor to Mary Fairfax—Lord Fairfax (who turned his hand also to paraphrasing Proverbs) was rendering the Song of Songs into verse.

Fairfax's "Songe of Salomon" appears, along with numerous religious lyrics ("The Songe of Mary The Blessed Virgin," for instance) in Bodleian MS. Fairfax 40. The paraphrase, itself neither better nor worse than most, emphasizes the erotic qualities of Solomon's Song: "Kiss me ô kiss me with thy mouth," "I am my spouse into my Garden Come," "I held him fast & would not let him goe." Miss Røstvig suggests the likelihood not only that Marvell read his patron's poetic efforts but that the two men shared their views on the esoteric subjects presently concerning each of them (at the time, Fairfax was also quite involved with the *Hermetica*).[8] Such an exchange of ideas would, of course, place an interest in the Song of Songs quite close to Marvell's thinking at the time he was writing "The Garden." For in Fairfax's "Songe of Salomon," we have a typical verse paraphrase describing the lusciousness of the tree which offers its fruit and shade to the Beloved, who passively enjoys her "delightfull seat." Again, in the allegorical context in which Fairfax was working, the qualities of the garden referred to aspects of the matchless Bride:

> My Love is as a Garding Loocked up
> Or springing fountaine that is sealed up
> Whose plants as orchards of pomgranets are
> With other fruits that pretious are and rare
> Cipresse & Spinknard wholsome safferron
> Calamus & Frankincense sweet cinamon
> Mirrh Aloes what else is of greatest price
> With numerous kinds of other cheifest spice
> A fount of Gardins Living springs that streme.[9]

More persuasive evidence that "The Garden" should be understood in this context is found in comparison between "The Garden" and Marvell's earlier Latin poem, "Hortus." Although for
centuries "The Garden" was believed to be an English translation
of the Latin poem, not since A. H. King's article in *English Studies*
in 1938 has close study been made of the relation between these
poems. It is generally agreed that "Hortus" was written about
a year before "The Garden." Margoliouth has pointed to the in-
convenience of the theory (held by Grosart among others)[10] that
"The Garden" is a translation of "Hortus"; despite their marked
similarities, the poems differ in both structure and imagery. Again,
long sections present in Latin do not appear in the English poem;
and the latter contains four stanzas for which no Latin counter-
parts exist. Serious consideration of these differences can lead to
but one conclusion: as Marvell "translated" his poem he also revised it, and in so doing he created an entirely new artifact, a
poem not only more Christian in content but bearing a markedly
meditative tone and structure. Finally, Marvell's revision introduced an entirely new linguistic context in which the English poem
must be read if it is to be properly understood.

Since this is a crucial point in my argument, it may be profitable
to consider these revisions in some detail. "Hortus" is in most respects a classical poem of retirement. Not so "The Garden." Many
of the most traditional sections of the Latin poem were eliminated
by Marvell's revision. This passage, for example:

> *Me quoque, vos* Musae, *&, te conscie testor* Apollo,
> *Non Armenta juvant hominum,* Circique *boatus,*
> *Mugitusve Fori; sed me Penetralia veris,*
> *Horroresque trahunt muti, & Consortia sola,*[11]   (ll. 16–19)

not only bears references to the Muses and Apollo but refers also
to the Roman Forum, to the bellowing "circus" of sycophants who
attached themselves to the great. Of all this no mention is made
in the revised poem. Again, the fourth stanza of "The Garden"
is highly compressed in comparison with the corresponding part
of the Latin text. During revision Marvell cut out half of the
mythological allusions, trimming seventeen lines to eight. As we
can see,

Hic Amor, exutis crepidatus inambulat alis,
Enerves arcus & stridula tela reponens,
Invertitque faces, nec se cupit usque timeri;
Aut exporrectus jacet, indormitque pharetrae;
Non auditurus quanquam Cytherea vocarit;
Nequitias referunt nec somnia vana priores.
Lætantur Superi, *defervescente Tyranno,*
Et licet experti toties Nymphasque Deasque,
Arbore *nunc melius potiuntur quisque cupita.*
Jupiter *annosam, neglecta conjuge,* Quercum
Deperit; haud alia doluit sic pellice Juno.
Lemniacum *temerant vestigia nulla Cubile,*
Nec Veneris *Mavors meminit si* Fraxinus *adsit.*
Formosæ pressit Daphnes *vestigia* Phæbus
Ut fieret Laurus; *sed nil quaesiverat ultra.*
Capripes & peteret quòd Pan Syringa *fugacem,*
Hoc erat ut Calamum *posset reperire Sonorum*   (ll. 32–48)

is hardly the Latin equivalent of

> When we have run our Passions heat,
> Love hither makes his best retreat.
> The *Gods*, that mortal Beauty chase,
> Still in a Tree did end their race.
> *Apollo* hunted *Daphne* so,
> Only that She might Laurel grow.
> And *Pan* did after *Syrinx* speed,
> Not as a Nymph, but for a Reed.

The comment of Marvell's first editor following the above seventeen Latin lines—"Desunt multa"—must be seen as something more than a little suspect. There is no evidence that anything is "missing" from "Hortus." The differences between the two poems (in the absence of a complete manuscript of "Hortus") must be explained as the result of the author's revision. This would seem a fortiori true since the four stanzas added to the English poem most markedly depart from the earlier Latin sequence. If this is so, clearly any attempt to explicate "The Garden" by ascertaining the sense of the Latin poem must fail. It happens that where the poems most dramatically diverge Marvell's revision identifies the context in which "The Garden" should be understood, and this context is not relevant to the Latin poem at all.[12] For this reason, when King attempts to gloss the English poem by imposing on the English word the nuance of the Latin usage, he begs the question. There is no such thing as a "meaning" of any word outside a given linguistic context. And where the context changes, so often does the "meaning"; when the context changes, so often do the function and tone of the "same" word. When these English stanzas are placed in their proper context, we see not only that the tone of the poem changes but that the meaning of the imagery of the poem is radically altered. Finally, when these changes are seen from a proper perspective, most of the difficulties created by modern criticism disappear.

In spite of their differences, on this much critics agree: in Stanza V (where the author's most radical revision begins) the speaker's role is undeniably passive. He may "lead" a "wond'rous Life in" the garden, but it is the fruits of the garden which "drop," "crush," "reach," and the flowers which insnare. True, the speaker falls, but even in falling he remains a passive agent. "Stumbling on Melons" as he passes, he continues to be acted upon by the multiplicity of garden forms. Finally, the flowers of the garden reach out for him, just as had the "Clusters of the Vine." If there is eroticism in this stanza, its strongest impulse is located in the figures —not of nature (the term is too inclusive)—but of the garden. Again, the notion of the speaker's fall into sin implies the exercise of the will. Yet it seems clear that during Stanza V the speaker remains in a passive, receptive state. Though in certain contexts "grass" means "flesh," the word is used here as one of a series of poetic figures, all having parallel functions in expressing the active love of the garden. Thus, the grass provides a comfortable bed for the speaker's "repose." In turn, this repose is both a prerequisite for and a prelude to the experience described in the succeeding stanzas, which are products, also, of the author's revision.

It must be admitted that in one sense both poems deal with eroticism, if we are to use that term in its broadest sense. That is, both poems describe the presence of lovers in the garden, the carving on the trees, the race of the pagan gods for the elusive nymphs. But in the handling of the love motif the greatest difference appears, and here is where the meaning of Marvell's revision begins to be seen. In "The Garden," the plants love man. Not so in "Hortus." In the Latin poem the vegetable world does not move toward the speaker in any way. Rather, it is as if the garden (almost capriciously) hides Quiet from him:

> *Alma Quies, teneo te! & te Germana Quietis*
> *Simplicitas! Vos ergo diu per Templa, per urbes,*
> *Quæsivi, Regum perque alta Palatia frustra.*
> *Sed vos Hortorum per opaca silentia longe*
> *Celarant Plantæ virides, & concolor Umbra.*　　(ll. 7-11)

In the revised poem, responsibility for the absence of Quiet belongs to the speaker. And at the same time, the "green plants" (*Plantæ virides*) are elevated to a religious category ("sacred Plants"). Again, whereas in the Latin work the comparison of the trees to the beauty of women is highly detailed, touching the hair, the arms, and voice of the mistress and the leaves, branches, and whispering of the trees, in "The Garden" the qualities of the trees are made much less particular. We are told only that their "Beauties" far exceed those of any mistress. Nor does Stanza V carry through the parallelism of the Latin poem, where the branches of the trees were the passive recipients of the speaker's adoration. Rather, in "The Garden," the trees assume the role of love's aggressor, as they thrust themselves upon a passive speaker.

But in the last analysis we find the best evidence that "The Garden" should be read in the context of the Song of Songs in comparison between Stanza V:

> What wond'rous Life in this I lead!
> Ripe Apples drop about my head;
> The Luscious Clusters of the Vine
> Upon my Mouth do crush their Wine;
> The Nectaren, and curious Peach,
> Into my hands themselves do reach;
> Stumbling on Melons, as I pass,
> Insnar'd with Flow'rs, I fall on Grass,

and this passage from Casimire:

> The Apple ripe drops from its stalke to thee,
> 　　From tast of death made free.
> The luscious fruit from the full Figtree shall
> 　　Into thy bosome fall.
> Meane while, the Vine no pruning knife doth know,
> 　　The wounded earth no plow.[13]

In Stanza V, the most radical departure from the Latin original, Marvell echoes Casimire's ode, "Out of Solomon's Sacred Marriage Song," which was only one of the many paraphrases of the Song of Songs available to him. Marvell does more, of course, than merely borrow the figure of "luscious fruit" falling on a passive speaker, for indeed that figure is a familiar one within the context of the Song of Songs. He adds a series of concrete details which suggest, rather than stipulate, the lusciousness of the garden forms. To be sure, the ripe apple drops, but now it is only one of many forms, dropping about the speaker's head. Now, too, the "Clusters of the Vine" assume a "luscious" quality, as they crush their wine upon the speaker's lips. The various forms of the garden reach out for the speaker, give themselves to him in an act of self-immolation. As many critics have observed, the garden appears almost to pursue the speaker. Unhappily, about this active love of the garden the critics have been generally confused.

"A GREEN THOUGHT IN A GREEN SHADE"

It might be argued that even if we allowed for an allegorical interpretation of "The Garden" in terms of the Song of Songs, we should not have explained the data in the poem. In particular, the bearing of this view on the passivity of the speaker is not at once clear. To this we must reply that we have just illuminated that passivity by identifying the speaker in the poem as the devout soul, who, by merit of her inclusion in the Mystical Body of the Church, is the Bride of Christ. In this context, the speaker's passivity is not at all problematic, for it implies the expected relation between Bride and Bridegroom. Thus, the context of the Canticles would adequately explain the aggressive role of the garden, which pursues, captures, and embraces the Beloved. But would it though? For if the garden is the soul, and if the soul is the Bride of Christ, in what sense may she be pursued by herself? The answer to this question may be easily given, but only insofar as a traditional ambiguity (as distinct from vagueness) of biblical commentary—ambiguity residing in the figure of divine marriage—is understood. In the first chapter, we discussed the way in which the Song of Songs was believed to describe the three marriages of Christ, two of which are relevant here. The first marriage took place with the quickening and fruitfulness of Mary's womb: the marriage between Word and flesh, for Mary was the Church as well as the Virgin-Mother of God. The second wedding was seen in the Sacrifice, which, like the Virgin Birth, was often represented in the context of hortus conclusus; as the earlier chapters show, above all the imagery of the Song of Songs was eucharistic, since only by partaking of the fruit of Sacrifice was man made secure behind the garden wall of the Mother Church. In this way, man recapitulated the life of Christ in a necessarily dependent role. The splendor of Solomon's wedding, the openly erotic description of physical beauty, the detailed narrative of Love's banquet (Stanza V)—all the richness in the Song of Songs—referred to the inscrutable mystery of the Sacrifice.

Marvell's revision introduces the associated meanings of this context into the poem, and this is nowhere more evident than in his manipulation of the figure of shade. Not that this figure is absent or of no value in the classical "Hortus"; in the second stanza of the Latin work, value is imputed to both shade and the figure "green" ("*Celarant Plantæ virides, & concolor Umbra*"). But note a critical difference. Here, the plant and shade are green; in the revised "Garden," a poem treating of religious ecstasy, greenness is the quality of the speaker's thought. Again, "*concolor Umbra*" is a weak assertion of the color of the shade. It is very clear, if we consider the Latin stanza as a whole, that the emphasis differs greatly from that in the line, "A green Thought in a green Shade." The green plants, linked in the Latin poem to a "like-colored" shade, become in the second stanza of "The Garden" "sacred Plants," while the "like-colored" shade is transmuted to the green dwelling place of "a green Thought." What does this manipulation of color imagery and of the figure of shade mean? It means that Marvell is invoking specifically eucharistic and mystical associations of the image of the garden shade.

It will be helpful here to bear in mind a structural function of Stanza V, which provides the link between the fourth stanza and all that is to follow. This function rests on a feature so simple as to escape notice, namely on Marvell's use of the color green. Certainly the most debated couplet in the poem ends the sixth stanza: "Annihilating all that's made/ To a green Thought in a green Shade." But though the critics have tended to follow Empson into speculation as to the "meaning" of this annihilation, the best hint as to the meaning of the passage lies in its use of color imagery: Stanza VI is linked to Stanza V by the imagery of shade and the color green. The "Thought" and the "Shade" share the color of the grass on which the speaker has fallen. But another, more subtle, relation holds: the single branches of Oak, Palm, and Laurel are green also. It must be, then, that greenness in itself does not present the final statement of value in the poem. Instead, that value is represented by shade when in conjunction with the color green. Careful reading will show that there are in "The Garden" degrees of shade, and that the system of value developed by the contrasts in the poem is a function of the image of shade. For this reason it is not enough to explain the "meaning" of the item "green"; the meaning of any linguistic item is determined by its context, in this case the allegorical tradition of the Song of Songs. We want to know how the imagery in "The Garden" functions in that context —in short, the contextual meaning of such figures as green, fruit, thought, flame, sun, shade. We want to know, above all, what Marvell means by his governing figure of the garden.

If this analysis is correct, Marvell is drawing on a contrast which is basic to the tradition of the Song of Songs—that between the garden and the not-garden. In iconography, the latter is most often seen as a desert or wilderness. In "The Garden," Marvell develops a series of contrasts which establishes a hierarchy of values. These, in turn, point up the primary and overriding antithesis between the garden and the not-garden. It is not the city and the country which Marvell poses as alternatives here, but shade and its absence, growth and its lack. In the first stanza, the limits of "uncessant Labours" emerge, not simply through contrast between labor and repose, but also by an implied comparison of the effects of the one with those of the other. Men frustrate themselves by seeking the tokens of worldly acclaim, for even when these are achieved they prove to be of little value.

The plain fact is that physical effort leads to a dearth of shade, and therefore to the opposite of value:

How vainly men themselves amaze
To win the Palm, the Oke, or Bayes;
And their uncessant Labours see
Crown'd from some single Herb or Tree.
Whose short and narrow verged Shade
Does prudently their Toyles upbraid;
While all Flow'rs and all Trees do close
To weave the Garlands of repose.

The "Toyles" of the men are inextricable from amazement or confusion. Their "uncessant Labours" must be seen as vain. In fact, pathos may be discerned here. The reader is aware that the Palm, the Oak, and Bay are rewards which go only to a limited number of fortunate human beings, to those who are victorious in the various arenas of competition. Yet these rewards, rather than suggesting the satisfactions of power and fame, bear witness to the meaninglessness of even the most effective human effort. For the highest reward the world may endow is a wreath which offers but a "short and narrow verged Shade." Yet it is for such spindly, single branches that the "Companies of Men" endlessly strive. Ironically, the very rewards of worldly success testify to men that their most diligent labors are meaningless, since these rewards cannot produce the one thing of undoubted value: shade. In the garden, where the speaker finds solitude, "all Flow'rs and all Trees do close/ To weave the Garlands of repose." That is, labor and repose are parallel and mutually exclusive functions leading to different and diametrically opposed ends. As early as the first stanza, passivity is linked with a quantity of shade, labor with dearth.

Writers on the Song of Songs had long held the labors of men to be of little value. Man's effort to redeem himself under the Law had proved futile, since no amount of labor could restore him to his lost estate. Since the Law represented the just demands of a righteous God, we often read of the "burning wrath" of its heat. That is why in iconography Adam's labors are pictured in scenes of desolation. He had been shut from the garden of plenty to toil in the blazing sands of the wilderness. Until the advent of Grace (the "shadow of the sacraments") man was, as we read in Vaughan's "The Search," completely at the mercy of nature, wholly dependent on his own designs.

Thus, in "The Garden," motion and effort are always linked

with heat, whether with the heat of vain, unceasing labors or with the heat of the race put on by Apollo and Pan for "mortal Beauty":

> When we have run our Passions heat,
> Love hither makes his best retreat.
> The *Gods*, that mortal Beauty chase,
> Still in a Tree did end their race.
> *Apollo* hunted *Daphne* so,
> Only that She might Laurel grow.
> And *Pan* did after *Syrinx* speed,
> Not as a Nymph, but for a Reed.

This stanza introduces another aspect of sexuality to "The Garden." But certainly Legouis must be mistaken; though a contrapuntal arrangement exists between Stanzas IV and VIII:

> Such was that happy Garden-state,
> While Man there walk'd without a Mate:
> After a Place so pure, and sweet,
> What other Help could yet be meet!
> But 'twas beyond a Mortal's share
> To wander solitary there:
> Two Paradises 'twere in one
> To live in Paradise alone,

misogyny is not the issue here. Instead, the two stanzas play upon a theme of solitude, which runs through the entire poem but emerges now and again with greater emphasis. It should be clear, however, that the speaker rejects—not woman—but company. Just as he was earlier misled in his belief that "Fair quiet" and "Innocence" were to be found among the "Companies of Men," the "Fond Lovers" remain confused over the proper means to satisfaction and the proper end of human life. Foolishly they defile the garden, preferring the passions of the body to the love of God, and so afflict themselves with "Passions heat." Again, rather than existing in contrast to the "Fond Lovers," as some have suggested, the pagan gods suffer the same "cruel" flame, since they, too, are found in hot pursuit of "mortal Beauty." The pagan gods and lovers alike "run" through "Passions heat," and in their chase for "mortal Beauty" they suffer with vain men the heat of frustration. The pagan gods end their race in possession of single branches, the "Fond Lovers" with the cruel heat of their love.

Much has been written about paradox in "The Garden." It seems to me, however, that if paradox exists at all in this poem it is found preeminently in Stanza III, not Stanza V (where critics usually find it). It is paradoxical indeed that, though the idea of love conjures expectations of tenderness, in fact, lovers are cruel:

> No white nor red was ever seen
> So am'rous as this lovely green.
> Fond Lovers, cruel as their Flame,
> Cut in these Trees their Mistress name.
> Little, Alas, they know, or heed,
> How far these Beauties Hers exceed!
> Fair Trees! where s'eer your barkes I wound,
> No Name shall but your own be found.

The flame here refers, of course, to the freezing fire of courtly love, a motif which, as we have seen, was long associated with the garden image. In cutting their mistresses' names on the trees, in distorting the original loveliness of the garden, foolish lovers betray their lack of discernment, and in this way reveal how little they truly know of love's nature. The trees (emblems of divine love and of its productive effects) represent the spiritual potentialities of man, which are more beautiful than the features of any woman. We get some idea of the ironic intent of Marvell's use of the garden image when we recall the allegorical gardens in such works as the *Roman de la Rose*, Nevill's *Castell of Pleasure*, and Beaumont's *Psyche*, where the figure is used to unfold a veritable anatomy of confusion in love. In these works, Solomon's retreat is in either explicit or implicit contrast to the bewildering paradise of natural love. Man is naturally inclined to pursue the overheated pleasures of this world; that is why concupiscence is so often described as flame. But the garden into which man enters for his body's pleasure is distinct from that entered by Marvell's speaker. The poet's irony stems from the juxtaposition of the apparent (or physical) with the essentially true. Caught up in passions that burn, the "Fond" lover, like the protagonists of the *Roman* and *Psyche*, is trapped in a confusing garden from which he cannot escape. But—and here the injunctions of the sundials must be borne in mind—for whatever amazement enters the mind, for whatever humiliation or ultimate defeat must be suffered, for whatever bizarre scene meets the eye (the vision of carved trees), the will is responsible. With this convention in mind, we are ready to grasp the full impact of the contrast between Stanzas IV and V:

> When we have run our Passions heat,
> Love hither makes his best retreat.
> The *Gods*, that mortal Beauty chase,
> Still in a Tree did end their race.
> *Apollo* hunted *Daphne* so,
> Only that She might Laurel grow.
> And *Pan* did after *Syrinx* speed,
> Not as a Nymph, but for a Reed.

> What wond'rous Life in this I lead!
> Ripe Apples drop about my head;
> The Luscious Clusters of the Vine
> Upon my Mouth do crush their Wine;
> The Nectaren, and curious Peach,
> Into my hands themselves do reach;
> Stumbling on Melons, as I pass,
> Insnar'd with Flow'rs, I fall on Grass.

The juxtaposition of Stanzas IV and V presents a vivid contrast between the single branches won by the pagan gods and the opulent garden growth. This contrast points up the difference between the heat of human effort—regardless of what sort—and the shaded repose of the garden, the one represented by single branches, the other by abundant fruit. The lovers and the pagan gods of Stanza IV (the latter with their all-too-human strivings) illustrate the elusive satisfactions of "Passions heat," lending a final picture of the wilderness of human nature, and preparing the reader for a glimpse of the enclosed garden of the Song of Songs.

In Stanza V we have a sequence of figures—drawn from the paraphrases of the Song of Songs—which represent the life-giving power of divine love: the language of the passage is, above all, eucharistic. When the Bride of the Song of Songs exclaimed, "I sate downe under his shadow with great delight, and his fruit was sweete to my taste," she gave voice to her gratitude for the Sacrifice. The tree was the apple tree ("As the apple tree among the trees of the wood, so is my beloved among the sonnes"), which was, in turn, a type of the Cross. In Chapter Three we discussed the dense associations of this figure, which, taken together, meant

Christ was the tree and its fruit also. He was the grapes which crush themselves, for the tree was a winepress; he was the fruit of the vine, and the liquor distilled through the Sacrifice. The apples fall in Marvell's poem—of course they do—just as they had in the "Exposition of the Songs," in *Pia Desideria*, and in Quarles' *Emblemes* (see our figs. 29–31), and their falling is a reminder that the Eucharist was freely given in an act of self-immolation. The speaker's passivity at this stage refers to the belief that to receive such delicious meat and drink man had but to "sit still." Thus, we find the Bride sitting beneath the tree, apples falling all about her, while in the tree her Saviour hangs, crucified. As in Quarles' emblem, the soul has grasped the eucharistic meaning of the tree's shade. In a moment of supreme surrender she has placed herself at last beyond the reach of the "burning sun of the wrath of God," which before had given her cause to complain:

> I know not where to go, nor where to stay:
>   The eye of vengeance burnes; her flames invade
>   My sweltring Soule: My soule has oft assaid
> But she can find no shrowd, but she can feele no Shade.[14]

Through meditation, as Prynne had written, the soul unfolds the mystery of the garden:

>   Christ hath *a shade most sweete*
> *Against all scalding Heates, all stormes we meete,*
> *Yea from his Fathers burning Wrath and Rage,*
> *Which none but he can quench, coole, or asswage:* . . . ,[15]

and come to know this shade as the author of her repose:

> *Here may they find, blest rest, repose, and ease,*
> *When nought else can them comfort or appease.*
> O let our soules for ever dwell and rest
> In its refreshing shade, which makes them blest.[16]

Here is protection from the burning sun of the Law, that divine umbrella which allows Marvell's speaker to refer late in the poem to "a milder sun." The sun is milder because, by God's Grace, its effect has been palliated. It is proper that the fruit of the garden come to the speaker without effort on his part. For the Sacrifice was brought about by man's own powerlessness to help himself. A gift, the Eucharist descended upon man without his effort and regardless of his worth. For if his worth were the measure of his salvation (as during the dispensation of Law it was) man would labor as endlessly and with as little hope of gain as do the "Companies of Men." The lush quality of the imagery in Stanza V, in contrast to the single branches of Stanza I, stipulates the difference between the state of nature and the state of Grace. It represents the contrast between the limited potentialities of natural man and the limitless power of God.

In this context, even the greenness of the grass unfolds a mystery. The grass where the speaker falls is that "bed of green" on which the matchless love of Bride and Bridegroom is consummated. In the King James version, the Latin "Lectulus noster floridus" was translated "our bedde is greene"; Giovanni Diodati translated the passage "il nostro letto etiando e verdeggiante." According to tradition, the greenness of this bed represented the fruitfulness of Christ's union with the Church, of which Solomon's marriage was a type. It was the sign of regeneration made possible by the eclipse of the sun of the Law; the Christ Tree, the apple tree, shaded man from the Law's condemnation, allowing a garden to spring where all had been desert. The wilderness, emblem of the breach between God and man, belonged to nature, for into nature man had fallen. But as we read in Herbert's "Sunday," at the Sacrifice, Christ enclosed a garden for his pleasure. Thus, T. S. translates "Also our fruitful bed is green," explaining that the bed was that place *"Where Christ conjoyns in spiritual union,"* producing *"great increase."* [17] William Baldwin expresses the same traditional view: *"Beholde our Bed, our peace most plentiful/ Of conscience, doeth florish through thy myght."* [18] As we have observed, poetic paraphrases of the Song of Songs lent their full weight to the perpetuation of such typical interpretations. In Gervase Markham's *Poem of Poems* (1596), we read:

> (Dearelie belov'd) double thou art as faire,
> And more then faire pleasure consorts with thee,
> Beautious pleasant; pleasant beautious deare,
> To this thou addest all eternitie;
>   And ever greene our bridall bed shall bee.[19]

The quality of green, in this context, refers to the flourishing of the bed where Christ and his Bride are joined in marriage. The block book *Canticum Canticorum* illustrates this idea, with its bed covered with roses (our fig. 33), and this iconographic example resembles a passage in Baldwin, where we read, "Our bed is decked with flowers." The same idea emerges in such Flemish paintings as Roger van der Weyden's "Annunciation" (fig. 4).[20] Earlier, we discussed the way in which the Annunciation functioned in the iconography of Speculum, linked in almost every instance with the enclosed garden of the Song of Songs (figs. 4, 5, and 17). In such paintings the artist drew upon the exegetical tradition which held that Mary was the first Bride of Christ, hortus conclusus of the Church, and paradigm of the devout soul. As the wall enclosing the flowers of the Elect from the weeds of the damned, Mary became, in her role as the Church, a model of the individual soul, who, as the "living stone" from which the walls of the Temple were built, was an enclosed garden in microcosm. Thus, the touchstone of the enclosed garden as an emblem (*hortus mentis*) of man's inner being. This is how the figure was used by St. Teresa and St. John, and how it was used by Herbert, Vaughan, and Marvell.

As we may see from comparison with dozens of paraphrases of the Song of Songs, Marvell is writing of the shadow of the apple tree, where the Spouse reclines in full enjoyment of the "shade of Grace." In this shadow, the soul transcends the limitations of human nature; there and only there does she flourish in virtue. In the shadow of the Christ-Tree, the Bride of the Song finds a "bed of green," where she enjoys the full delight of spiritual union. This is that delicious "repose," that ineffable passivity described by St. Teresa. As we read in Chapter Three, unfolding the true sense of that mysterious Scripture, "I sat down under the shadow of him whom I desired and his fruit is sweet to my palate," she wrote: "A person in this state has no need, for any purpose, to move her hand, or to rise (I mean by this to practise meditation), for the Lord is giving her the fruit from the apple-tree with which she compares her Beloved: He picks it and cooks it and almost eats it for her."[21] As in Marvell's poem, the fruit comes to the speaker without effort, since the aim of meditation has been achieved: "For here all is enjoyment, without any labour of the faculties"; moreover, "While the soul is enjoying the delight which has been described, it seems to be wholly engulfed and protected by a shadow."

We are now in a better position to consider the structural function of Stanza V, which precedes this highly problematic stanza:

> Mean while the Mind, from pleasure less,
> Withdraws into its happiness:
> The Mind, that Ocean where each kind
> Does streight its own resemblance find;
> Yet it creates, transcending these,
> Far other Worlds, and other Seas;
> Annihilating all that's made
> To a green Thought in a green Shade.

Critics have often asked what Marvell meant by "pleasure less." While this is an interesting question, another seems to me to be more profitably advanced: What is the sense of "Mean while"? This is a convenient question because, as a glance at Casimire will show, Marvell's model uses the term in a manner clearly synonymous with "all the while." In other words, "Mean while," or during the speaker's sojourn in the garden (and perhaps even longer), "the Vine no pruning knife doth know,/ The wounded earth no plow." All this may seem too simple, but the point may help explain Marvell's figure of withdrawal, and thereby place Stanzas V and VI in a meaningful relation to the first four stanzas (which, we must remember, have been viewed by critics as being somehow cut off from them). In Casimire's poem, the speaker is saying that the mystical garden has prospered for a great length of time by supernatural means. Similarly, the mind of Marvell's speaker has been withdrawing from the moment of his entrance into the temporal garden. In Stanza VI, following successful meditation, his mind is elevated, his affections moved. As we read in St. Teresa, the soul has no further need of meditation. The significance of the temporal object has been understood, the analogy between the garden and the potentiality of the soul recognized. Now the goal of meditation—the contemplative state—has been achieved. In that state, such handbooks as *The Mind's Road to God* or *The Spiritual Canticle* insist, the soul finds the closest approximation possible in this life to that union for which the enclosed garden of the Song of Songs is the emblem.

Now, the images of green and shade converge. The speaker's thought (or state of mind) is the purest expression—the fruition —of the devout life, which is, in turn, the desideratum of the dispensation of Grace. In this state is the highest expression of spiritual ascent; the "sacred Plants" of "Fair quiet" and "Innocence" (the issue, now, of meditation) flourish in what many of Marvell's contemporaries and literary progenitors had come to think of as the "shade of Grace." It may appear that such a comment derives from an excessive reading back of later upon earlier stanzas. But this is not the case, for the image of shade has functioned powerfully throughout the earlier stanzas of "The Garden." The "sacred Plants" are those "flowers of virtue" sought by the saints as the desired end product of meditation. And they grow "Only among the Plants," only in the solitude of the garden of meditation, what Casimire called in Marvell's model poem "the sacred Green." As "The Garden" unfolds, the reader learns that the alternative to "uncessant Labours" is not idleness; the speaker's passivity must not be confused with sloth.[22]

"LOVE"

Marvell's allusiveness to garden allegory (we have touched briefly on this subject) may explain the contrast in "The Garden" between "uncessant Labours" and a subtle form of effort which is the actual predicate of repose. Though we must recognize repose as the alternative to labor, we can by no means leave it at that. There is a sense in which repose depends on action, be it as it may action of a particular kind. Students of medieval allegory are familiar with the role played by Idleness in such works as the *Roman de la Rose* and the *Chastel du Labour*.[23] In that context, and in terms of the contrast we are considering, Idleness never leads to repose; rather, as the father of lust, he is the progenitor of love's cruel flame. As such, in the *Chastel du Labour*, Idleness is the archenemy of New-Married, the regenerate soul.

Now we are talking about the role of the senses in this allegorical tradition. Clearly, the themes of meditation and love are an inextricable part of any such discussion. The one is an activity of mind which is preparatory to, and the predicate of, repose, while the other is an affection which, no matter what its object, is the understood content of the garden image. In this sense, we have returned to the place where this study began, namely, to discussion of the ambiguous nature of the term "love" as it was understood in the literature of the Renaissance and seventeenth century. Love was instinctive, irrepressible, neither good nor evil; but the will, endowed with the responsibility for investing that affection, must be one or the other. The problem entering human deliberations stemmed from the fact that man's will, though free, was prone to express those most prominent features in his nature, so that man bestowed his love in much the same way as he bestowed his life. Placed on earth to choose a proper object for his love, man had been given a perfect model for that choice in the Saviour's prayer, "Thy will be done." But again, the will was free; life presented alternative paths for the will to follow. And here a note of warning resounded from the Sermon on the Mount: "Enter ye in at the strait gate, for wide is the gate, and broad is the way that leadeth to destruction, and many there be which goe in thereat: Because strait is the gate, and narrow is the way which leadeth unto life, and few there be that finde it." This Scripture might well serve as a relevant gloss on the value of solitude,[24] and on the negative quality of the "Companies of Men."

Just as the multitude labor, compete, pursue, at times they fall idle. It might be thought that such a departure from "uncessant Labours" would be of value. But not so. For though they remain physically still, in no case do their spirits come to rest. Consider the garden scene in Bruyant's *Le Livre du Chastel du Labour* (1499), where Indolence and Sloth gather with two companions in a walled pleasance[25] (which reminds us distantly of the bands of couples thronging the miniatures of the *Roman*). In contrast, above the Vices in the *Chastel*, spiritual husbandmen toil to improve the ground of the hill. Similarly, Marvell's lovers retreat into the garden, but in contrast, they do not come alone to meditate upon its meaning for the spiritual life (for this would presuppose their isolation from the world and from each other). Instead, they come to dally, to mar the trees, and only when exhausted, to rest. But here Marvell's language is deeply ironic. The lovers rest, to be sure, but there is no indication that they escape the heat. Instead, the sequence on the pagan gods suggests that the heat of passion cannot be escaped. The lovers generate the flames of inordinate passion, which then torment them. And in the case of the gods, the single branches of the metamorphosed nymphs are the projection of the fruitlessness of their hot race.

As for the lovers, it seems that they are blinded to the very thing they most desire. Pursuing "Beauty," they fail to recognize its manifestation in the garden. It is as if their senses have become distorted. Or rather, as if the senses distort the images received in such a way as to coincide with the lover's will, which is already disposed to cherish the lesser object.[26] The contrast between the plurality of lovers and the isolated speaker points up a crucial ambiguity in Stanza IV, arising from Marvell's use of the term "Love." Syntactically, it is not certain whether "Love" refers to the affections of the lovers or to the principle dwelling in the garden. But once the imagery of Stanza IV is taken seriously, and the implication of the sardonic parallel (not contrast) between the lovers and the gods is understood, Marvell's irony makes perfect sense. It is ludicrous to imagine that one may approach the love banquet (described in Stanza V) after the body and soul have been enervated by a debilitating lust, or that one may approach such delights in anything but rapt solitude. If "Love" follows the "Fond Lovers" into the temporal garden (and he very often does in the miniatures depicting the voyeurism of David as Bathsheba takes her bath),[27] he must be recognized in his pagan, purblind, cherubic form.

How is it that man enters an attractive garden only to find himself bewildered and powerless to escape? The answer is given in just such miniatures, and in such works as the *Roman de la Rose*, *The Merchant's Tale*, and William Nevill's *The Castell of Pleasure* (1518), works whose broad features of garden allegory persist in the seventeenth century in such poems as Beaumont's *Psyche*. Let us briefly consider a single case, Nevill's *The Castell of Pleasure*. The protagonist of this poem falls asleep while reading a passage from Ovid in which Cupid's power is shown in his triumph over Phoebus. Morpheus pays a visit, persuading him that he seeks "mortal Beauty" and this alone; the dreamer launches upon a pilgrimage to paradise: the fulfillment of desire. In the mock language of devotion, he prays to the god of the mountain for Courage, before approaching the gate of Desire, where he confronts a clear choice:

> Who as in to this place wyll take his entrynge
> Must of these wayes have fre eleccyon
> Yf he lyst be lusty lepe daunce and synge
> Or yf in worldly welthe he set his affeccyon
> In honour ryches or prosperous invencyon
> He shall be conveyed yf he wyll so ensewe
> Elles to the scrypture underneth let hym gyve intencyon
> Whiche is set out in letters of yndye blewe.[28]

The Castle of Pleasure offers the values of wealth, power, and love. Dismissing the possibility offered by the second inscription (an injunction to pursue a life of virtue), the protagonist decides to choose between love and riches. Ironically, he chooses love on the grounds that it endures. Now "enflamed with loves fyre," he follows Chaucer's Januarie (and his many predecessors) in his blasphemy. Just as Januarie exploited the sacrament of marriage and the Church itself for his own lascivious end, the dreamer addresses Christ in a prayer that his folly may be perpetuated. He has become a saint, a star in the constellation of Love's heaven, and as such he is led into the presence of Desire, to become acquainted with Vice and Beauty. By now his senses have been overwhelmed:

> This sayd I was nye the gardyn of affeccyon
> Whiche apperyd to my syght bothe gay and gloryous
> Envyronde with emyraudes to it a free proteccyon
> The percynge dyamonde the amatiste amorous
> The stedfast Saphyr the blew turkes ryght precyous
> With many other stones I lacke connynge them to shew
> Me thought it was a new paradyse delycate and delycyous
> It shone so fresshly and bare so grete avewe.[29]

The dreamer soon discovers, though, that his paradise is really Hell. Once free to choose, now he is "locked . . . in loves chayne." He finds that the garden wall (made of myrtle trees) represents not his protection but his bondage. In the imagery of such poems, as C. S. Lewis has eloquently stated, is an ironic representation of the court, with its idle poets and sardonic amorality.[30] This garden, like the values of the court itself, is a mirror image of the garden of *Caritas*. In this garden, which is almost uniformly lovely, only the apple tree looks out of place. The only tree that fails to flourish in this landscape, it strikes the dreamer's eye as "playn." This bit of irony completes the picture: here is the enclosed garden of the Song of Songs, but with a few important changes. Here is love—true love—that most natural and intense of all human emotions. But here too is the corruption of the soul which follows once the will has attached this strong affection to an inappropriate object. The dreamer finds himself, like the overheated "Lovers" of Marvell's "Garden," outside the shade of the flourishing apple tree.

A token of inclusion beneath the "shade of Grace" is seen in man's spiritual endeavor. After all, Christ, divine Cupid of figure 37, was the paragon of gardeners, whose loving care restored what Eden's "foolish gardener" had brought to ruin. As we have read in Hagthorpe's *Divine Meditations* (1622):

> Man hath a garden thats not very large,
> nor very narrow, and it is his charge.
> To dresse the same, to prune and looke unto it,
> Least weeds (instead of wholesome hearbs) oregrow it.[31]

St. Teresa's handbook of devotion, the *Life*, employing imagery similar to that in figure 37, indicates the breadth of this meditative tradition: the Imitatio Christi, the refinement of the spiritual life, is like the watering of a garden.[32] The four drawings from the well represent the four stages of the mystical experience (these being comparable, in turn, to the levels of biblical meaning, and so of history in its broadest and most particular forms).[33] The soul moves from the body now, by steps through understanding to the bodiless, timeless moment of union with divinity.

Perhaps Marvell has this tradition in mind when, in "Appleton House," he writes of one whose love of gardens (seen in the topiary forms of turrets) must be understood allegorically:

> And yet their walks one on the Sod
> Who, had it pleased him and *God*,
> Might once have made our Gardens spring
> Fresh as his own and flourishing.
> But he preferr'd to the *Cinque Ports*
> These five imaginary Forts:

> And, in those half-dry Trenches, spann'd
> Pow'r which the Ocean might command.   (ll. 345–52)

In rejecting political ambition, Fairfax did more than achieve a gentleman's peace of mind; he triumphed over the world, the flesh, and the devil. In other words, he conquered human nature. As the Old Testament dispensation had shown beyond all doubt, it is natural for man to love the world inordinately. Only the few, like Fairfax and the speaker in "The Garden," succeed in the Imitatio Christi. For them, the garden becomes a mirror of God's love, reflecting God's creative power. Such a man has given birth to those flowers ("sacred Plants") of virtue which bloom eternally:

> For he did, with his utmost Skill,
> Ambition weed, but Conscience till.
> Conscience, that Heaven-nursed Plant,
> Which most our Earthly Gardens want.
> A prickling leaf it bears, and such
> As that which shrinks at ev'ry touch;
> But flowrs eternal, and divine,
> That in the Crowns of Saints do shine.   (ll. 353–60)

As Marvell writes, it is the saint who recognizes and meditates, with the speaker in "The Coronet," his own role in afflicting the head of Christ. Through his spiritual endeavor he attempts to replace the Saviour's crown of thorns with a garland of flowers. At first, he finds the Serpent entwined in "wreaths of Fame and Interest" ("Fond Lovers" and the "busie Companies of Men" will always fail to "weave the Garlands of repose"). But such failure indicates an improper response to the gift of Sacrifice. Blindly, man seeks his own ends, whether in worldly success or in sexual gratification; but the true rewards go to the one who separates himself from the world and its mundane values. Unhappily, in the world the many share the rewards of the many, which are few, while upon the one (in his solitude) are lavished the manifold splendors of the saintly life.

COMPUTING TIME

Clearly, the four stanzas added to "The Garden" require and clarify our rereading of the earlier ones, regardless, now, of the latter's similarity to parts of "Hortus." Such rereading, in turn, illuminates the revised portions. In the context of the Song of Songs, the early stanzas (I–IV) concern the movement of the soul from sensitive perception of a physical object *toward* the state for which that object traditionally stands. The earlier stanzas are now seen as the preliminary stages of meditation, where the soul discovers the application of the garden to human conduct. The insight gained at this (moral) level corresponds to the tropological meaning of Scripture, and represents the first departure of the soul from the literal understanding of Creation. Immediately following this new awareness comes the meaning of the object with reference to the speaker's own soul; in the de contemptu mundi tradition, the soul apprehends its mistaken pursuit of worldly values (II) and ponders the general folly of others (III–IV). Finally, the soul ends its allegorical rumination: as in Prynne's "Christian Paradise," the garden has painted before the speaker's eyes the figure of the crucified Christ. Of course Stanza V is ambiguous, but not necessarily because of any sexual attitude Marvell did or did not have. Within the context of the Song of Songs, this ambiguity is a traditional aspect of the language, deriving from the possible juxtaposition of allegorical and anagogical levels of meaning for exactly the same pattern of images: the image-cluster of the enclosed garden. Not only do the eucharistic figures of tree, fruit, and shade suggest the riches of Love's banquet, they shadow forth the mysteries of spiritual union as they were known in their highest, experiential form.

As the mystics write, in this highest of all possible conditions it is as if the soul has departed from the body:

> Here at the Fountains sliding foot,
> Or at some Fruit-trees mossy root,
> Casting the Bodies Vest aside,
> My Soul into the boughs does glide:
> There like a Bird it sits, and sings,
> Then whets, and combs its silver Wings;
> And, till prepar'd for longer flight,
> Waves in its Plumes the various Light.

Apparently, the "Here" refers to the preceding stanzas, which describe the shaded garden bed where the speaker has fallen. In experience, the speaker has meditated on the object of his love in such a way as to have become momentarily fused with it. The soul, in its active capacity, "glides" into the boughs of the tree in whose shade it has flourished. This gliding movement (an invention of the author's revision) represents a logical development of the two preceding stanzas, and indeed of the preceding poem as a whole, with its movement *toward* the anagogic or mystical level of meaning. At last, it seems as if the body has disappeared, as if all the universe has merged with the object of the speaker's contemplation. As in figure 34, the speaker's entire being has ascended into the tree, to become wholly separated from the world. In this miniature, a monk (lover of "delicious Solitude") retreats from the world, which stretches beneath him as a dualism between light and dark; on our right, a huge black rat and the open jaws of a wide-eyed beast are in contrast to the peaceful unicorn, the white rat, and the general brightness of the opposite side of the painting. As in Marvell's "Garden," the contrasts here reflect the potentiality of withdrawal from the world. And here, as in the "Zacheus" poems of Quarles, man climbs the physical tree in Imitatio Christi, and in so doing ascends the ladder of perfection.

This is what Marvell means by his figure of annihilation. As we saw in Chapter Four, in John Hall's "Emblem 14" (drawn from Augustine's text, "I will pierce heaven with my mind, and be present with thee in my desires") the subject is the exertion of the will directing love toward heaven. The point of that example is worth repeating. In the Hall emblem divine Cupid aims an arrow at heaven, as another already bends upon striking the blazing heart of God's love. Nearby, the Spouse sits in her usually passive position. The soul in her role as Spouse becomes aware of an expansion, as if she would become an "Ocean where each kind/ Does streight its own resemblance find":

> Swell heart into a world and keep
> That humid sea:
> Become, my bosome, one great deep
> That it may lodge in Thee:
> That glorious sun with his Celestiall heat
> will warm't, and mak't evaporate.[34]

The heart swells, becoming more and more amenable to the rays of God's love, until finally all division between the object and that love has disappeared:

> Spring-head of life, how am I now
> Intomb'd in Thee?
> How do I since th' art pleas'd to flow,
> Hate a dualitie?
> How I am annihilated? yet by this
> Acknowledge my subsistence is.

The speaker is "Intomb'd" because he has died to the present world. Hating all division from its true essence, which is spiritual and therefore divine, the soul rises from one moment in time into the timeless:

> Still may I rise; still further clime
> Till that I lie
> (Having out-run-short-winded time)
> Swath'd in Eternitie.[35]

Critics rightly point to the death motif in Stanza VII of "The Garden." The "longer flight" refers to that ultimate separation of soul and body (the two are apart now only momentarily), which transpires only once "That subtile knot, which makes us man" has been forever untied. Of course, the mere fact that a shorter flight is in progress testifies to the regenerative process which has taken place, and which the garden represents. This is the meaning of Vaughan's allusion to hortus conclusus in "Regeneration." However, whereas Vaughan's speaker had heard the whispering of the wind in the mystical garden (assurance of regeneration and sign that the highest level of experience has been achieved), now Marvell's speaker feels himself divested of his clothing of flesh, as if the knot of humanity with all its restrictions has already been undone. He feels a motion in his soul, as of a bird gliding into the branches of the soul's beloved tree. Once perched in its boughs, the bird sends forth a song of reciprocal love. We recall, of course, how springtime in the Song of Songs was heralded by the "time of the singing of birds," notably, by "the voice of the turtle." The dove, represented in Hawkins' emblem of the enclosed garden, appears also in Speculum, bearing the sprig of olive to the ark as a reminder of God's mercy. Perhaps, as in the paraphrases, this is the bird which "sits" in the tree "and sings":

> the flowrs appear shew summer's near
> Each chirping bird doth sit and sing,
> The turtles voice doth make a noise,
> All which bespeak a glorious spring.[36]

Meditation, the primary source of movement in the garden, is the crux for the exercise of the will. Of course, this point immediately suggests another familiar implication of the bird image: meditation is itself a bird on whose wings the soul is lofted into union with the divine essence: the soul, animated by a desire "to give it selfe to the beloved object," is drawn as on "the winge of the dove, to flie to her repose, . . . [to] her beloved."[37] As we saw in Stanza IX, the alternative to "uncessant Labours" is not sloth but spiritual industry. The annihilation of time and the objects of time is predicated on the proper exercise of the soul, which resembles the profitable employment of the bee:

> How well the skilful Gardner drew
> Of flow'rs and herbes this Dial new;
> Where from above the milder Sun
> Does through a fragrant Zodiack run;
> And, as it works, th' industrious Bee
> Computes its time as well as we.
> How could such sweet and wholsome Hours
> Be reckon'd but with herbs and flow'rs!

As the emblem tradition would have it, the bee presents man with an emblem of the proper way of counting (computing, spending) time. He is, as Wither writes, "laborious in an honest way,"[38] neither idle nor unceasing in his work. As Marvell's figure of the floral sundial reminds the reader, Time presents man with the choice of how to spend his time. If he is wise, he emulates the bee. For, in the last analysis, asks John Wall,

> What is the Church but as a garden? What are we but as spirituall Bees? O let us sucke the flowers and draw the sweetnesse, and never rest, till we have made a hive of our soules and bodies: that our hearts may be as waxe, softened, and mollified, for the impression of this seale, and nothing but this.[39]

And as St. François de Sales writes, where is the spiritual bee led in meditation except to those divine passions described in the Song of Songs?

> Thus the celestiall Spouse, as a mysticall bee, flies to the Canticle of Canticles, now upon the eyes, now upon the lippes, cheekes and head haire of the well-beloved, to draw from thence the sweetnesse of a thousand passions of love; . . . .[40]

Emulating the profitable employment of the bee, man makes a proper use of the temporal garden, employing it as setting for and emblem of meditation (see fig. 41). Because of this, he escapes the blazing sun of God's justice, which, in the state of nature—independent of Grace—prevails. Again, Marvell's revision was accomplished within the allegorical tradition of the Song of Songs. The Latin "*candidior*" becomes "milder," the new form suggesting that the effect of the sun in "The Garden" bears not only upon the sight but upon all those parts of man's being which are capable of perceiving either the sun's mildness or its lack. In the context of the Song of Songs, the mildness refers to the intervention of God's mercy, to the "shade of Grace" in which the speaker safely dwells. Because his time has been well spent in solitary meditation, the speaker "computes" his "time" in the manner of the bee, responding to the garden, which, as Prynne writes, "paints" before his eyes the figure of Christ, which "tenders" to his "thoughts" the "Soule-ravishing,/ Sweete, heavenly Meditations which doe spring/ From Gardens." [41] The soul is lifted "high on *Contemplation's* Wings" [42] "Above the Spheares in a delightfull Trance." [43] Longing for that ultimate union which the garden typifies, the soul glides into the tree whose shadow (like a heavenly embrace) is a "milder Sun."

CONCLUSION

If the foregoing analysis is correct, "The Garden" is no more disunified than the final stanza "est une sorte de post-scriptum," [44] and that stanza represents the traditional (and, given the limits of human experience, necessary) return of the soul to the physical place where meditation began. Though Bonaventure offered no advice on the disposition of the soul once transcendence had been achieved, the return frequently appears in such works as Bishop Hall's meditation, "Upon a fair Prospect," and in those poems which embody ("To our bodies turn we then") the *Itinerarium Mentis* structure.[45] When "The Garden" is read in the context of the Song of Songs, the poem is richer than most recent criticism has allowed, but that richness is seen as the product of a distinctly seventeenth-century sensibility, one not in all respects like our own. For this reason, we beg the question when we assume that one perceives the meaning of "The Garden" and the "meaning" of a Rorschach inkblot in the same way, namely, by an immediate apprehension of the object, followed only by the play of the viewer's imagination. The critic cannot assume that he carries a perfect dictionary around in his head, one containing all potentially relevant examples, regardless of what part of the language he may confront. For the very question at issue when a critic construes a poetic text is this: What is the linguistic context in which that text should be construed? Only after a text is properly construed may a critic talk about the richness of a poem, for only then does he have a poem to talk about.[46] It makes no sense to talk about "The Garden" as if its author were conversant with the works of Freud or Sartre or Heidegger. Specifically, it makes no sense to say with William Empson that "The chief point [of Marvell's poem] is to contrast and reconcile conscious and unconscious states, intuitive and intellectual modes of apprehension," [47] for that is an anachronistic description of the meaning of Marvell's text. And in this case the description is made all the more incomprehensible when the critic adds that the "chief point of the poem . . . is never made, perhaps could not have been made" in the poem. If the history of an idea ought never to replace the poem, neither should the reverie of a modern critic.

In this culminating chapter, I have tried to isolate the particular way in which the image-cluster of the enclosed garden functions in "The Garden": it does not function in this poem in the same way it does in "The Mower against Gardens." At the same time, by treating the allegorical aspect of "The Garden," I have tried to show that the speaker's fall on grass has nothing to do with "carnal sin"; nor do I detect (or even understand what King might mean by) "the normal sin-associations" of Marvell's poem.[48] "The Garden" is not a poem about sexual aberration or sexual frustration or sexual ambivalence—it is not a poem about twentieth-century guilt either—but rather one in which erotic imagery functions to suggest the innocent fulfillments of the spiritual life. That imagery had been so construed for centuries. So it was construed by preachers, artists, and poets in the early seventeenth century, and so (as the revision of "The Garden" shows) did Marvell himself construe and use it. Thus, regardless of how strange it may appear to the modern mind, in "The Garden," eroticism and innocence go hand in hand, for both were essential aspects of that love described by Solomon. Celebrated for their passion in the "holy of holies" of Scripture, depicted by artists and poets through the centuries, two lovers ecstatically enjoyed each other in a lovely, perfumed garden, sheltered from the storm of time by an indestructible wall, and by the plentiful shade of a fruit-bearing tree: "I sate downe under his shadow with great delight . . . ."

Reference Matter

Appendix: "Hortus"

The following graceful translation of "Hortus" is reprinted from William A. McQueen and Kiffin A. Rockwell, *The Latin Poetry of Andrew Marvell* (Chapel Hill, N.C., 1964), by permission of the University of North Carolina Press.

THE GARDEN

What madness so stirs the heart of man?
Alas, madness for the Palm and the Laurel, or for the simple
    grass!
So that one tree will scarcely crown his curbless efforts,
Nor wholly circle his temples with its scanty leaves.
While at the same time, entwined in garlands of tranquil   5
    Quiet,
All flowers meet, and the virgin woods.
    Fair Quiet, I hold you! And you, sister of Quiet,
Innocence! You a long time in temples, in cities
I sought in vain, and in the palaces of kings.
But you in the shaded silences of gardens, **far off,**   10
The green plants and like-colored shadow hide.
    Oh, if I am ever allowed to profane your retreats,
Wandering about, faint, and panting for a better life,
Preserve your new citizen, and me, having attained my wish,
Leafy citizens, accept in the flowery kingdom.   15
    Me also, you *Muses*—and I call you, omniscient *Apollo*, as
    witness—
Herds of men do not please, nor the roaring of the *Circus*,
Nor the bellowing of the Forum; but me the sanctuaries of
    spring,
And silent veneration draw, and solitary communion.
    Whom does the grace of maidenly beauty not arrest?   20

187

Which, although it excels snows in whiteness and purple in
    redness,
Yet your green force (in my opinion) surpasses.
Hair cannot compete with leaves, nor arms with branches,
Nor are tremulous voices able to equal your whisperings.
25   Ah, how often have I seen (Who would believe it?) cruel
    lovers
Carving the name of their mistress on bark, which is more
    worthy of love.
Nor was there a sense of shame for inscribing wounds on
    sacred trunks.
But I, if ever I shall have profaned your stocks,
No *Neaera, Chloe, Faustina, Corynna* shall be read:
30   But the name of each tree shall be written on its own bark.
O dear *plane tree, cypress, poplar, elm!*
        Here Love, his wings cast aside, walks about in sandals,
Laying aside his nerveless bows and hissing arrows,
And inverts his torches, nor does he wish to be feared;
35   Or he lies stretched out and sleeps on his quiver;
Nor will he hear, although Cytherea call;
Nor do idle dreams report previous iniquities.
        The Gods rejoice, the Tyrant ceasing to rage,
And although they have known *nymphs* and *goddesses* many
    times,
40   Each one achieves his desires better now in a *tree.*
Jupiter, forgetful of his wife, languishes for the aged oak;
Juno has not suffered thus for another rival.
No traces dishonor the bed of *Vulcan,*
Nor is Mars mindful of *Venus* if the *ash* be present.
45   *Apollo* pursued beautiful *Daphne*
That she might become a *laurel;* but he had sought nothing
    more.
And though goat-footed *Pan* fell upon fleeing *Syrinx,*
This was that he might procure a sounding reed.

Desunt multa

And you, maker of the garden shall not depart without a
    grateful song:
50   You who in the brief plants and joyous flowers have indicated
The growing hours and intervals of the day.
There the sun more bright passes through the fragrant signs;
And fleeing the fierce *Bull,* the *Crab's* threatening claw,
Glides toward the safe shadows of roses and violets.

And the sedulous bee, intent on its sweet labor,   55
Seems to mark its duties with the thyme as horologe.
O sweet lapse of time! O healthful ease!
    O hours worthy to be numbered in herbs and flowers!

Notes

Unless otherwise noted, all books published before 1700 bear a London imprint. Throughout the text and notes, in quotations from manuscripts and early printed books, I have regularized the use of *i* and *j* and *u* and *v*, disregarded meaningless capitals, and expanded contractions. Where an entire poem originally appeared in italics, I have eliminated the italics completely.

INTRODUCTION

1 E. D. Hirsch, Jr., "Objective Interpretation," *PMLA*, LXXV (1960), 463–79.

CHAPTER I: THE SONG OF SONGS

1 Lily B. Campbell, *Divine Poetry and Drama in Sixteenth-Century England*, London, 1959.
2 In his "Invocation To the Divine Father of sacred Muses," Barnaby Barnes makes this point clear:

> No more lewde laies of Lighter loves I sing,
> Nor teach my lustfull Muse abus'de to flie,
> With Sparrowes plumes and for compassion crie,
> To mortall beauties which no succour bring.
> But my Muse fethered with an Angels wing,
> Divinely mounts aloft unto the skie.
> Where her loves subjects with my hopes doe lie:
> For Cupids darts prefigurate hell's sting.
>
> (*A Divine Centurie of Spirituall Sonnets* [1595], sig. A4)

3 St. Bernard of Clairvaux, *On the Song of Songs*, tr. and ed. by a Religious of C.S.M.V. (London: A. R. Mowbray, 1952), p. 23.
4 St. François de Sales, *A Treatise of the Love of God*, tr. by Miles Car (Douay, 1630), p. 32; cf. R. K., *The Canticles, or Song of Solomon*,

Reduced into a Decasyllable . . . (1662), p. 1: "An holy Cantick paralell'd by none, ..."

5 Richard Sibbes, *Bowels Opened* (1639), p. 2. The first engraving in the Huntington Kitto Bible (1836) meant to illustrate the Song of Songs is an iconographic analogue of these literary examples. Here an angel plays the organ, reading notes from the musical score of Solomon's Song. Behind the Bride (center) the Bridegroom enters beneath the banner of Canticles ii.16 (XXV, fol. 4650). The engraving was executed in the early decades of the seventeenth century. For detailed discussions of the early history and medieval heritage of biblical allegory, see R. P. C. Hanson, *Allegory and Event: A Study of the Sources and Significance of Origen's Interpretation of Scripture* (Richmond, Va., 1959), and Beryl Smalley, *The Study of the Bible in the Middle Ages* (Oxford, 1952).

6 Michael Drayton, *The Harmony of the Church* (1591), ed. by Alexander Dyce for the Percy Society, *Early English Poetry* (London, 1843), VII, sig. B2.

7 Ibid., sig. B2ᵛ.

8 Henry Ainsworth, *Solomons Song of Songs in English Metre* (1623), bound with *Annotations Upon the Five Bookes of Moses, the Booke of Psalmes, and the Song of Songs* (1627), pp. 3 ff. Paraphrase of the Song of Songs found its way into the liturgy; Claudio Monteverdi's magnificent *Vespers of 1610* is an example of the perpetuation of this tradition. Jean Bonnard cites an interesting medieval analogue of a paraphrase molded into the form of the Stabat Mater: Jean Bonnard, *Les Traductions de la Bible en vers français au moyen âge* (Paris, 1884), p. 158. Bonnard reprints passages from three other verse paraphrases of the Canticles, all dating from around the 13th century (p. 151). He finds in these little of originality: "les explications allégorique sont celles que l'on trouve partout."

9 Luis de la Puente, *Meditations upon the Mysteries of our Holie Faith,* tr. by John Heigham (St. Omers, 1619), I, 7.

10 Casimire Sarbiewski, *The Odes of Casimire,* tr. by G. Hils (1646), pp. 31, 41, 83.

11 Joseph Beaumont, *The Minor Poems of Joseph Beaumont,* ed. by Eloise Robinson (Boston: Houghton Mifflin, 1914), p. 16, quoted by permission. All citations from *The Minor Poems* in my text are from this edition.

12 William Loe, "The Song of Songs," in *Songs of Sion* (Hamburg, 1620), pp. 73–92.

13 George Wither, "The Song of Songs," in *The Hymnes and Songs of the Church* (1623[?]; STC 25909), pp. 31–59. The typography of the three 1623 editions of Wither's *Hymnes* varies; I use this edition throughout.

14 Ibid., p. 31.

15 Campbell, p. 57.

16 William Baldwin, *The Canticles or Balades of Salomon* (1549), sig. Aiii^v.

17 Jude Smith, *A misticall devise of the . . . love betwene Christ . . . and the Church* (1575), sig. Aii.

18 Loe, pp. 100–10[1].

19 Richard Rowlands, *Odes. In Imitation of the Seaven Penitential Psalmes* (Antwerp, 1601), p. 51.

20 Francis Quarles, *Sions Sonets* (1625), sig. C2^v.

21 In a direct address to the practitioners of *"that sacred Art,"* Quarles replies in advance to critics of his unusual "sonets" by saying that their *"Muse is out of heart."* His sonnets present the very essence of that which *"creates a Poet." Sions Sonets*, sig. A4^v.

22 John Weemes, *Exercitations Divine*, bound with *The Workes of Mr. J. Weemes* (1634), III, 158, hereafter cited as *Workes*.

23 Simon Wastell, "A Dialogue Between the Church and her Daughters," in *Microbiblion* (1629), pp. 29–30.

24 Modern scholars seem to agree that the Song of Songs is not a song at all, but rather, as Morris Jastrow writes, "a collection of lyrics, little popular pieces, conceived in various places, at indefinite dates, and . . . finally collected in the third century B.C." They were chosen "as part of Sacred Canon" not for anything "intrinsic to the works" but simply because they "were on the lips of all and beloved of all." *The Song of Songs*, tr. by Morris Jastrow (San Francisco: Robert Grabhorn, 1922), p. 4.

25 Biblical citations in my text are to the Authorized Version of the English Bible (1611), ed. by William Wright (5 vols., Cambridge: Cambridge University Press, 1909). I have omitted the italics of the King James Version from my text.

26 T[homas] W[ilcox], *An exposition uppon the Booke of the Canticles, otherwise called Schelomons Song* (1585), p. 4.

27 William Gouge, *An Exposition of the Song of Solomon: called Canticles* (1615), sig. A3^v.

28 Theodore Beza, *Sermons Upon the Three First Chapters of the Canticle of Canticles*, tr. by John Harmar (Oxford, 1587), sig. A4, pp. 2, 3.

29 St. John of the Cross, *The Complete Works of St. John of the Cross*, tr. and ed. by E. Allison Peers (Westminster, Md.: Newman Press, 1953), II, 24, quoted by permission of the Newman Press and Burns & Oates Ltd., London. My citations from St. John of the Cross are from this edition. His *Spiritual Works which lead a soul to perfect union with God*, which lacked *The Spiritual Canticle*, was published in 1618.

30 St. François de Sales, *A Treatise of the Love of God*, p. 645.

31 Morton Bloomfield, *Piers Plowman as a Fourteenth-Century Apocalypse* (New Brunswick, N.J., 1961), p. 30. For an example of the

perpetuation of the four levels of interpretation, at least in purport, see Louis Richeome's *Holy Pictures of the mysticall Figures of the most holy Sacrifice . . . of the Eucharist,* tr. by C. A. (1619), p. 3. Similarly, in a sermon entitled "The Bridegrome and his Bride," John Rawlinson claims that his text, taken from the Song of Songs, and all other texts in Scripture contain both "*Literæ cortex, the shell of Literal,* or *Historical sense,* and *Nucleus spiritualis intelligentiæ, the kernel of a Spiritual* or *Moral sense.*" *Quadriga Salutis* (Oxford, 1625), sig. N4ᵛ.

32 Weemes, *Workes,* I, 229.

33 Ibid., I, 230.

34 Ibid., I, 232.

35 Ibid., I, 234.

36 Ibid.

37 In commenting on chapter 6, verse 8, of the Canticles, for example, Robert Allen writes that the Church, "generally considered," is "but one." But at the same time, as the popular analogy of the Church with "the naturall bodie" would indicate, the Church, "though it have many members," is "yet but one bodie." *The Doctrine Of The Gospel* (1606), Bk. III, 25. St. Augustine wrote that the Church was made "not of timber and stones, but of living soules." *Of The Citie Of God,* tr. by J. Healy, with a commentary by John Vives (1610), p. 634.

38 See the Appendix of Helen Gardner's edition, *The Divine Poems* (Oxford: Clarendon Press, 1952), pp. 121–27. Citations from *The Divine Poems* in my text are from this edition, by permission of the Clarendon Press, Oxford.

39 See Miss Gardner's note on l. 12, p. 80. Similar uses of the figure of the soul as the Spouse are too numerous to mention, but see Walter Montagu, *Miscellanea Spiritualia* (1648), p. 175.

40 Beaumont, *The Minor Poems,* p. 46.

41 Gervase Markham, *The Poem of Poems* [1596], sig. E1.

42 Robert Crofts, *The Lover: Or, Nuptiall Love* (1638), sig. E6. See also Robert Wilkinson's sermon on the joining of Lord Hay and his wife, *The Merchant Royall* (1607), p. 5.

43 Joseph Hall, "An Open and Plaine Paraphrase, upon the Song of Songs, Which is Salomons," in *Salomons Divine Arts* (1609), sig. N2ᵛ.

44 St. François de Sales, *A Treatise of the Love of God,* p. 390.

45 Citations from Crashaw in my text are from *The Poems English Latin and Greek of Richard Crashaw,* ed. by L. C. Martin (Oxford: Clarendon Press, 1957), by permission of the Clarendon Press, Oxford. The present example is from "On a prayer booke sent to Mrs. M. R.," pp. 128–29.

46 Francis Quarles, *Emblemes* (1635), pp. 245–46. All quotations from the *Emblemes* in my text are from this edition.

47 William Gouge, *The Saints Sacrifice* (1632), pp. 9-11.

48 Luis de Granada, *A Memoriall of a Christian Life*, [tr. by Richard Hopkins] (Rouen, 1599), p. 761.

49 Origen, *The Song of Songs: Commentary and Homilies*, tr. by R. P. Lawson (London, 1957), pp. 36, 60.

50 Francis Rous, *The Mysticall Marriage* (1635), p. 13.

51 Ibid., p. 14.

52 Ibid., p. 15.

53 John Saltmarsh, *Poemata Sacra* (Cambridge, 1636), sig. C8.

54 Ibid., sigs. C8–C8ᵛ. Similarly, Nathaniel Richards writes:

> Make me to feele, those wonted holy fires,
> Which rapt my soule in sanctifide desires,
> (Ravisht all sense) and with admir'd amaze,
> Expos'd me, to that blessed burning blaze. . . .
>
> (*The Celestiall Publican* [1630], sig. B4ᵛ)

55 St. François de Sales, *A Treatise of the Love of God*, p. 32.

56 John Dove, *The Conversion of Salomon* (1613), p. 8.

57 Ibid., p. 11. See also Alonso Roderigues, *A Treatise Of Mentall Prayer*, tr. by I. W. (St. Omers, 1627), p. 28.

58 Henoch Clapham, *Three Partes of Salomon his Song of Songs, expounded* (1603), p. 7.

59 John Cotton, *A Brief Exposition With Practical Observations Upon the whole Book of Canticles* (1655), p. 3.

60 John Davies, *The Muses Sacrifice* (1612), fols. 69–69ᵛ.

61 St. François de Sales, *A Treatise of the Love of God*, sig. A8ᵛ.

62 Dove, p. 15.

63 Davies, fols. 7ᵛ–8.

CHAPTER II: THE ENCLOSED GARDEN

1 *The Sarum Missal*, tr. by Frederick E. Warren (London, 1913), II, 465.

2 *Pontificale Romanum* (Mechliniae, Belgium: H. Dessain, 1934), pp. 284, 285, 286. The "Roman Pontifical" originated in the tenth century; for a brief but thorough treatment of its place in liturgical history, see Michel Andrieu, *Le Pontifical romain au moyen-âge* (Vatican, 1959), I, 3 ff. The subject of the Assumption suggested the same passage to Richard Crashaw:

> Shee's call'd againe, harke how th' immortall Dove
> Sighs to his silver mate: rise up my Love,
> Rise up my faire, my spotlesse one,

The Winter's past, the raine is gone:
The Spring is come, the Flowers appeare,
No sweets since thou art wanting here.

("On the Assumption," *Poems of Crashaw*, p. 139)

Cf. "In the Glorious Assumption of Our Blessed Lady," pp. 304–6.

3 Beaumont, *The Minor Poems*, p. 41.

4 Jerome Porter, *The Flowers Of The Lives Of The Most Renowned Saincts* (Douay, 1632), pp. 119–20. Again, Christ "drawes the image of the spouse he came to take, in the figure of perfect beauty, as the best sensible Character can be made of her; and makes this quality the object of Christs love, *As she is all faire, and no spot to be found in her:* and thus, as beauty is chosen for a simbol of spirituall purity," man must understand "the allegory of it." Walter Montagu, *Miscellanea Spiritualia* (1648), p. 39.

5 Francis Rous, *The Mysticall Marriage* (1635), p. 17. Pierre Cotton voices a prayer entitled "To the holy Virgins, Men and Women," which begins: "Vessels of honour, Fountaines sealed up, Parkes walled round about, Lillies of the territorie of *Eden*," and goes on to name the six virtues which grow from the stem of the lily. *The Interiour Occupation Of The Soule* (Douay, 1618), sig. G10ᵛ. Similarly, we read in William Evans' *A Translation of the Booke of Nature, into the Use of Grace* (Oxford, 1633), "*That there is but one Church.* Thus saith the *Lord* speaking of his Church, *My dove, my undefiled is but one, the only one of her Mother.*" He of course cites the Song of Songs, vi.9 (p. 45).

6 T[homas] W[ilcox], *An exposition uppon the Booke of the Canticles, otherwise called Schelomons Song* (1585), p. 14: "... *I am like to them that dwell under Solomons Tapistry,* ... but by one parte of *Solomons* householde, as his tapistrie or curteines, shee [the Bride] ment all the glorye and furniture of his house, whatsoever, of which you maye read at large I.Kinges.10.1,2&c."

7 According to John Weemes, Solomon was a "speciall type of Christ," for "It was hee who fell not away untill his old age, and although the Lord threatned him, that hee would rent his Kingdome for this his Idolatrie, yet hee continued still in it, I King. 9.11." *Workes*, III, 249. See Wilcox, p. 3; Origen, *The Song of Songs: Commentary and Homilies*, tr. R. P. Lawson (London, 1957), p. 51.

8 Thomas Walkington, *Salomons Sweete Harpe* (1608), p. 13.

9 Origen, p. 40. The view was current in the early 17th century. For example, in Walkington (p. 8), we read: "Thus spake he [Solomon] in his three-folde Philosophie, as *Origen* tearms it; *Morall, Naturall, Theoreticall:* morall, in the *Proverbs:* naturall, here in *Ecclesiastes:* and contemplative in that heavenly *song of songs.*"

10 John Dove, *The Conversion of Salomon* (1613), p. 166; see also p. 130.

Reference was often made to Ephesians v.23: "They shall be one flesh." For the prototype of this idea, note Origen, p. 51.

11 Otto van Veen, *Amoris Divini Emblemata* (1660), p. 118.

12 Robert Whitehall, *Sive Iconum* (Oxford, 1677), Icon 141.

13 Henoch Clapham, *Three Partes of Salomon his Song of Songs, expounded* (1603), p. 9.

14 Luis de la Puente, *Meditations upon the Mysteries of our Holie Faith*, tr. by John Heigham (St. Omers, 1619), I, 269.

15 Speculum humanae salvationis (England, c. 1390), Morgan MS. M.766.

16 "Psautier Illustré" (Paris, 1906), reprod. from Bibliothèque Nationale MS. Latin 8846, fol. 18. Analogues to this example are numerous. In the Huntington Kitto Bible, see II, fol. 249, and III, fols. 349–69 passim.

17 Mary was known in the "Ave's" as the "port of parradice." *Devotional Pieces in Verse and Prose*, ed. by J. A. W. Bennett (Edinburgh, 1955), p. 295. Again, the Huntington Kitto Bible provides numerous examples of many of the scenes described in this paragraph; see esp. XXV, fols. 4654a–b, 4656, 4657, 4683ᵛ.

18 Adam of St. Victor, *The Liturgical Poetry of Adam of St. Victor*, tr. by Digby Wrangham (London, 1881), II, 229. In Henry Hawkins' *Partheneia Sacra* (Rouen, 1633), we get a good idea of the perpetuation of this tradition: "She was a *signed fountain*, because she was likewise an *enclosed Garden*. She was a *Garden*, because *Her* understanding was ful of fayth, and knowledge of GOD, with infinit varietie of flowers of al kinds; and *closed* it was, because no errour or ignorance might enter therinto. She was a *Garden*, because her affect was ful of love to GOD and her Neighbour; and *closed*, because no terrene love or base desire of the flesh or world, could find accesse to her hart. She was a *signed Fountain*, because her Virginal womb was ful of the water of Celestial grace; and *signed*, because *sealed* with the irrevocable Vow of perpetual and immaculate *Virginitie*" (pp. 215–16).

19 Gervase Markham, *The Poem of Poems* [1596], sigs. C8–C8ᵛ. See Adam of St. Victor, III, 33, 35.

20 Richard Rowlands, "Epithetes of Our Blessed Lady," in *Odes. In Imitation of the Seaven Penitential Psalmes* (Antwerp, 1601), p. 48. See Adam of St. Victor, III, 127.

21 John Donne, *The Poems of John Donne*, ed. by Herbert J. C. Grierson (Oxford: Clarendon Press, 1958), I, 434–35, quoted by permission of the Clarendon Press, Oxford. For a discussion of the poem's relation to the Donne canon, see II, clii–liii.

22 Hawkins, pp. 13–14.

23 Ibid., p. 11.

24 For an extended discussion of the importance of the seven-part division of the meditation, see Louis L. Martz, *The Poetry of Meditation* (New Haven, 1954), ch. 2.

25 Hawkins, pp. 170-71.

26 Ibid., p. 228.

27 Erwin Panofsky, *Early Netherlandish Painting* (Cambridge, Mass.: Harvard University Press, 1953), I, 131-34. See Panofsky's fig. 104 (Vol. II). For much of the following argument I am indebted to Panofsky. Since I refer often to the figures in Volume II of this work, it will be a great help to the reader to have a copy of it available.

28 Ibid., I, 132.

29 Erwin Panofsky, "Gothic and Late Medieval Manuscripts" (unpub. MS at the Pierpont Morgan Library, 1935), p. 59. In a discussion of the House of David and Solomon, Hugh Broughton makes the same comparison: *A Comment upon Coheleth* (1605), pp. 11-12.

30 Panofsky, *Early Netherlandish Painting*, I, 136. See his fig. 199 (Vol. II).

31 "Hours of Isabelle of Brittainy," from photographs in the Pierpont Morgan Library, fol. 48^v.

32 "Hours of the Virgin" (Paris, c. 1503), Morgan MS. M.732, fol. 30^v.

33 Cf. "Kildare Book of Hours" (Paris, c. 1415), Morgan MS. M.105, fol. 113^v.

34 *Heures de Milan*, ed. by George H. de Loo (Brussels, 1911), fol. 30.

35 Panofsky, *Early Netherlandish Painting*, I, 133 ff.

36 Ibid., I, 146 ff. See II, fig. 306.

37 Ibid., I, 144 ff. See II, figs. 236, 237.

38 Ibid., I, 146.

39 Ibid., II, fig. 82.

40 Ibid., II, fig. 198. We find a similar treatment of the setting in a miniature of St. Catherine in *Le Bréviaire du Musée Mayer van den Bergh . . . étude du texte et des miniatures*, ed. by Camille Jaspar (Brussels, 1932), fol. 611^v.

41 Panofsky, *Early Netherlandish Painting*, II, figs. 485, 486.

42 Ibid., II, fig. 255.

43 William Dunbar, *Poems*, ed. by James Kinsley (Oxford, 1958), p. 9.

44 Speculum humanae salvationis, Morgan MS. M.766, fol. 30^v.

45 William Prynne writes:

> *Gardens enclosed are with walls, pales, bounds,*
> *Hedges, dikes, and more fenc'd than other grounds:*
> *So God his Church and chosen doth enclose,*
> *And fence with walls, pales, dikes against all foes, ...*

> ("A Christian Paradise," in *Mount-Orgueil* [1641], p. 152)

46 J. B., *Virginalia* (1632), p. 31. Iconographically, the wall of the city surrounds the Virgin just as does the wall of hortus conclusus. Thus, in figure 21 the Spouse and her friends are assaulted by mounted knights, but the crenellated wall surrounding the city reminds the viewer of the inevitable outcome of the struggle.

47   Christopher Harvey, *The Synagogue* (1639), p. 4.
48   Benedict von Haefton's *Schola Cordis* was first published in Antwerp in 1629, and may well have been known in England through this edition.
49   Christopher Harvey, *The School of the Heart* (1664), p. 125. Harvey's adaptation of *Schola Cordis* was first published in 1647.
50   Ibid., p. 126.
51   Ibid., p. 125. For an example which might well be used as a gloss on this passage, see Henry Ainsworth, *Solomons Song of Songs in English Metre* (1623), bound with *Annotations Upon the Five Bookes of Moses, the Booke of Psalmes, and the Song of Songs* (1627), p. 34: "Vers. 12. *A garden*] understand from the verses before and after, *Thou art a garden;* which is (by signification) a place closed and fenced; and is sowne and planted with hearbs and trees, for use and pleasure. So in Esa. 5. the Church of Israel is likened to a fenced vineyard. *locked*] or, *barred:* that is, close shut; as the Greeke translateth it *shut:* which is for safetie and defense, that no evill should come thereon, no enemies should enter." Similarly, in *The Conversion of Salomon* John Dove says of the Church: "God hedgeth it in on every side, that the wilde Boare may doe no hurt. It is as a Towne walled about for defence against the enemies, that it cannot bee conquered, as Jerusalem was compassed about with Hils, *They which doe trust in the Lord shall be as Mount Sion which cannot be moved, and standeth for ever, the Hils compasse Jerusalem round about, so is the Lord about his people from henceforth for ever more*" (pp. 201-2). See John Cotton's interpretation of the same passage from the Song of Songs, *A Brief Exposition With Practical Observations Upon the whole Book of Canticles* (1655), p. 103.
52   Cotton, p. 104. We find a relevant gloss on this use of "wilderness" in Thomas Wilson's *A Christian Dictionary* (1614), p. 851: "[Wildernesse] A vast, barren, desolate place. 2 The old man, with his lusts and affections, which are to be forsaken of such as will come to Christ. Cant. 8,5. *Who is this that commeth out of the Wildernesse?*"
53   See Eric Partridge, *Origins* (London, 1958). This is not, however, the scientific derivation of the word. See also James Hastings, *Encyclopaedia of Religion and Ethics* (New York, 1926), I, 84, and *OED*.
54   Thus the wall surrounding the garden in Richard Baxter's *The Saints Everlasting Rest* (1650) is made of jasper and is called "Salvation" (p. 850).
55   Citations from Herbert in my text are from *The Works of George Herbert*, ed. by F. E. Hutchinson (Oxford: Clarendon Press, 1941), by permission of the Clarendon Press, Oxford. Herbert may have been influenced in his poetic identification of Temple and garden by examples like the following, which were numerous in the early part of the century:

When I have given due sacrifice of prayse,
    then up I rise, and to thy Temple goe:
There do I seeke out thy divinest wayes,
    and walke where thou the seedes of love doost sowe.
That fruite I taste of, which doth make my hart
Beare chearefull musicke in the highest part.

Therefore doe I view thy rare and wondrous deedes,
    and thinke how dearely thou redemedst man:
Oh then poore hart how suddenly it bleedes,
    as from a sluce or conduit, streames have run.
Then cry I Lord come helpe me from the ground,
Or I shall dye of this continuall wound.

                          St. Peters Teares (1602), sig. B3ᵛ.

56 Nehemiah Rogers, [*A*] *Strange Vineyard In Palæstina* (1623), p. 73.
57 Ralph Austen, *The Spiritual Use of a Garden* (1657), p. 6. This work is bound with Austen's *A Treatise of Fruit-Trees.*
58 Ibid., p. 83.
59 John King, *The Fourth Sermon Preached at Hampton Court* (Oxford, 1606), p. 4.
60 Prynne, p. 136.
61 St. John of the Cross, *Complete Works*, II, 144–45.
62 St. Teresa writes: "I speak of pruning, for there come times when the soul feels like anything but a garden: everything seems dry to it and no water comes to refresh it, and one would think there had never been any kind of virtue in it at all. The soul suffers many trials, for the Lord wants the poor gardener to think that all the trouble he has taken in watering the garden and keeping it alive is lost. Then is the proper time for weeding and rooting out the smaller plants, and this must be done, however small they may be, if they are useless; for we know that no efforts of ours are availing if God withholds from us the water of grace, and we must despise ourselves as nothing and as less than nothing." *The Life of the Holy Mother Teresa of Jesus*, from *The Complete Works of Saint Teresa of Jesus*, tr. and ed. by E. Allison Peers from the critical edition of P. Silverio de Santa Teresa, C.D. (London and New York: Sheed & Ward, 1944), I, 87. Citations from St. Teresa in my text are from this edition, published in three volumes by Sheed & Ward, Inc., New York.
63 Daniel Price, *The Spring* (1609), sig. B1.
64 Ibid., sig. B1ᵛ.
65 Ibid., sigs. B2–B2ᵛ.

CHAPTER III: SHADE

1   St. Augustine, *S. Augustines Praiers,* tr. by Thomas Rogers (1581), p. 91.
2   Henry Hoddeson, *A Treatise, Concerning the Death and resurrection of our bodies* (1606), sig. H4ᵛ.
3   T. S., *The Book of the Song of Solomon in Meeter* (1676), p. 2.
4   The Holy Bible, tr. by John Wycliffe, ed. by Josiah Forshall and Frederick Madden (Oxford, 1850), III, 73. In *A Guide to Goe to God* (1626), William Gouge explains that the Church, since it was still a mixture of flesh with spirit, was "Blacke by reason of her infirmities, and imperfections, as well as of her afflictions and persecutions" (p. 53).
5   John Dove, *The Conversion of Salomon* (1613), p. 38.
6   Ibid.; cf. Matt. xiii.21.
7   Francis Quarles, *Emblemes,* p. 239.
8   George Wither, *The Hymnes and Songs of the Church,* p. 34. Similarly, in Francis Quarles' *Sions Sonets* (1625) we read:

> What if Afflictions doe dis-imbellish
> My naturall glorie, and denie the rellish
> Of my adjourned beautie, yet disdaine not
> Her, by whose necessarie losse, you gaine not;
> I was enforc'd to swelter in the Sunne,
> And keepe a strangers Vine, left mine alone;
> I left mine owne, and kept a strangers Vine;
> The Fault was mine, but was not onely mine.   (sig. B1ᵛ)

In a footnote Quarles explains that the Bride had been deceived by false prophets, forced into idolatry, and therefore could not be held fully responsible. Similarly, in George Sandys' *A Paraphrase Upon The Song Of Solomon* (1641), responsibility is shifted in an equally forceful manner:

> Despise not my discoloured look:
> This Tawney from the Sun I took.
> My Mothers Sons envy'd my worth,
> And swoln with malice, thrust me forth
> To Keep their Vines in heat of Day,
> While, ah, my own neglected lay.   (pp. 2–3)

9   John Wall, *Alæ Seraphicæ* (1627), p. 4. See also Dove, p. 29; Henoch Clapham, *Three Partes of Salomon his Song of Songs, expounded* (1603), p. 32.
10 Joseph Fletcher, *The Historie of the Perfect-Cursed-Blessed Man*

(1629), pp. 26–27; cf. figs. 23 and 24 with the Huntington Kitto Bible, III, fols. 450 and 451.

11   Francis Thynne, *Emblemes and Epigrames*, ed. by F. J. Furnivall (London, 1876), p. 35.

12   William Gouge, *An Exposition of the Song of Solomon: called Canticles* (1615), p. 79. Thomas Adams writes: "Job had no water of snow, nor David of hyssop, nor had the pool of Bethesda, though stirred with a thousand angels, power to cleanse us. Let nature do her best, we dwelt at the sign of the *Labour-in-vain*." *The Works of Thomas Adams* (Edinburgh, 1862), I, 398.

13   Gouge, *An Exposition*, p. 80; see also p. 116; and John Deacon and John Walker, *Dialogicall Discourses of Spirits and Divels* (1601), p. 134.

14   Gouge, *An Exposition*, p. 80.

15   Adams, I, 398. Similarly, John Dove writes that the black Bride is "as it were, besmeared with originall sin, derived from *Adam*" (p. 32).

16   See St. Bernard, *On the Song of Songs*, tr. and ed. by a Religious of C.S.M.V. (London: A. R. Mowbray, 1952), ch. 8; Origen, *The Song of Songs: Commentary and Homilies*, tr. R. P. Lawson (London, 1957), Bk. II, secs. 1 and 2; Henry Ainsworth, *Solomons Song of Songs in English Metre* (1623), bound with *Annotations Upon the Five Bookes of Moses, the Booke of Psalmes, and the Song of Songs* (1627), p. 8; Gouge, *A Guide to Goe to God*, p. 53.

17   Adams, I, 398. After having written that natural man "dwelt at the sign of the *Labour-in-vain*," Adams asserts that "A medicine of water and blood, John xix.34, let out of the side of Jesus by a murdering spear, hath made the daughter of Zion fair."

18   Edward Lord Herbert of Cherbury, *The Poems English & Latin of Edward Lord Herbert of Cherbury*, ed. by G. C. Moore Smith (Oxford: Clarendon Press, 1923), pp. 34–38, by permission of the Clarendon Press, Oxford. See Smith's note on Mrs. Cecyll, pp. 152–53. I do not believe that "Another Sonnet to Black it self" is part of the compliment to Diana Cecyll.

19   Origen writes: "This blackness, then, for which you reproach me, is in me because the sun has looked askance at me by reason of my unbelief and disobedience. But when I shall stand upright before Him and shall be crooked in nothing, . . . then He who is Himself upright will look on me, and there will be in me no crookedness, nor any cause for Him to look askance at me. And then my light and my splendour will be restored to me, and that blackness for which you now reproach me will be banished from me so completely, that I shall be accounted worthy to be called *the light of the world*" (pp. 108–9). See also St. Bernard, *On the Song of Songs*, pp. 78–79.

20   Joseph Beaumont, *Psyche* (1648), p. 22.

21   Ibid., p. 23.

22 Ibid., p. 25. For a similar poetic idea, see Henry Lok's Sonnet 53, *Sundry Christian Passions* (1593), p. 36; cf. Robert Southwell's two uses of the shade image in *Saint Peters Complaint* (1605), pp. 64–65, and *Maeoniae* (1595), p. 13.

23 Beaumont, *Psyche*, p. 25.

24 Ibid., p. 85.

25 Ibid., p. 392.

26 In *The Glasse of Time* (1620) Thomas Peyton identifies the worm of conscience "With coales of fire, which never shall go out" (p. 56). Anne Collins writes that the soul out of "Communion with Christ" is "scorched with distracting care." *Divine Songs and Meditacions* (1653), p. 28. All citations from Anne Collins in my text will be from the apparently unique volume of her work now in the Huntington Library. Selected verses from this work are available in my edition published by the Augustan Reprint Society (William Andrews Clark Memorial Library, 1961).

27 George Abbot, *Exposition Upon The Prophet Jonah* (1600), pp. 601–2. See Dove, p. 85.

28 In *Noahs Dove* (1627) Henry Valentine writes: "Now with *Jonas* she [the Church] sits in the arbour of peace, shaded and shrowded from the heat of the Sunne: anon, the *gourd* is withered, the Sunne beats upon her, and she complaines of her *blacknesse*" (p. 18). See also Thomas Jackson, *Davids Pastorall Poem* (1603), pp. 57, 62.

29 Fray Luis de Granada, *Of Prayer, and Meditation* [tr. by Richard Hopkins] (Douay, 1612), fol. 55.

30 William Loe, *Songs of Sion* (Hamburg, 1620), p. 87. This idea was popular in the songs of the time:

> My Jesus is an Apple-Tree,
>   And others Barren Wood.
> He is a Shadow from the Heat
>   Of Conscience, Wrath and Hell.

[John Mason], *Spiritual Songs, or, Songs of Praise To Almighty God . . . Together with The Song of Songs Which is Solomons . . .* , 5th ed. (1696), p. 69.

Elsewhere in the same work, which was first published in 1683, Mason writes:

> What are the common Trees o'th'Wood
>   Unto the Apple Tree?
> What is the Rich and Noblest Blood,
>   My lovely Lord, to Thee?
>
> I sate Rejoycing in Times past
>   Under his cooling Shade

His Fruit was sweet unto my Tast,
O what a Feast I made!   (pp. 65–66)

In the same vein Venantius Fortunatus, the great medieval composer of hymns, writes in "De Cruce Domini," "Heat is there none that can burn beneath thy shadowy covert." *Hortus Conclusus*, ed. by Stephen A. Hurlbut (Washington, D.C., 1934), III, 14–15. See also Alexander Grosse, *The Happines of Enjoying, And Making A True use . . . of Christ* (1647), p. 17.

31 George Gifford, *Fifteen Sermons Upon the Song of Salomon* (1600), p. 77.

32 Gouge, *An Exposition*, p. 16.

33 St. John of the Cross, *Complete Works*, II, 137. For analogues to this passage, see Dove, p. 83; Joseph Hall, *The Works of Joseph Hall*, ed. by Phillip Winter (Oxford, 1839), III, 295; the glosses in the English Bibles, 1600 and 1611 editions.

34 T. S., *The Book of the Song of Solomon in Meeter*, p. 2. Likewise Sandys, *A Paraphrase Upon The Song Of Solomon:*

You Daughters of Jerusalem,
You Branches of that holy Stem,
Though black, in favour I excell:
Black as the Tents of Ismael;
Yet gracefull, as the burnisht Throne,
And Ornaments of Solomon.   (p. 2)

And according to John Dove, "such ornaments as she [the Bride] received from her husband, she was by grace made comely, but by nature shee was not so" (p. 30).

35 Gouge, *An Exposition*, p. [87?].

36 T[homas] W[ilcox], *An exposition uppon the Booke of the Canticles, otherwise called Schelomons Song* (1585), p. 14.

37 William Prynne, "A Christian Paradise," in *Mount-Orgueil* (1641), p. 124.

38 Ibid., p. 5.

39 Ibid., p. 136.

40 *Hymns Ancient and Modern for Use In The Services Of The Church . . .* (London: William Clowes, 1909), pp. 150–51. See also Peyton, pp. 62, 71.

41 "The Gardin," from Beaumont, *The Minor Poems*, pp. 450–51.

42 This is the rhetorical thrust of the juxtaposition of *A Treatise of Fruit-Trees* (1657) and *The Spiritual Use of a Garden*; the latter work is avowedly allegorical in method and homiletic in tone.

43 For the following remarks, I am indebted to John Ashton's Introduction to *The Legendary History of the Cross* (London, 1887) and to

the Introduction by J. Ph. Berjeau to *Geschiedenis van het heylighe Cruys; or, History of the Holy Cross* (London, 1863).

44 Jacobus de Voragine, *The Golden Legende,* tr. by William Caxton (Westminster, 1483), fol. clxvii.

45 Ibid., fol. clxiii^v.

46 Ashton, p. xxi. This section is missing from the third edition of the *Golden Legend.* Ashton follows the first edition.

47 Ashton, p. cxv.

48 Tr. by Thomas Frognall Dibdin, *Bibliotheca Spenceriana* (London, 1814), III, 356. The original reads:

> Hier doet dauid ter selver vren   9 *ems*
> Sijn hof vaste ende wel bemueren
> Oeck suidi dat claerliken verstaen
> Dat hi hier sijn ghebet heest ghedaen.

49 This sequence may be followed in any of the works cited in notes 42–47.

50 *Poems of Crashaw,* p. 278.

51 Berjeau, p. vii.

52 Ashton, pp. lxv ff.

53 Daniel Price, *The Spring* (1609), sig. C3^v.

54 *Spiritual Songs from English MSS of Fourteenth to Sixteenth Centuries,* ed. by Frances M. M. Comper (London: The Society for Promoting Christian Knowledge, 1936), p. 28, by permission of the Society for Promoting Christian Knowledge. Citing Isaiah xi.7 and Cant. ii, Louis Richeome writes: "*A rodd shall rise out of the roote of Jesse, and from the roote thereof shall spring a flower.* This Rod is the B. Virgin, sayth S. *Hierome,* having no other shrubbe joyned with her: The flower is her Sonne Jesus Christ, The flower of the field, as he is called, issued from this Virgin, whereof the same Prophet sayd, cap. 7. *Behold a Virgin shall conceave, and bring forth a sonne.*" *The Pilgrime of Loreto,* tr. by E. W. (Paris, 1629), p. 190.

55 Comper, p. 28. "Spray" here means "to branch."

56 Ibid. See Comper's note.

57 From an excerpt tr. by H. E. Luxmore, cited in Eleanour Sinclair Rohde, *The Old-World Pleasaunce* (New York: Dial Press, 1925), p. 37.

58 A reproduction of this painting appears in Eleanour Sinclair Rohde, *The Story of the Garden* (Boston, 1933), fig. facing p. 45.

59 See Arthur Watson, *The Early Iconography of the Tree of Jesse* (London, 1934), fig. 27; discussion, p. 126.

60 "Hours of Isabelle of Brittainy," from photographs at the Pierpont Morgan Library, fol. 21^v.

61 George Wither, *A Collection of Emblemes, Ancient and Moderne*

(1635; STC 25900ᶜ), p. 217. Typographically, the five states of the first edition of Wither's *Collection of Emblemes* vary; I have used this issue throughout.

62 "An Exposition of the Song of Songs" (c. 1450); facsimile edition at the Morgan Library, fol. 26.

63 *The Poems of Edward Taylor*, ed. by Donald E. Stanford, with a Foreword by Louis L. Martz (New Haven: Yale University Press, 1960), p. 375. This kind of paraphrase is very common. For example, in "The Magnificence" Du Bartas writes:

> Among the Trees, my Love's an Apple-Tree,
> Thy fruitfull Stem bears Flowr and Fruit together:
> I'll smell thy Flowr, thy Fruit shall nourish mee,
> And in thy Shadow will I rest for ever.

Guillaume Du Bartas, *Divine Weekes And Workes*, tr. by Josuah Sylvester (1621), p. 464.

Anthony Stafford's seventh meditation reads: "Our Master hath left us two Sacraments. One of which tell's us that wee are Christians: the other biddes us live like Christians. This later is that Tree of Life; the passage whereto is guarded by no Cherubin, nor by any brandished Sword: but whosoever will, may come thither; and, eating worthily, may live for ever. When therefore I eate of this Tree, I will remember out of whose bloud it sprang. The memory whereof will suggest unto mee, that I eate not this fruit worthily, I am unworthy to be a branch of the Tree: that is, if I eate not his body worthily, I am then unworthy to be a member of that body whereof he is the head." *Meditations, and Resolutions, Moral, Divine, Politicall* (1612), pp. 6–8.

64 "An Exposition of the Song of Songs," fol. 28. Similarly, in the Huntington Kitto Bible, Christ is shown, crowning his Bride, beneath the flourishing, fruit-laden Tree; the scene is surrounded by a garden wall (XXV, fol. 4664ᵛ).

65 William Baldwin, *The Canticles or Balades of Salomon* (1549), sig. c.ii.

66 This untitled poem by Thomas Page is prefixed to John Gerhard, *A Golden Chaine of Divine Aphorismes*, tr. by Ralph Winterton (Cambridge, 1632), sig. ¶¶ 2ᵛ.

67 St. Teresa, *Complete Works*, II, 389.

68 Citations to Hugo in my text will be to *Pia Desideria*, tr. by Edmund Arwaker (1686), pp. 163–67. For a discussion of the place of Herman Hugo in emblematic literature, see Rosemary Freeman, *English Emblem Books* (London, 1948), ch. 5. The immediate problem of Hugo's influence on Quarles is treated by Gordon Haight: "Beginning with Book III, the plates of the *Emblemes* are all copied from Hugo and in the same order. Thus the original of Emblem III, 2 is found in

Pia Desideria, I, 2, etc." "The Sources of Quarles's Emblems," *The Library*, XVI (1936), 196.

69 Quarles, *Emblemes*, p. 249.

70 *Poems of Crashaw*, pp. 254–61.

71 Francis Quarles, *Divine Fancies* (1632), p. 35.

72 Ibid., p. 36.

73 Rowland Watkyns, *Flamma Sine Fumo* (1662), p. 51. In Luis de la Puente's *Meditations upon the Mysteries of our Holie Faith*, tr. by John Heigham (St. Omers, 1619), we read: "And Christ our Lord himselfe, upon this motive did in the memorie of his passion, call in the booke of Canticles this day wherin his mother the Sinagogue crowned him with a crowne of thornes, the day of his espousalls, and of the exultation of his hart; and therfore he entred into Hierusalem . . . to celebrate on the bed chamber of the Crosse, the espousalls with his Church" (II, 7). Again, Puente writes that on this day the wedding of Christ and the Church was solemnized "upon the nuptiall bed of the Crosse" (II, 228).

74 *The Works of George Herbert*, pp. 63–64.

75 Quarles, *Sions Sonets*, sig. B2.

76 Richard Baxter, *The Saints Everlasting Rest* (1650), p. 28.

77 Grosse, p. 17.

78 For typical examples of this interpretation, see St. Bernard's *The Steps of Humility*, tr. by George Bosworth Burch (Cambridge, Mass., 1942), and Gouge, *An Exposition*, p. 17.

79 Sandys, p. 7. See St. Bernard, *The Steps of Humility*, p. 163.

80 Robert Crofts, *The Lover* (1638), sig. E7. See Baxter, p. 45. In his *Treatise of Mentall Prayer* tr. by I. W. (St. Omers, 1627) Alonso Roderigues writes that the Spouse is "inebriated . . . taken, and absorpt in God" in such a way as all memory of the self passes (pp. 22, 23); and in Quarles' *Sions Sonets*, we read:

> I Thirsted; and, full charged to the brinke,
> He gave me boules of Nectar, for my drinke,
> And in his Sides, he broacht me (for a signe
> Of dearest love) a Sacramentall wine;
> He freely gave; I freely dranke my fill; . . . .   (sig. B4)

This is why Mason (p. 69) speaks of "The shadow of his Sacraments."

81 Puente, II, 270.

82 Sandys, p. 5.

83 Consider such examples as are found in contemporary dictionaries and paraphrases. In Thomas Wilson's *A Christian Dictionary* (1614) (which is actually four dictionaries, not one), we find an explication of this text in the section entitled "For the Canticles or Song of Salomon":

Greene Bed. See Bed.

[Our Bed is green] The protection of Children unto God in Christ, in the spirituall birth, by the immortall seed of the word. For the Church is so a Virgine, as she is the Mother of all Gods Children. Cant. I, 15. *Our Bed is green.*

And in Joseph Hall's "An Open And plaine Paraphrase upon the Song of Songs, Which is Salomon's," bound with *Salomons Divine Arts* (1609), we find much the same thing (p. 12):

The Church

15. *My wel-* *beloved, be-* *hold, thou art* *faire & plea-* *sant: also our* *bed is greene.*	Nay then (O sweet saviour and spouse) thou art alone that faire and pleasant one indeed, from whose fulnesse I confesse to have received al this little measure of my spiritual beauty: and behold, from this our mutuall delight, & heavenly conjunction, there ariseth a plentifull and florishing increase of thy faithfull ones, in all places & through all times.

84 T. S. explains his paraphrase in *The Book of the Song of Solomon in Meeter:* "*Where Christ conjoyns in spiritual union*" there follows "*great increase*" (p. 4). In *The Canticles or Balades of Salomon* William Baldwin writes in paraphrase: "*Beholde our Bed, our peace most plentiful/ Of conscience, doeth florish through thy myght*" (sig. B4).

85 William Alabaster, *The Sonnets of William Alabaster*, ed. by G. M. Story and Helen Gardner (London: Oxford University Press, 1959), p. 7; by permission of the Clarendon Press, Oxford.

86 St. Teresa, *Complete Works*, II, 392. Note the hierarchy of analogous states in Alonso Rodrigues: "In this most speciall kind of *Prayer*, and *Contemplation, S. Bernard* placeth three degrees. The first, he compareth to *Eating*, the second to *Drinking* (which is done with more facility & delight then *Eating*, for there is no trouble in the chewing) and the third, in being *Inebriated.* And he brings to this purpose, that of the Spouse in the *Canticles, Comedite amici, & bibite, & inebriamini charissimi.* He sayth first, come *Eate*; secondly, come and *Drinke*; and thirdly, come and *Inebrietate* your selves, with this Love" (p. 23).

87 John Collop, *The Poems of John Collop*, ed. by Conrad Hilberry (Madison: University of Wisconsin Press, 1962), p. 43.

88 In *The Garden Of Our B. Lady* (St. Omers, 1619), Sabin Chambers writes: "When we have arrived by the contemplation of heaven unto the delights therin, our understanding presently butteth upon Almighty God, who is a *Non plus ultra*, and the end of all that we can thinke of, since in him all this Beatitude is contayned, as in a place inaccessible unto mans understanding" (pp. 248-49).

89 "So say the Mistikes, that this highest portion of man's soule is the Spouse his bed, Salomon's coutch, his Cabinet, and the place of his more particular delights. Ther is the Divine essence united to the essence of the soule; there the spirituall marriages (marriages the fullnesse of our eternall felicitie) celebrated, wherof so much mention is made in the holy Scripture." Jean Camus, *A Draught of Eternitie*, tr. by Miles Car (Douay, 1632), pp. 216–17. And in Puente, II, 864, we read: "*O my beloved, most sweet tree, brought from heaven, for the health of the world, now I content not my selfe, only to say as did the spouse. Under his shadowe whom I desired, I sate, and his frute was sweet unto my throate: but I further desire that thou enter within me, and that thou make me one thing with thee, that in virtu of of [sic] thee, I may bring forth most sweet frutes like unto thine, which may remayne unto life everlasting, Amen.*"

CHAPTER IV: TIME

1 Erwin Panofsky, *Early Netherlandish Painting* (Cambridge, Mass.: Harvard University Press, 1953), I, 146 ff.; Panofsky's fig. 104.

2 See Georges Poulet, *Studies in Human Time*, tr. by Elliott Coleman (Baltimore, 1956), pp. 13–16, and the chapter on Montaigne (ch. 1).

3 This inscription is cited by Eleanour Sinclair Rohde, *The Old-World Pleasaunce* (New York: Dial Press, 1925), p. 139.

4 A picture of this impressive dial is reproduced in *Gardens Old and New* (London, n.d.), I, 232.

5 H. Inigo Triggs, *Formal Gardens in England and Scotland* (London, 1902), II, 6.

6 Ibid., I, 20.

7 Rohde, *The Old-World Pleasaunce*, p. 178.

8 Aurelian Townshend, *Aurelian Townshend's Poems and Masks*, ed. by E. K. Chambers (Oxford: Clarendon Press, 1911), p. 6, by permission of the Clarendon Press, Oxford. See Samuel Chew, *The Pilgrimage of Life* (New Haven, 1962), pp. 12–17.

9 *The Works of George Herbert*, pp. 122–23; cf. "Time" and "In Solarium," where the speaker betrays the same tone: "Contemplare, miser, quantum terroris haberet . . ." (p. 417).

10 Louis L. Martz, *The Poetry of Meditation* (rev. ed., New Haven, 1962) ch. 3.

11 Francis Quarles, *Emblemes*, p. 174. Thomas Forde writes: "As in a Sun-Diall, the shadow moves from one houre to another till the Sun set, yet we cannot perceive it to move, so our life passeth away, and though it be insensibly, yet it does constantly, till the Sun of our life be quite down, and we over-taken with the black night of death." *Lusus Fortunae* (1649), p. 21.

12 See A. C. Hamilton, "The Argument of Spenser's *Shepheardes Calender*," *ELH*, XXIII (1956), 171–82.

13 *The Complete Poetical Works of Spenser*, ed. by R. E. Dodge (Cambridge, Mass.: Houghton-Mifflin, 1936), p. 54.

14 See Robert Allen Durr, "Spenser's Calendar of Christian Time,"
ELH, XXIV (1957), 269–95.

15 This anonymous inscription is cited in Rohde, *The Old-World
Pleasaunce*, p. 172.

16 Carrying through the figure of the calendar, there are such examples
as this in the commonplace books:

> Time flyes away fast;
> Our houres doe waste
> The while we never remember,
> How soone our life, here,
> Growes old with the year
> That dies with the next December.

Thomas Grocer, "Dayly Observations both Divine and Morall"
(1657), Huntington MS. 93, p. 17.

17 Anne Collins, *Divine Songs and Meditacions*, p. 56.

18 Henry Vaughan, *The Works of Henry Vaughan*, ed. by L. C. Martin
(Oxford: Clarendon Press, 1957), p. 397, by permission of the Clarendon Press, Oxford.

19 Ross Garner, *Henry Vaughan: Experience and the Tradition* (Chicago,
1959), pp. 60–61.

20 From *The Life of the Holy Mother Teresa of Jesus*, in *Complete
Works*, I, 86.

21 From *Spiritual Canticle*, in St. John of the Cross, *Complete Works*,
II, 270.

22 Of this wind Gaspar Loarte writes in *Instructions And Advertise-
ments, How To Meditate The Misteries of the Rosarie of the most
holy Virgin Mary* [tr. by J. Fenne; Rouen, 1600]: "O my soule, if thou
wouldest dispose thy selfe to taste of this sweete wine, howe soure
would al worldly thinges be to thee, which at this instant seeme so
savourie? If thou wert so happie, as that this holye winde might
breath upon thee, refresh thee, and guide thee, O, howe much more
securely mightest thou saile and arrive to the desired port? This is that
wind which the Spouse desired and craved in the Canticles, when she
saide: *Gett thee gone thou wind of North; and come thou wind of
South; breath upon my garden, and it shal become odoriferous and
fruitful*" (fols. 95–95ᵛ).

23 Nicholas Breton, *The Pilgrimage to Paradise* (1592), p. 1.

24 Martz, *The Poetry of Meditation*. The reader will recognize that for
much of the material in this chapter I am greatly indebted to this
important work.

25 For the following remarks on gardening I am indebted to Eleanour Sinclair Rohde, *Garden-Craft in the Bible and Other Essays* (London, 1927), and her *The Story of the Garden* (Boston, 1933); Ralph Dutton, *The English Garden* (rev. ed., London, 1950); Sir Frank Crisp, *Mediaeval Gardens* (2 vols., London, 1924).

26 G. G. Coulton, *Five Centuries of Religion* (Cambridge: Cambridge University Press, 1923), I, 14.

27 Cited in Rose Standish Nichols, *English Pleasure Gardens* (New York: Macmillan, 1925), p. 53.

28 Ibid.; Miss Nichols cites Durand.

29 E. Allison Peers, *Spirit of Flame: A Study of St. John of the Cross* (New York: Morehous-Gorham, 1945), p. 115.

30 St. François de Sales, *Introduction to the Devout Life*, tr. by John K. Ryan (New York: Doubleday, 1957), p. 93.

31 Martz, pp. 58–59.

32 Andrew Marvell, *The Poems and Letters of Andrew Marvell*, ed. by H. M. Margoliouth (Oxford: Clarendon Press, 1952), I, 48, by permission of the Clarendon Press, Oxford.

33 John Melton, *Astrologaster* (1620), p. 2.

34 William Prynne, "A Christian Paradise," in *Mount-Orgueil* (1641), p. 126.

35 Ibid., pp. 117, 121.

36 Ibid., p. 125.

37 Rowland Watkyns, *Flamma Sine Fumo* (1662), p. 98.

38 Henry Hawkins, *Partheneia Sacra* (Rouen, 1633), p. 7.

39 Ibid., p. 9.

40 Ibid., pp. 13–14. Such distinctions between the enclosed garden of the Song of Songs and all other gardens were commonplace in the handbooks of devotion. In one of these, for example, we read: "The Gardens of the *Hesperides* warded and guarded by those three daughters of *Atlas*, were pleasant; the Gardens of *Lucullus* fragrant; the Grove of *Ida* eminent; yet not comparable to those exquisite pleasures, which the divine pastures comprehend; there is that *hedged Garden*, that *sealed Well*, that *Bethesda*, that *Eden*, that *Syloe*; here may the delight of every *Sence* be renewed; the thirstie satisfied, the hungry filled, the sicke cured, the labourer cheered, and the exquisite mirrour of all perfection; torrent of ever-flowing bounties, *Jessaes* branch, *Aarons* rod, and that flowrie garden of *Engaddi* represented . . . . This it is to be joyned to an heav'nly spouse, sending from Paradice pomgranats, with the fruits of apples; Cypresse, Nard . . . and Cinnamon, with all the woods of Libanon . . . ." Richard Brathwaite, *Essaies upon the Five Senses* (1620), pp. 60–61.

41 Hawkins, pp. 15, 16.

42 Ibid., p. 27.

43 Ibid.

44 Ibid., pp. 32–33.

45 Ibid., pp. 33–34.

46 Ibid., p. 215.

47 Ralph Austen, *The Spiritual Use of a Garden*, bound with *A Treatise of Fruit-Trees* (1657), p. 21. Religious associations with the act of gardening proper were traditional enough. See William Lawson's, *A New Orchard and Garden* (1623), p. 1; Leonard Meager, *The New Art of Gardening* [1683?], sigs. A2–A2ᵛ; John Parkinson, *Paradisi in Sole* (1629), sigs. **3–**3ᵛ; Sir Anthony Fitzherbert, *The Book of Husbandry*, reprinted from edition of 1534, ed. by Walter Skeat (London, 1882), passim.

48 Austen, p. 83.

49 Henry Lok, *Sundry Christian Passions* (1593), p. 9. In a book addressed to Catholics who had been imprisoned, Robert Southwell wrote that the garden of the Church, planted by Christ, was watered by the blood of the martyrs. *An Epistle of Comfort* (Paris, 1604?), p. 93.

50 Austen, sig. ttᵛ.

51 George Wither, *A Collection of Emblemes*, p. 140.

52 Ibid., p. 144.

53 Ibid. Benjamen Carier writes that "if we will exclude the devill, let us also be alwaies tilling the Paradise of our soules by one good worke, or other, that GOD may delight to walke therein: . . . ." *A Sermon preached before the Prince* (1606), sig. B3.

54 Wither, *A Collection of Emblemes*, p. 144.

55 John Hagthorpe, *Divine Meditations, And Elegies* (1622), pp. 4–5.

56 St. Teresa, *Life*, in *Complete Works*, I, 65. See Fray Luis de Granada, *Of Prayer, And Meditation* [tr. by Richard Hopkins] (Douay, 1612), fols. 169ᵛ–70.

57 Robert Southwell, *Saint Peters Complaint* [1605], p. 65.

58 Ibid., p. 64.

59 Thomas Adams, *The Works of Thomas Adams* (Edinburgh, 1862), II, 436.

60 Casimire Sarbiewski, *The Odes of Casimire*, tr. by G. Hils (1646), p. 87.

61 Loarte, fol. 95ᵛ.

62 Prynne, p. 117.

63 Ibid., p. 121.

64 Ibid., p. 124. See my Chapter I.

65 Ibid., p. 117.

66 Rev. xxi.2.

67 This song, supposedly based on *The Song of Peter Damian* (cf. *The Song of S. Peter Damiani*, ed. from the Vatican MS and tr. by Stephen A. Hurlbut [Washington, D.C., 1928]), is entitled "The Description of heavenly Jerusalem," and appears in the anonymous *The Song of*

Mary the Mother of Christ (1601), pp. 30, 31. Similarly, in "A Glimpse of Heavenly Joyes: Or New-Hierusalem" (bound with Du Bartas' *Divine Weekes*), Sylvester translates a hymn from Augustine:

> The Gates and goodly Walls about,
>   Of rich and orient Gemms:
> The Streets, all pav'd with purest Gold,
>   As smooth as any Glass-is:
> No Foile, no Soile, no Sorrow there;
>   No Sicknesse thither passes.
> No Winter's Frost, no Summer's Toast,
>   Doth there Distemper bring:
> But, Flowers, perpetuall flowring there,
>   Make there perpetuall Spring.
> There, *Balsam, Saffron, Lilly, Rose,*
>   Doe sweat, sent, shine, and blush:
> There, Mead, & Field, spring, spire, & yeeld;
>   Rills, Milke and Hony gush:
> There *Aromaticks* breath-about
>   Their odoriferous Aire:
> There, ever dangle dainty Fruits
>   On Trees still blooming faire . . . .

Guillaume Du Bartas, *Divine Weekes And Workes,* tr. by Josuah Sylvester (1621), p. 1114.

See also Nicholas Breton's "The City of God," *A Bower of Delights* (London, 1893), pp. 46–49; originally published in 1591.
68 Thomas Peyton, *The Glasse of Time* (1620), p. 50.
69 Ibid., p. 51.
70 Robert Hill, *Lectures upon the Three First Chapters of the Revelation* (1604), p. 298.
71 St. Bernard, *On the Song of Songs,* tr. and ed. by a Religious of C.S.M.V. (London: A. R. Mowbray, 1952), pp. 62–63. George Wither reiterates the same argument when he writes that *"in this* Song of Salomon *(wherein is mystically expressed the mutuall affection betwixt Christ and his Church, ... the chiefe passages therof throughout all Ages from* Abel *to the last Judgement . . ."* are to be found. *The Hymnes and Songs of the Church,* p. 31.
72 Alice Sutcliffe, *Meditations Of Man's Mortalitie* (1634), p. 96.
73 Luis de Leon, *The Names of Christ,* tr. by Edward Schuster (St. Louis: Herder, 1955), p. 212. This work was first published in 1595 in Spain.
74 Ibid., p. 216.
75 John Cotton, *A Brief Exposition With Practical Observations Upon the whole Book of Canticles* (1655), pp. 236, 238; see also Francis

Rous, *The Mysticall Marriage* (1635), p. 169; Robert Wilkinson, *The Merchant Royall* (1607), p. 12.

76 Hill, p. 293.

77 [John Mason], *Spiritual Songs, or, Songs of Praise To Almighty God . . . Together with The Song of Songs Which is Solomons . . .* , 5th ed. (1696), p. 112.

78 Morton Bloomfield, *Piers Plowman as a Fourteenth-Century Apocalypse* (New Brunswick, N.J., 1961), p. 9.

79 T. S., *The Book of the Song of Solomon in Meeter* (1676), p. 32.

80 This part of the paradox is stated very clearly by William Gouge: "the *times of restitution,* or perfection . . . is to come. God will have his creatures waite for it." *A Guide to Goe to God* (1626), p. 53.

81 Panofsky, *Early Netherlandish Painting,* I, 139. See Panofsky's fig. 244.

82 It was part of the tradition that time entered the world at the Fall. We will remember that in *Paradise Lost,* the wreath which Adam had woven for his Bride withered quite suddenly once the Fall had taken place. Similarly, in Peyton's *Glasse of Time,* we find a woodcut depicting the Fall, with Adam and Eve reaching into the Tree, while between them stands the figure of Time (p. 31), with his scythe and winged glass, his large wings, and swift cloven hooves. Time watched while Adam allowed his Bride to move aside from him "Even but a little," for Sin and Death (coincident with Time) were about to be endowed with power on the earth (p. 32).

83 Panofsky, *Early Netherlandish Painting,* II, fig. 82.

84 Louis Richeome, *Holy Pictures of the mysticall Figures of the most holy Sacrifice and Sacrament of the Eucharist,* tr. by C. A. (1619), p. 1.

85 *Ibid.,* p. 3.

86 Phineas Fletcher, *The Purple Island* (Cambridge, 1633), p. 10.

87 *Ibid.,* p. 147.

88 Francis Quarles, *Divine Fancies* (1632), p. 8.

89 John Hall, *Emblems With elegant Figures* [1658], p. 96.

90 *Ibid.,* p. 98.

91 *Ibid.,* p. 53.

92 *Ibid.,* p. 54.

93 Pedro de Alcántara, *A Golden Treatise of Mentail Praier,* tr. by Giles Willoughby (Brussels, 1632), pp. 151–52. The disappearance of the external world emphasized in the quotations from John Hall is recognized by Augustine Baker to be the desideratum of the contemplative life, which aims at "an Habituall & almost uninterrupted perfect union with God in the *Supreme Point of the spirit;* and such an union as gives the soule a fruitive possession of him, & a reall, experimentall perception of his Divine Presence in the depth & center of the spirit, which is fully possessed and filled with him alone; not only all deliberate affections to creatures being excluded, but in a manner all

Images of them also, at least so far as they may be distractive to the soule." *Sancta Sophia* (Douay, 1657), pp. 21-22.

94   Otho Casmann, *Vade mecum*, tr. by H. T. (1606), sig. B5ᵛ; see also St. François de Sales, *A Treatise of the Love of God*, tr. by Miles Car (Douay, 1630), pp. 15-16. Similarly, Henry Montagu writes that meditation, by "exciting our wils, produceth some holy resolution. We meditate, saith one, to know God; wee contemplate to love God." *Contemplatio Mortis et Immortalitatis* (1631), p. 4.

95   Alonso Roderigues, *A Treatise of Mentall Prayer*, tr. by I. W. (St. Omers, 1627), p. 21.

96   Ibid., pp. 22, 23.

97   William Struther, *Christian Observations And Resolutions* (Edinburgh, 1628), pp. 101-2.

98   In *The Terrestriall Paradise* (1639) Robert Crofts writes:

> So as through earthly pleasures, our dull sight
> May (as through Spectacles) by reasons light
> Look up to Heaven, to God himself and spie
> Some glimpses of his glorious Majestie
> And so may taste already, in some measure
> The Ocean of his sweet and heavenly pleasure.   (p. 91)

99   *Le Bréviaire de Phillippe le Bon* (Brussels, 1909), plate 24. Reproduced from the MS at the Bibliothèque Royale de Belgique.

100   Joseph Hall, *Meditations and Vows* (1605), p. 21.

101   Ibid., p. 34.

102   St. François de Sales, *A Treatise of the Love of God*, p. 428.

103   Ibid., p. 431.

104   Ibid.

105   William Fuller, *Mourning of Mount Libanon* (1628), p. 18. Fuller's parishioners at St. Giles asked for his removal partly on the grounds that he was a "popish innovator" (*DNB*).

106   "Heures de Turin" (Paris, 1902), plates 17-20, after originals in Bibliothèca Nazionale, Turin, and the Louvre.

107   George Ferguson, *Signs and Symbols in Christian Art* (New York, 1961), pp. 179-80.

108   George Widley, *The Doctrine of the Sabbath* (1604), p. 25.

CHAPTER V:
MARVELL AND "THE GARDEN ENCLOSED"

1   *The Poems and Letters of Andrew Marvell*, ed. by H. M. Margoliouth (Oxford: Clarendon Press, 1952), I, 48-50, by permission of the Clarendon Press, Oxford.

2 For the view that all literature is "more or less allegorical," see Angus Fletcher, *Allegory: The Theory of a Symbolic Mode* (Ithaca, 1964), Intro.

3 For some idea of the range of critical opinion, see Harold Wendell Smith, "Cowley, Marvell, and the Second Temple," *Scrutiny*, XIX (1953), 184–205; Anthony Hecht, "Shades of Keats and Marvell," *The Hudson Review*, XV (1962), 50–71. Briefly stated, Hecht sees the subject of both poems as "an exquisite secular and sensuous ecstasy . . . which is self-induced and autoerotic." See also Pierre Legouis, *André Marvell: poète, puritain, patriote* (Paris: Henri Didier, 1928), pp. 123 ff; William Empson, "Marvell's 'Garden'," *Scrutiny*, I (1932), 236–40 (this essay is included as a chapter in *English Pastoral Poetry* (New York, 1938), pp. 119 ff.); A. H. King, "Some Notes on Andrew Marvell's Garden," *ES*, XX (1938), 118–21; Milton Klonsky, "A Guide through the Garden," *SR*, LVIII (1950), 16–35; M. C. Bradbrook and M. G. Lloyd Thomas, *Andrew Marvell* (Cambridge, 1940), pp. 59–64; Ruth Wallerstein, *Seventeenth-Century Poetic* (Madison, 1950), pp. 319–35; Frank Kermode, "The Argument of Marvell's 'Garden'," *EC*, II (1952), 225–40; Pierre Legouis, "Marvell and the New Critics," *RES*, VIII (1957), 382–89; Lawrence Hyman, "Marvell's Garden," *ELH*, XXV (1958), 13–22; Maren-Sofie Røstvig, "Andrew Marvell's 'The Garden': A Hermetic Poem," *ES*, XL (1959), 65–76. See also Miss Røstvig's "Benlowes, Marvell, and the Divine Casimire," *HLQ*, XVIII (1954), 13–35, to which I am greatly indebted; Geoffrey H. Hartman, "Marvell, St. Paul, and the Body of Hope," *ELH*, XXXI (1964), 175–94; Harold E. Toliver, *Marvell's Ironic Vision* (New Haven, 1965), pp. 88 ff., 138–51, et passim.

4 René Wellek and Austin Warren, *Theory of Literature* (New York, 1956), p. 31.

5 Wallerstein, pp. 319–40. The reader will recognize my indebtedness to Miss Wallerstein; my differences with her will be equally clear throughout the chapter.

6 Don Cameron Allen, *Image and Meaning* (Baltimore, 1960), ch. 6.

7 Ibid., ch. 7.

8 Røstvig, "Andrew Marvell's 'The Garden': A Hermetic Poem," *ES*, XL (1959), 65–76.

9 Bodleian MS. Fairfax 40, p. 443, quoted by permission of the Bodleian Library, Oxford. A small portion of Fairfax's paraphrase appears in *The Poems of Thomas Third Lord Fairfax*, ed. by Edward Bliss Reed (New Haven, 1909), pp. 259–60.

10 Marvell, *Poems & Letters*, I, 219.

11 For a translation of "Hortus," see the Appendix.

12 For another point of view, see George Williamson, "The Context of Marvell's 'Garden'," *MLN*, LXXVI (1961), 590–98.

13 Casimire Sarbiewski, *The Odes of Casimire*, tr. by G. Hils (1646), pp.

83–89. I am indebted to Miss Røstvig, who first pointed out the connection between Sarbiewski and Marvell in "Benlowes, Marvell, and the Divine Casimire," *HLQ*, XVIII (1954), 13–35, and in *The Happy Man: Studies in the Metamorphoses of a Classical Ideal, 1600–1700* (Oslo, 1954), I, 240–66, esp. p. 259. In relation to "The Garden," Miss Røstvig emphasizes the influence of the *Hermetica*; cf. the argument of the present chapter with her "Andrew Marvell's 'The Garden': A Hermetic Poem," *ES*, XL (1959), 65–76.

14   Francis Quarles, *Emblemes*, p. 237. Again, the lusciousness of the scene draws upon such examples as this from John Davies' *The Muses Sacrifice* (1612):

> O! juycie *Bunch* of *Soule*-refreshing *grapes*,
>   (hard pressed in the *Wine-presse* of the *Crosse!*)
> Make druncke my thirstie *Soule*, that (gasping) gapes
>   for thy pure bloud, to purge mine, being to grosse.
>
>   (fol. 22)

15   William Prynne, "A Christian Paradise," in *Mount Orgueil* (1641), p. 124.

16   Ibid., p. 136.

17   T. S., *The Book of the Song of Solomon in Meeter* (1676), p. 4. See Don Cameron Allen, "Symbolic Color in the Literature of the English Renaissance," *PQ*, XV (1936), 81–92.

18   William Baldwin, *The Canticles or Balades of Salomon* (1549), sig. B4.

19   Gervase Markham, *The Poem of Poems* [1596], sig. B4.

20   This painting, now hanging in the New York Metropolitan Museum, depicts an interior Annunciation. The bed in the right half of the painting is covered with roses. Through the window we may see an enclosed garden, and at a distance the Tower of David, with its gate now opened.

21   St. Teresa, *Conceptions of the Love of God*, in *Complete Works*, II, 389.

22   Here I must take strong exception to Hecht, who writes that "the joke at the expense of labor is very lightly stated, and [that] if the poet seems to be recommending a kind of sloth, it is sanctified by nature." Hecht, "Shades of Keats and Marvell," *The Hudson Review*, XV (1962), 51.

23   In the latter work we read:

> Ydell people ever troubled are with thought
> With indygence mysaventure and necessyte
> And in the snare whan they are cought
> They are envyroned with poverte
> Than cometh dysconfort in theyr adversyte

And also dyspayre them doth manace
And thought and trouble ever doth them chace.

Jean Bruyant, *The Castell of Labour*, tr. from the French of Pierre Gringore, reprinted in facsimile from Wynkyn de Worde's edition of 1506, with an intro. by Alfred W. Pollard (Edinburgh, 1905), sig. A2.

24   For a relevant discussion of the value of solitude, see Augustine Baker, *Sancta Sophia* (Douay, 1657), pp. 16-18.

25   Jean Bruyant, *Le Livre du Chastel du Labour* (privately printed, 1909), plate 11.

26   See the discussion of the way in which the senses act as impediments to devotion in Pedro de Alcántara, *A Golden Treatise of Mentail Praier*, tr. by Giles Willoughby (Brussels, 1632), pp. 151-52.

27   For example in the "Book of Hours of Claude I" (Rouen, c. 1500), Morgan MS. 356, we find King David spying on Bathsheba. The fountain in which Bathsheba bathes is dominated by a statue of Cupid, who is in the act of shooting an arrow. Lest the meaning of this escape the viewer, a side panel is provided which serves as a graphic commentary on the painting. Here are two scenes showing the outcome of this garden experience. Above, King David and Bathsheba lie abed; below, a battle rages, where (in the front line) Bathsheba's husband receives an enemy spear through the chest (fol. 30^v).

28   William Nevill, *The Castell of Pleasure*, ed. by Roberta D. Cornelius (London: *EETS*, 1930), pp. 84-85.

29   Ibid., pp. 89-90.

30   C. S. Lewis, *The Allegory of Love* (New York, 1958), pp. 13-21. See also D. W. Robertson, Jr., "The Doctrine of Charity in Medieval Literary Gardens," *Speculum*, XXVI (1951), 24-49.

31   John Hagthorpe, *Divine Meditations* (1622), pp. 4-5.

32   "Thou shalt not onely labour to lop the branches of evill affections: but also shalt endevour contrariwise to plant or griffe in, the graffes of good affections: For the minde is never free from motions, either stormy and evil, or calme and good, let it therefore be occupied with good, that it be not overwhelmed with ill: to wit, Let thy minde be occupied in divine and spirituall things." Otho Casmann, *Vade mecum*, tr. by H. T. (1606), sig. E5^v.

33   St. Teresa describes the fourth water: "His help is very necessary, even more so than it was for describing the last water, for in that state the soul still feels that it is not completely dead—and we may use this word in speaking of it, since it is dead to the world. As I said, it retains sufficient sense to . . . [make] use of exterior things for the expression of its feelings, even if this is only possible by signs. In the whole of the prayer already described, and in each of its stages, the gardener is responsible for part of the labour; although in these later stages the

labour is accompanied by such bliss and consolation that the soul's desire would be never to abandon it. . . . In this state of prayer . . . there is no feeling, but only rejoicing, unaccompanied by any understanding of the thing in which the soul is rejoicing. . . . In this rejoicing all the senses are occupied, so that none of them is free or able to act in any way, either outwardly or inwardly." *The Life of the Holy Mother Teresa of Jesus*, in *Complete Works*, I, 105.

34 John Hall, *Emblems With elegant Figures* [1658], p. 53.

35 Ibid., p. 54.

36 T. S., *The Book of the Song of Solomon in Meeter*, p. 6.

37 St. François de Sales, *A Treatise of the Love of God*, tr. by Miles Car (Douay, 1630), p. 373.

38 George Wither, *A Collection of Emblemes*, p. 250.

39 John Wall, *Alæ Seraphicæ* (1627), p. 24.

40 St. François de Sales, *A Treatise of the Love of God*, p. 328.

41 Prynne, p. 117.

42 In a pastoral dedication to Drummond, Lauder uses the phrase in his description of poetic ecstasy. *The Poetical Works of William Drummond*, ed. by L. E. Kastner (Edinburgh: William Blackwood and Sons, 1913), I, cxii.

43 Prynne, p. 117.

44 Legouis, *André Marvell*, p. 127.

45 See Helen Gardner's "The Argument about 'The Ecstasy,'" in *Elizabethan and Jacobean Studies Presented to Frank Percy Wilson* (Oxford, 1959), pp. 279–306.

46 E. D. Hirsch, Jr., applies the distinction between meaning and relevance to the act of criticism in his important essay, "Objective Interpretation," *PMLA*, LXXV (1960), 463–79.

47 Empson, "Marvell's 'Garden'," *Scrutiny*, I (1932), 236.

48 The view is all but pervasive, but this particular locution belongs to King, "Some Notes on Andrew Marvell's Garden," *ES*, XX (1938), 118–21.

Index